NATIONAL GIRO
MODERN MONEY TRANSFER

UNWIN PROFESSIONAL MANAGEMENT LIBRARY

Company Organization: Theory and Practice
PA Management Consultants Limited
M. C. Barnes, A. H. Fogg, C. N. Stephens, L. G. Titman

Marketing and Higher Management
PA Management Consultants Limited
Esmond Pearce

Effective Industrial Selling
Vic Markham

Planning the Corporate Reputation
Vic Markham

Managing the Training Function
Christopher Gane

Managing for Profit – The Added Value Concept
R. R. Gilchrist

The Organization Gap
R. B. Kemball-Cook

Computers, Management and Information
David Firnberg

Decision Strategies and New Ventures
W. G. Byrnes and B. K. Chesterton

Systems Analysis in Business
John Graham

NATIONAL GIRO
MODERN
MONEY TRANSFER

GLYN DAVIES
Sir Julian Hodge Professor of Banking and Finance
University of Wales Institute of Science and Technology

Foreword by
The Rt Hon. James Callaghan, MP

London
GEORGE ALLEN & UNWIN LTD
RUSKIN HOUSE   MUSEUM STREET

First published in 1973

© Glyn Davies 1973

ISBN 0 04 332054 6

Printed in Great Britain
in 11 point Times New Roman
by William Clowes & Sons, Limited
London, Beccles and Colchester

Foreword

by The Rt Hon. James Callaghan, MP

I am very grateful to Professor Glyn Davies for giving me this opportunity of writing a Foreword to his important book about the National Giro—one of the oldest, simplest and yet most efficient means of transmitting money from one person to another. Even so, as he himself says, many people in this country still regard it as a strange and foreign-sounding intrusion.

His book is valuable at many levels. He describes a fascinating piece of social history; he gives us an account of the workings of the system since it was introduced in 1968, together with a description of some of its customers; and, more than this, he points the way to even more significant developments in the future.

That the Giro has not caught on faster since it was established in 1968 is due to three main factors. It began at a difficult time economically and financially; then, after two years, its future was thrown into jeopardy by the election of the Conservative Government, notoriously unsympathetic to the Giro and under whose previous régime the idea had been rejected. Finally the very propaganda in favour of establishing it had at last led the clearing banks, which for years had leaned up against each other, to start competing. Nevertheless, nearly half a million customers have discovered its advantages for paying bills and transmitting money round the country and they now include a number of our largest companies and nationalised industries as well as at least two major government departments. Fortunately after eighteen months of indecision by the Conservative Government following its election in 1970, the Giro was given the signal to go ahead, and doubts about its future have now been resolved. I agree with Professor Glyn Davies' conclusion that with this cloud removed, it will continue to make substantial progress.

The Postal Clerks' Association, the forerunner of the Union of Post Office Workers, was one of the earliest and strongest advocates of a National Giro, and the trade union movement as a whole, recognising that the joint-stock banks were essentially facilities for the middle classes, placed the weight of the movement behind the agitation for the National Giro over fifty years ago. It was intended to be the trade unionists' bank but, sadly, since its establishment by the Labour Government in 1968, few of the major trade unions have taken a serious interest in it despite its undoubted advantages which have been recognised by people as diverse as the Gower Rural District Council, which collects its rents through Giro, and the Essex dairyman who uses it for his customers to pay their milk bills.

I was converted to the idea of a National Giro long before Labour took office in 1964 and among its other foremost advocates was Douglas Jay, who became President of the Board of Trade. When Tony Wedgwood Benn was told by Harold Wilson in 1963 that he would become Postmaster General if Labour was returned to office, he too took up the idea with enthusiasm. The time was ripe, for the Radcliffe Report on the Monetary System in the late 1950s had reported favourably on the idea although it was rejected by the then Government, despite the support of Mr Bevins, the Conservative Postmaster General. So when the Labour Government took office in October 1964, conditions were favourable for a reassessment.

The Giro has had to put up with much political prejudice as well as the antagonism of the clearing banks although, more lately, they seem to have come to terms with it. In consequence the Giro was established much later in this country than on the Continent.

Readers will find particularly interesting Professor Glyn Davies' ideas for future development, especially his proposal that the activities of the former Post Office Savings Bank (now the National Savings Bank) should be combined with those of the Giro. Such an institution would then have complete facilities for the transfer of funds, the taking of deposits from the public and the lending of funds—indeed all the facilities of the clearing banks and on a comparable scale. Both the Giro and the National Savings Bank enjoy the overwhelming advantage of the Post Office being available in or near every high street and housing estate. Such a development would bring the advantages of banking almost to the doors of millions of people who now never cross the threshold of the clearing banks. My hope is that either this Government or the next Labour Government will take up this proposal and so permit the new Bank/Giro to compete with the 'Big Four' Banks. I am sure it would give them a run for their money in the speed and efficiency of its service to its customers and in the cheapness of its facilities.

Professor Davies' book points firmly in this direction and I hope that one of the results of his work will be that the Post Office will turn itself into a fully fledged financial institution with all the functions of a bank. Certainly he has helped to clear away a lot of the ignorance about the system and he gives the Giro a fresh impetus. There may even be lessons in it for those who believe that the right way forward is to nationalise all the clearing banks.

House of Commons
10 July 1973

To Grethe

Preface

There are a number of reasons why I thought a book on National Giro might be necessary. First in importance was the fact that whereas books on money and banking abound, the one single book on this topic had been published in 1964 before National Giro was founded. A book written a decade later would be able to compare promise with performance in the context of a rapidly changing technology and of a financial environment which has similarly shown revolutionary changes in the recent past. Second, although there was a paucity of books on the subject, National Giro was nevertheless frequently at the centre of storms of controversy in Parliament and Press. The subject of Giro seems to be particularly prone to give rise to extreme comments: it has suffered equally from the excessive hopes of protagonists and the exaggerated fears of competitors. In most of these exchanges it was the short-term political aspects which were mainly emphasised, while longer-term economic and social factors were perhaps too often relegated to the background or completely ignored. Third, the campaign for a British Giro has roots that go far deeper than are revealed by a superficial examination, while the institution is also part of a concept that has world wide ramifications, which in view of the increasing integration of European economies, is becoming of growing importance.

It therefore seemed to me a useful, indeed a necessary exercise, to try to put the story of the origins and operations of National Giro into its historical and geographical perspective. Although perspectives can vary according to the standpoint of the viewer, I have attempted to give full factual evidence for justifying my position.

Economists quite rightly tend to take a wide and unblinkered view of the topics they investigate, bringing into the discussions aspects that others might not at first sight consider to be quite relevant. As an economist I have been an outsider looking in, but one that has been invited by Giro, by business firms large and small, and by central and local government departments to come in and take a closer but still unblinkered look. I have tried to relate what I have seen inside Giro to the changing economic and financial circumstances which are likely to influence its growth in the future, emphasising in particular the inter-relationships between Giro and its competing and complementary financial institutions.

National Giro was the first public sector bank to be established in Britain for over a century and it was the first bank in the world to be set up from its beginnings so as to give a fully computerised nationwide service. Its story deserves to be more widely known.

Glyn Davies

Acknowledgements

When Sir Julian Hodge endowed the Chair of Banking and Finance at UWIST he made provision also for a fund for furthering research into the science and practice of banking and finance. I am therefore pleased to begin at this primary source with my expressions of thanks for all the assistance which has been so generously given by numerous individuals and organisations in order to make this book possible.

The staff of National Giro have not only given me the utmost of co-operation, but have done so with an unfailing warmth, patience and kindness for which I am glad to take this opportunity of thanking them. I would particularly like to mention the help of Mr Donald Wratten, Director of National Giro; Mr Alastair Hanton, the Director of Organisation; Mr Harold Robson, Director of Marketing; Mr F T Roberts, Investment Controller; Mr John Stiles, Publicity Manager, and also his predecessor Mr Bob Hickman with whom I discussed my project in its early days. I hope that the many others within the Post Office in general, including the Post Office Records Office, and within National Giro, who have similarly been unstinting with their aid will fully appreciate that it is only considerations of space rather than lack of gratitude on my part that causes me to refrain from mentioning them individually.

The staff of postal Giros in Europe, Israel and Japan have similarly been most helpful, not only in sending me their reports and statistics, but also in answering a number of detailed enquiries, including a questionnaire on the profitability of their organisations. The resultant material had for the most part to be compressed into a single chapter, but I hope that in accepting my thanks the staff concerned will forgive me for having to condense their material into a space that fails to do justice to the generous provision of material.

A considerable part of the book is based on detailed case studies requiring individual interviews which naturally demanded much sacrifice of time and energy on the part of a number of individuals and organisations. In this connection I would like to thank Mr Clifford Jones, Borough Treasurer of Gower Rural District Council; Mr Tickle and Mr Purdy of Tickle's Dairies, Grays, Essex; Mr P B Wood and Mr E J

Smith of Associated British Foods Limited; Mr V A Maskens of J H Dewhurst Limited; Mr C J E James of the Provident Clothing and Supply Company; and Mr G H Wills and Mr M C Swift of Imperial Chemical Industries Limited; and the officials of the various government departments such as those for Health and Social Security and of Employment, who according to civil service convention remain anonymous.

To *The Banker, Euromoney* and the *Financial Times* I wish to express my thanks for permission to draw from four of my articles on Giro which they published during 1970–72. My indebtedness to other writers is indicated in the various references and footnotes. In addition however I would like to make special mention of *Hansard* and *Which* for permission to use material from these most helpful sources. I wish also to thank the Librarians of the Institute of Bankers, the British Museum and the Trades Union Congress for permission to make use of their admirable facilities.

I owe an especial debt of gratitude to the Rt Hon. James Callaghan for his kindness in contributing the Foreword, which is all the more fitting and welcome since, as Chancellor of the Exchequer when the vital decision was taken to establish the Giro, he retains a keen parental interest in its progress.

The excellent secretarial assistance of Miss Rosslyn Jones is most gratefully acknowledged—a model of co-operation with a gift for retrieving vital papers which seem to have an uncanny knack of disappearing underneath other papers as soon as they arrive on my desk.

On a personal, domestic note I would like to acknowledge that the index is provided thanks to the professional services of my eldest son, Roy Davies, BSc, while my wife, in addition to translating from the Scandinavian languages, has consistently encouraged and occasionally prodded me towards the completion of this work, despite the many sacrifices involved for herself and the family.

Contents

Figures

Tables

CONTENTS

Chapter 1

Giro in Historical Perspective

'Money is the wheel round which consumption follows production
and production follows consumption.'
Edward Solly, *Principles of Political Economy*, London, 1821.

BETTER LATE THAN NEVER

National Giro, the United Kingdom's new postal money transmission
service, began its business in October 1968—at least 100 years late! Of
all countries, Britain was easily the first to attain the position where a
modern, viable Giro system could have been established, yet it was the
last of the major European countries to do so. The first agricultural,
commercial and industrial revolutions had wrought their fundamental
changes a generation sooner in Britain than in any other country. Our
island had escaped the devastation of internal wars that had periodically
ravaged the European continent: our industrial and financial institutions,
though exposed to periodic commercial crises, enjoyed the enviable experience of operating against a background of peace and security lacking
abroad. In a survey made in the 1930s into the relative economic standing of the Great Powers at the end of the Napoleonic Wars, it was
claimed that: 'England had practically fifty years start of France. It had
about 200 years start of Germany'. [1] This view may have been exaggerated, but not all that much. More recent evidence taking into account
the results of the very considerable research into the economic progress
of continental countries that has been carried out since the 1930s given
by D S Landes in the *Cambridge Economic History of Europe*, confirms
the enormous lead that Britain had over most of the world in most
economic sectors throughout most of the nineteenth century. In mid-
century 'this little island, with a population half that of France, was

19

turning out about two-thirds of the world's coal, more than half of its iron and cotton cloth. . . . Her merchants dominated in all the markets of the world; her manufacturers feared no competition. . . . She was, in short, the very model of industrial excellence and achievement . . . a pace-setter to be copied and surpassed.' [2]

The two basic physical ingredients for the successful operation of a modern Giro system were an established Post Office with a network of branches covering the country, and a railway system linking all the main centres: these had achieved a high pitch of excellence in Britain before they did in any other country. Yet we were the last of the major European countries to establish a postal Giro system; seventy-five years after Austria; over sixty years behind Germany and Switzerland; and fifty years later than France, Italy and the Netherlands. Of course, British supremacy did not cover every field and our lead was overtaken in sector after sector after the third quarter of the nineteenth century. Nevertheless, nowhere during this period did our lead remain more pronounced than in the field of banking and finance. When other countries were going off silver on to gold, or debating the merits of bi-metallism, the Pound stood supreme and apparently unshakable. The Bill on London was becoming the main instrument of international trade, and the old unit country banking system was undergoing increasing amalgamation until the 'Big Five' banks emerged to hold two-thirds or so of the country's total deposits by 1918. Indeed, it was this clearly demonstrated excellence of the British banking system compared with that obtaining in most other countries that was partly, but only partly, the reason why Britain did not set up the kind of money transfer system that seemed so logical to so many on the Continent. In this regard continental emulation of British achievements culminated in the establishment of Giro systems long before Britain became convinced of the merits of flattery through imitation and availed herself of advantages in this direction, which had plainly been hers for the taking far longer than was the case elsewhere. But it took such an unnecessarily long time that there was ample justification for F P Thomson's scathing comment, written in 1964 in a book that did so much to present the British public with the case for Giro, that 'Whilst continental Europe is on the threshold of an internationally streamlined and super-efficient money-movement system which already has proved of immense financial, economic and social benefit to every country operating a post Giro system, Britain and the Commonwealth continue to be weighed down with archaic and inefficient methods which do not measure up to the needs of a scientific age.' [3]

However, in being the last major European country to establish a Giro, we became the first in the world to profit from the advent of the second industrial revolution by setting up a system which, from the outset, was geared to the possibilities of electronic accounting. The other major financial institutions had to adapt existing manual procedures to the new methods: National Giro was the first of the world's major financial institutions to establish itself right from the beginning along electronic lines. Whether a belated ultra-modern system with its corresponding costs and which has yet to expand its circle of customers up to viable proportions, will turn out to be as profitable as an old-fashioned system which has already built up a large clientele, but which has to modernise a system built on pre-computer lines, cannot yet be answered, though what evidence there is would seem to point to the interim conclusion that it is the custom that counts far more than the technical methodology. However, you cannot jump a gap in two hops: to obtain the glittering advantages of scale which the new system promised, National Giro geared itself for a million-sized market, considerably larger as it turned out, than could be attained in its first few years, but a market which when attained would guarantee its success. With a million or so customers National Giro would be a household word: with half a million or less its meaning remains obscure to most people— a strange and foreign-sounding intrusion into the British financial establishment.

MEANING OF GIRO

With Giro systems operating in over fifty countries ranging from the very poor like the Congo Republic and Madagascar, to the very rich like Britain and Sweden, and exhibiting a great diversity in financial customs and institutions, it is understandably difficult to define the concept concisely and unambiguously. But there are certain basic similarities in all the various kinds of Giro systems, which allows one to give a fairly typical illustration of what Giro essentially stands for. The word 'Giro' comes from the Greek 'Guros' meaning a ring, circle, revolution or circuit, a most apt designation, for the essential and distinguishing feature of Giro is the rapid transmission and circulation of money claims

21

to and from a single centre. Whereas typically, cash payment is anonymous and immediate and does not necessarily require the keeping of any accounts, all other forms of payment must normally be definitely identified by the name or number of the payer, or the recipient, or both: that is accounts have to be kept; and even at the fastest such payments, including the processes not only of recording but also of informing both parties to the transaction, are not quite immediate.

The overriding purpose of Giro is to create a payment system that is the safest, quickest and most economical non-cash payment system that can be devised with any given stage of technology. Typically, each Giro customer has a named or numbered account at the centre of the Giro system, allowing him to build up or draw down by means of a mailed instruction his own deposit as recorded at the Giro centre. Transfers to other named or numbered accounts or from other customers to his own account are made in similar fashion. All customers' monies are recorded and the bulk is kept at a single centre. The typical Giro is a single-centred, one-bank institution enabling a time-saving recording system for money transfers. But it normally has many more peripheral offices serving this single centre than even the largest of the commercial banks. For example, the British Post Office has over 20 000 offices equipped for Giro, compared with the average of 3000 branches for each of the 'Big Four' banks. Giro accounts are not kept at the local Post Offices, but at Giro centre, where the results of all transactions after electronic recording may be remitted by post direct to the participants' own home or office. Until very recently bank accounts were kept at the local branches: now they are, mostly, recorded electronically at the banks' major computer centres, while the results of each transaction are remitted to the customers' accounts either at the local bank offices or head office and are not normally remitted to the participants' own home or office.

It is important to bear in mind that whereas the ordinary banks provide an extraordinary range of services, the postal Giro system is essentially and primarily, though not exclusively, a simple money-transfer system. Admittedly, the banks are currently considering how to shed some of their more costly or exotic services, while Britain's National Giro is moving in the opposite direction and urgently exploring ways of combining this money transmission system with a number of other new services. Nevertheless, there is likely to remain a wide gap between the two kinds of institutions. Although strongly competitive over minor sectors and over part of their major money transfer service, basically the institutions are complementary rather than competitive and are likely to remain so in essence, simply because their main business has sufficient points of difference to render peaceful co-existence and co-operation a mutually advantageous policy. Though the circulation of money through the Giro system involves numerous tributaries and distributaries, who form the bank's peripheral customers, it is the single central pool or reservoir which provides the means whereby the whole system is operated, from which is derived any profit and through which speedy documentation and recording takes place. Decentralised postal transfer and centralised electronic accounting combine to attract those customers who attach a high value to speedy, simple, accurate and cheap financial transfers.

There is a close connection between the area which the central accounting office can cover and the speed of delivery of the documents recording the monetary orders of the debtors and creditors. Extensive nationwide centralisation of transfers could not become the rule until the railways speeded up the transfer process in a revolutionary fashion. Apart from the Ancient Egyptian system mentioned below, most of the Giro systems operating before the industrial revolution were therefore localised, with occasional dealings over wide areas limited to a few merchants of such exceptional wealth as to be of outstanding international credit-worthiness. The modern concept of Giro which has been in operation since 1883 is consequently dependent upon systems of communication the speed of which exceeded the wildest dreams of earlier generations. Generally speaking, it was therefore not until a rapid communications system had been built up, by which is meant both a railway network and a widely diffused Post Office system, that the modern system of Giro, so basically simple in concept, could become a physical possibility over areas large enough to comprise a whole country, and so become national institutions. But the principle of Giro, usually operating over more limited areas, extends back through the Middle Ages to the world of the ancient civilisations of Mesopotamia, Assyria, Egypt, Greece and Rome. The fact that the Greeks had a word for it, testifies not only to the basic simplicity of the Giro concept, but also is a pointer to the antiquity of the precursors of the modern system.

23

ORIGIN AND GROWTH OF GIRO

Giro in Egypt

'Money,' said Keynes, 'like certain other essential elements in civilisation, is a far more ancient institution than we were taught to believe some few years ago. Its origins are lost in the mists when the ice was melting, and may well stretch back into the paradisaic intervals in human history of the interglacial periods, when the weather was delightful and the mind free to be fertile of new ideas—in the Island of the Hesperides or Atlantis or some Eden of Central Asia.' [4] However, when it comes to authenticated records it was those dual cradles of civilisation, Egypt and Babylon, that were probably the centres in which embryo Giro systems first developed quite independently of each other. The origin of transfer payments to order developed naturally by stages arising from the centralisation of grain harvests in state warehouses in both Babylon and Egypt. Written orders for the withdrawal of separate lots of grain by owners whose crops had been deposited there for safety and convenience, or which had been compulsorily deposited to the credit of the king, soon became used as a more general method of payment for debts to other persons, the tax gatherers, priests, or traders. This system of warehouse banking reached its highest peak of excellence and geographical extent in the Egyptian Empire of the Ptolemies (323–30 BC). Private banks and royal banks using money in the form of coins and precious metals had long been known and existed side by side with the grain banks, but the former banks were used chiefly in connection with the trade of the richer merchants and particularly for external trade. Obviously, anything in strong demand by the state, the value and condition of which were carefully measured and guaranteed by a well-trained bureaucracy, became almost universally accepted in payment of debt. Long established private merchant-banks were almost entirely foreign and dominated in particular by the Greeks.

There was a wide gap between this smooth working system and the monetary habits of the native Egyptian population. The native Egyptian's reluctance to accept metallic money probably suited the Ptolemies' economic strategy very well. They seemed to be for ever short of the precious metals which were indispensable for foreign purchases and especially for external military expenditures, for which purpose they wished to drain Egypt internally of its precious metals (very much as the internal gold coinage of Europe disappeared to meet the demands of the First World War). Yet the Ptolemies wished to stimulate economic activity within Egypt and were fully aware that this would require more rather than less money. If they were short of monetary metal, which not only appeared too precious to be used widely for internal monetary use, but which in any case was not very popular with the natives, there was of course an abundance of grain—and grain had for centuries possessed a quasi-monetary character in Egypt. If the Greek expertise in banking could be adapted by the Egyptian bureaucracy to the peculiar preferences and habits of the indigenous population, then the Ptolemies would have the best of both worlds. This they did. Thus it was partly in order to economise on coinage that much greater use was made internally of grain for monetary purposes: and this meant a much fuller development of the system of warehouse-banking and grain transfers than had ever been previously achieved anywhere. Consequently, although some rudimentary elements of a Giro system of payment had developed much earlier in Babylon and Greece than in Ptolemite Egypt, undoubtedly the honour for the first full and efficient operation of that most important financial innovation that enabled a nationwide circulation and transfer of credit, belongs to the Egypt of the Ptolemies.

We have seen that most of the external and some of the internal trade of Egypt was carried on with the aid of Greek and other foreign bankers. It was with their aid that the Ptolemies transformed a scattered local warehouse-deposit system into a fully integrated state Giro of such a high standard of efficiency and sophistication so as to be almost beyond credence by modern man, who too readily assumes that the use of grain as money must necessarily imply a primitive economic system. However, Einzig in his survey of 'Primitive Money' shows that despite the fact that 'By that time private banks dealing in coined money were already highly developed,' nevertheless 'The Government granaries engaged in credit transactions of an even more diversified character than those of the private banks.' [5] It is perhaps for this reason that Preisigke, one of the most authoritative writers on banking developments in the ancient world, entitled his work 'The Giro System in Hellenistic Egypt'. [6] Rostovtzeff, another eminent Egyptologist, in his monumental study of *The Social and Economic History of the Hellenistic World* gives conclusive evidence that by means of the grain banks, the banking habit

25

had been greatly extended in Egypt: 'The accounts of the bank are especially interesting because they show how popular recourse to the banks became with the people of Egypt . . . the system of paying one's debts through the bank had the additional advantage of officially recording the transactions and thus providing important evidence in case of litigation' and of course greatly assisted the state in matters of economic and fiscal control. Rostovtzeff explains in considerable detail the accounting system of the private and royal grain banks, in order to make it crystal clear that 'the payments were effected by transfer from one account to another without money passing'. [7] Double entry bookkeeping had of course not yet appeared, but a system of debit and credit entries and credit transfers was recorded by varying the case endings of the names involved, credit entries being naturally enough in the genitive or possessive case and debit entries in the dative case. As already stated Rostovtzeff found it necessary to mention 'this detail in the bank procedure, familiar in modern times, because many eminent scholars have thought it improbable that such transfers were made in ancient times'. [8] The numerous scattered government granaries were transformed by the Ptolemies into a network of corn banks with what amounted to a central bank in Alexandria where the main accounts from all the state granary banks were recorded. The separate crops of grain harvested by the farmers were not separately earmarked, but amalgamated into general deposits, except that the harvests for separate years, and therefore of different qualities, were stored in separate compartments. [9] Seed corn was directly under the control of the state by means of an official appropriately termed the *Oeconomus*, whose duty it was to see that seed corn would not be used for any other purpose. Vagaries of the weather, though on occasions disastrous, were of course much less of a hazard in the Nile Delta than with us: so that inflation or deflation could to some extent be controlled and the monetary scarcity of one year be compensated by the bounty of the next. [10] Thus the Giro system in Egypt had come about because of the need to economise on coins and the precious metals, by the need to supplement the existing private banks with a state bank system and above all by the desire to spread the banking habit throughout the community. It also gave to the rulers a closer control over the economy for fiscal purposes, while providing a general stimulus for trade more widespread than had previously been possible, particularly among the poorer classes. In the new economic organisation of the

Ptolemies 'two systems were ... blended, so as to form one well-balanced and smoothly working whole: the immemorial practice of Egypt and the methods of the Greek State and the Greek private household.' [11] Grain may have been primitive money—but the world's first Giro system transformed it into an efficient medium of payments partaking of many of the most desirable features of modern money.

Banking in Babylon

As Egypt was the originator of Giro, so Babylon was probably the birthplace of banking—well over 3500 years ago. As in Egypt security for deposits was more easily assured in the temples and royal palaces than in private houses and so it was natural enough that the first banking operations were carried out by royal and temple officials. Grain was the main form of deposit at first, but in the process of time other deposits were commonly taken: other crops, fruit, cattle and agricultural implements, leading eventually and most importantly to deposits of the precious metals. Receipts testifying to these deposits gradually led to transfers to the order not of the depositors but to a third party. 'This was the way in which loan business originated and reached a high stage of development in Babylonian civilisation.' [12] In the course of time private houses began to carry on such deposit business and probably grew to be of greater importance internally than was the case in contemporary Egypt. Some of these were partnerships such as that of the famous house of Igibi and Maraschu. Literally hundreds of thousands of cuneiform blocks have been unearthed by archaeologists in the various city sites along the Tigris and Euphrates, many of which are deposit receipts and monetary contracts, confirming the existence of simple banking operations as everyday affairs, common and widespread throughout Babylonia. The Code of Hammurabi, law-giver of Babylon, who ruled from 1728–1686 BC, gives us categorical evidence, available for our inspection in the shape of inscriptions on a block of solid diorite standing over 7 ft high now in the Paris Louvre, showing that by this period 'Bank operations by temples and great landowners had become so numerous and so important' that it was thought 'necessary to lay down standard rules of procedure'. [13] In Babylon, however, the use of precious metals and later of coinage, became much more generally accepted than was the case in Egypt and consequently the peculiar kind of state Giro system based on grain did not reach so high a pitch of development in Babylon as it did in the Egypt of the Ptolemies.

Greece and Rome

Whether or not the invention of coinage by Gyges, King of Lydia, around 687 BC was, as Keynes remarked, merely an 'act of ostentation appropriate to the offspring of Croesus and the neighbours of Midas' [14], coinage became increasingly fashionable among the various states in the Middle East in the succeeding centuries and so created a demand for international money merchants among whom the Greeks, as we have seen in the case of Ptolemite Egypt, rose to a position of prominence. Early Greek bankers (known as Trapezites from the Greek name for their rectangular tables, much as our term 'Bank' comes from the Italian word for bench) were at first then little more than money changers, taking in deposits for safe-keeping and in course of time investing the proceeds either directly themselves or through loans to other merchants for various commercial purposes. As in most other things Athens was prominent in developing its banking facilities particularly to supplement its international trade. The continued close association of this primary aspect of banking with temple life is well known to us all through the episode of Christ's overturning the tables of the money changers in Jerusalem at the dawn of the Christian era. [15] Typical of the earliest Greek bankers was Pasion, who achieved a position of some importance in Athens in the fourth century BC. Roger Orsingher in his history and analysis of the major banks of the world shows how financial expertise in Ancient Greece developed from the cash fixation of bankers like Pasion to the much more flexible Giro system of the Bank of Delos of the later Helenic period. 'Banking in the Athens of Pasion was carried on exclusively in cash: deposit contracts, Giro transfers and receipts in writing do not appear to have been known at this period.' [16] However, by the time the Bank of Delos was in operation 'it was particularly interesting that transactions in cash were replaced by real credit receipts and payments made on simple instructions, with accounts kept for each client'. [17]

Delos rose to prominence during the late third and early second centuries BC. Its importance in banking history can hardly be exaggerated. As a barren off-shore island its people had to live off their wits and make the most of the island's two great assets—its magnificent harbour and the famous temple of Apollo. Around these its trading and financial activities grew to support a large and very cosmopolitan city of some 30 000 inhabitants, developing first as a centre of Aegean and later of Mediterranean commerce and banking and one of the principal clearing houses of the ancient world. It was an entrepot for the Macedonian trade in timber, pitch, tar and silver, the best place for the slave trade and the main western depot for eagerly sought oriental wares brought along the ancient caravan routes from Arabia, India and even China. We have well-documented continuous accounts as kept by its magistrates, recording its main banking and trading activities for over 400 years. Its economy was typical 'of that prevailing in the other temples which stood in close connection with the city' [18] but was probably the best of its type and one of the most enduring. Its direct interest to us stems from its being both an historical and geographical link in the development of banking business in general and Giro transfers in particular. It connected the early Greeks with the later Hellenistic and Roman banking eras and it provided the bridge which joined Italian traders and bankers of the West with those of the eastern Mediterranean and beyond. The Italian merchants who were attracted first for purely trading purposes became domiciled and rose to prominence as citizens of Delos, eventually taking over from the Greeks and becoming the most important bankers in the city, maintaining the closest links with the main centres of the rising Roman Empire.

In matters of culture and commerce, the Hellenistic and Roman Empires merged into each other with mixed results, some baneful and some beneficial. The early Greek colonies in Sicily and Southern Italy were replicas of Corinth and Delos; and we have seen how Roman citizens became increasingly important as merchants and bankers in Delos and over the Aegean islands. Their activities spread in similar fashion throughout the central and western Mediterranean, gradually extending into the interior of Gaul and Spain. For political reasons Rome destroyed Carthage and Corinth, the main commercial rivals of Delos, and in contrast until well into the first century BC strongly supported the economy of Delos, strengthening its position as one of the chief free ports of the Mediterranean. Consequently, it was a most natural outcome that the Bank of Delos became the model most closely and consciously imitated by the banks of Rome. The Greek 'Giro' or 'Incasso' system of transferring money claims without movement of

29

cash became, along with the other Greek banking methods, very well developed. The Roman bankers normally acted as intermediaries either to accept or make payments . . . if a sum paid in at Rome had to be paid out at some other town this could be done (simply) by an exchange of liabilities. [19]

However, despite the advanced development of private banking partly in conscious imitation of that of the Greeks and the Egyptians, no centralised state Giro system developed in the Roman Empire to compare with that which had been the case in Egypt. The Romans, however, were determined to try to unify the monetary system as far as possible and following their conquests they replaced the forty or more separate coinage systems of the Aegean in favour of the Attic standard. Consequently, Attic silver coinage became as popular over much of the Middle East and Asia Minor as the Maria Theresa dollar was to become in modern times. But the Romans either failed or did not attempt to establish a unified state banking system, despite evidence that Roman statesmen were well aware of the advantages that Egypt had gained from its Giro and from its royal state banking system. 'It is interesting', says Rostovtzeff, 'that the idea of a central state bank survived' and had it received more support it might well have become 'a credit institution for the whole of the Roman Empire'. [20] Rome and Constantinople became the main inheritors of the banking wisdom of the ancient world, which by means of the Roman conquest had become 'knitted together into one economic unit by the establishment of lasting and uninterrupted social and economic relations between the united West and the equally united East'. [21] The barbarian invasions brought the first prolonged and general breakdown of this unity and for some centuries after the fall of Rome the volume of trade declined drastically while banking over much of the Mediterranean reverted to little more than money changing. However, trade contacts with the East were renewed and maintained wherever possible, for piracy and wars in depleting the supply of oriental goods greatly increased their value. Foremost in renewing and maintaining such contacts were the Italian merchants, supplemented during the period of the Crusades onwards, by traders from further north and west, when, for example, the Knights Templar rose to prominence, not only as merchants but also as embryo bankers. But it is not without significance that it is to the city states of Northern Italy that we must go if we wish to see the re-emergence of banking on a level at all comparable with that which had been achieved by the Hellenistic and Roman Empires.

EMERGENCE OF MODERN BANKING

Economists and historians have tended for a number of reasons to underestimate the extent to which credit was used in medieval trade. However 'there cannot be many topics in the economic history of the Middle Ages on which the evidence is as copious as on credit'. [22] Examination of this evidence, especially by Professor Postan, has shown that credit, particularly for external trade, was so common as to be an everyday affair, and exhibited itself in a great variety of ways that testified to the skill and versatility of those involved. Wool was England's golden fleece and 'as far back as we can trace the activities of the English exporters . . . the transactions were commonly based on credit'. [23] From the tenth century onwards Lombard merchants began to trade with the Low Countries and with England and during the thirteenth and fourteenth centuries as well as the Flemings the great Italian houses achieved a position of prominence as merchants and bankers, particularly the Lombard houses of Bardi, Bocacci, Frescobaldi, Peruzzi and Ricardi, etc. Credit in anticipation of the wool crop was commonly made for a year or two ahead and sometimes even for as many as twelve years. The Italians became tax collectors for papal dues and bankers assisting the transactions of the medieval fairs. They helped to establish banks in the major towns of western Europe in imitation of those established in the city states of Northern Italy.

The periodic unreliability of some of these private banks and the recurrent complaints of their profiteering caused a reaction in favour of state or public banks, which supplanted or supplemented the private banks. One of the most important of these early banks 'whose business was very similar to that of modern banks' [24] was the Bank of Genoa, founded in 1585, which 'became a state within a state . . . the East India Company never held in England a position a quarter as great as that which (the bank) occupied at Genoa'. [25] Still more interesting from our point of view as a perpetuator of the term 'Giro' was the state institution set up after the failure of the private banks in Venice in 1587 and named, at first, the 'Banco di Rialto'. It was replaced in 1619 by the famous 'Banco del Giro' which carried on operations continuously right up to the nineteenth century when it was suppressed in 1806.

31

The third example of Italian banks, for these more than any others were the fathers of modern banking, was that of the House of Medici. Like other banks of the period, they commonly lent on the security of merchandise and evidence as to their activities both in Holland and London is given by W R Bisschop, a Dutch expert on early modern banking: 'Their method of lending money has been preserved, coupled with the name of the Lombards, in the Dutch word *lommerd*; and the arms of the house of Medici, viz. three gold balls, still denotes the abode of an ever helpful friend.' [26] Although indigenous banking developments were taking place in most of the principal towns of Europe as a natural step, this process was undoubtedly speeded up by the activities of foreigners—the Jews, the Italians and the Dutch—and by the middle of the sixteenth century the banking habit had so far developed in Lyons, for example, that Orsingher could claim that their 'system of accounts tended to reduce to a minimum the circulation of hard cash' so that the Lyons banks had already achieved 'an objective identical with that of the contemporary system of cheques and clearing houses'. [27]

England was one of the last of the western European countries to develop a comparable banking system and here again the Lombards and other foreigners operating from the street named after them played an important part. 'A strange quirk of Fate! Lombard Street, at one time a street reserved almost exclusively for foreigners, has today become a street of prestige, a synonym for power, the general headquarters of British high finance.' [28] Three features may be singled out for brief attention from among the many schemes for continental-type banks proposed in the second half of the seventeenth century: money transfer, pawnbroking and public ownership or at least public guarantee. The shocking state of our coinage made improvements in transfer imperative and these the new banks could offer. 'That admirable invention of a Bank', wrote Hartlib in 1653, 'is no other thing than the transmitting of the Ownership of money . . . from hand to hand by assignation only; without the danger and trouble of keeping, carrying or telling it'. [29]

Pawnbroking and banking were, as we have seen, closely connected, but in the half century of monetary experiments that preceded the foundation of the Bank of England in 1694, this system of making loans on the security of goods was preached almost as a gospel for extending the banking habit among the poorer section of the community. Such institutions were termed 'Lombard' or more commonly 'Lumbard' banks. Receipts for up to about two-thirds of the value of goods deposited in such banks came to be passed and accepted as money. Many of these originated as Banks of Piety or Charity Banks, though not all the Lombards had this welfare motivation. It was in particular the desire for a public or national bank like that of the fashionable Bank of Amsterdam that led eventually to the foundation of the Bank of England. As early as 1678 Dr Mark Lewis proposed a 'model' (the term has a distinctly modern ring) for a large public bank to rescue customers from the clutches of the goldsmiths. Even in the case of the Bank of England the two aspects of pawnbroking and internal money transfer were strongly advocated with varying results. The bank did in fact carry out a fairly considerable amount of pawnbroking in its first couple of years, but this appears to have been rather more a matter of meeting the liquid requirements of the rich than pawnbroking for the poor. Its power to accept pawns existed right up to the Bank Act of 1946, when all previous by-laws ceased to be effective: but it is interesting to see how powerful the Lombard lobby was in the last decade of the seventeenth century in that it could thus influence the business of the Bank of England itself. [30]

That underrated economist Daniel Defoe in his 'Essay on Projects' (1697) suggested a scheme for money transfer throughout Britain using the Inland Bill of Exchange, which would be accepted by all the participating banks strategically situated across the land. Like Lewis and other contemporary writers he proposed that a series of strong banks similar to the Bank of England should be set up in each of the main trading centres of the country and that the Bank of England should establish a separate department to deal with the Inland Bills which the growing business of these provincial banks would generate. However, despite repeated demands from the provinces, the Bank of England remained firmly fixed in London for another 130 years, so that Defoe's idea of a national integrated banking and money transmission service remained a dream. He was correct, however, in his anticipation of a vast increase in the use of Inland Bills of Exchange, but these were traded between the weak unit banks of England and Wales (in contrast to the strong joint-stock Banks of Scotland) and the London money market and not directly with the Bank of England. By the time the Banco del Giro ended and the Bank of England at last began to set up branches in the provinces, early experiments in steam locomotion were beginning to show their

33

revolutionary possibilities. Eventually, after the legislative reforms of 1826, 1833 and 1844, the country banking system gave way to a more united amalgamated joint-stock banking system. The Inland Bill slowly declined as the cheque system expanded. The postal reforms of Rowland Hill took only partial advantage of the coming of the railways: they were never carried to their logical conclusion in the money transfer field, partly no doubt (as we shall see in the next chapter) because the British railway system, despite his powerful advocacy, failed to become state owned until after the Second World War. The chequing facilities of the banks remained the prerogative of the middle and upper classes: the working class in general had no accounts with the clearing banks and had to make do with a postal money transfer service which, compared with what it might have been, remained half-baked, cumbersome and expensive. So National Giro came on the scene a century late—whether in so doing it arrived too late to be profitable is a matter to which we return in a later chapter.

FULL CIRCLE

The concept of a simple money transfer service for a large part of the population has recurred in various forms throughout recorded history. A tenuous line, almost unbroken, connects the Giro of Ancient Egypt with that of modern times. Despite all the differences between these various concepts of Giro, there were certain recurring common elements, though the particular emphasis given to one or other of these differed from time to time and place to place. Among these were as we have seen: the need to economise on cash payments; to fill gaps left by the private banking sector; to increase competition and reduce profiteering among the private banks; to give the state greater command over the financial resources of its subjects; to provide a glorified pawnbroking system, and so on. The first four of these motives have been prominent as determinants of our modern Giro system: and when due allowance is made for the different economic background of seventeenth and twentieth century England, even pawnbroking as a method of attracting the poorer classes may be considered as not too dissimilar in its basic concept to National Giro's indirect link with the hire purchase of consumer durables. But there is one fundamental way in which the modern system differs from those of earlier ages. In previous times a simple money transmission service was inevitably part and parcel of a number of other banking services. Only with the coming of the railways was it possible for a system of money transfer alone, divorced from other banking services, to be profitable. This does not mean that Giro services have to be separate from other banking services, merely that modern communications systems made it possible for them to operate profitably, even when separately accounted for. But this discovery we owe to the Austrians, for though we had all the ingredients, we deliberately refrained from putting them together. The Austrians looked with considerable envy at the British Post Office and particularly at its Savings Bank idea: they also realised that the new speed of communications made possible by the railways—'England's gift to the world' [31]— could complete the cycle of money transfers faster and cheaper than ever before. The wheel had turned full circle: modern Giro had arrived.

REFERENCES

1   KNOWLES, L C A, *Economic Development in the Nineteenth Century* (London, 1932), p. 160.
2   LANDES, D S, *Cambridge Economic History of Europe* (Cambridge, 1966), p. 274.
3   THOMSON, F P, *Giro Credit Transfer Systems* (London, 1964), p. xiii.
4   KEYNES, J M, *A Treatise on Money* (London, 1935), Vol. 1, p. 13.
5   EINZIG, PAUL, *Primitive Money* (London, 1966, 2nd Ed.), p. 201.
6   PREISIGKE, F, *Girowesen in Griechischen Aegypten* (Strasbourg, 1910).
7   ROSTOVTZEFF, M, *The Social and Economic History of the Hellenistic World* (Oxford, 1941), p. 1285.
8   ROSTOVTZEFF, M, *ibid.*, p. 1285.
9   PREISIGKE, F, *op. cit.*, p. 69.
10   ROSTOVTZEFF, M, *op. cit.*, p. 279.
11   ROSTOVTZEFF, M, *ibid.*, p. 272.
12   ORSINGHER, ROGER, *Banks of the World: A History and Analysis* (Paris, 1964; English translation London, 1967), p. 1.
13   ORSINGHER, ROGER, *ibid.*, p. viii.
14   KEYNES, J M, *op. cit.*, p. 12.
15   ST MATTHEW, Chapter 21, verse 12.
16   ORSINGHER, ROGER, *op. cit.*, p. 4.
17   ORSINGHER, ROGER, *ibid.*, p. 4.
18   ROSTOVTZEFF, M, *op. cit.*, p. 233.
19   ORSINGHER, ROGER, *op. cit.*, p. 9.
20   ROSTOVTZEFF, M, *op. cit.*, p. 1288.
21   ROSTOVTZEFF, M, *ibid.*, p. 1019.
22   POSTAN, M M, 'Credit and Medieval Trade', in *Essays in Economic History*, edited by E M Carus-Wilson (London, 1954), p. 63.

23 POSTAN, M M, *ibid.*, p. 67.
24 ANDREADES, A, *History of the Bank of England* (London, 1966, 4th Ed.), p. 76.
25 ANDREADES, A, *ibid.*, p. 79.
26 BISSCHOP, W R, *The Rise of the London Money Market: 1648–1826* (London, 1968), p. 36.
27 ORSINGHER, ROGER, *op. cit.*, p. 18.
28 ORSINGHER, ROGER, *ibid.*, p. 38.
29 RICHARDS, R D, *The Early History of Banking in England* (London, 1929), p. 105.
30 HORSEFIELD, J K, *British Monetary Experiments: 1650–1710* (London, 1960), p. 111. See also R D Richards' *The Early History of Banking in England* (London, 1929), p. 173, where he states that 'It is interesting to note that under its by-laws the Bank can still, if it so desires, take pawns'. I am indebted to Mr Leslie Dicks-Mireaux of the Bank of England for pointing out that although Richards was correct when he wrote this book in 1929, the Act of 1946 has finally put paid to the Bank's pawnbroking powers.
31 TREVELYAN, G M, *English Social History* (London, 1944), p. 535.

Chapter 2

The Silent Demand

'The principle of the Post Office at its establishment, as is
distinctly laid down in 12 Charles II, was to afford advantage
to trade and commerce. The direct revenue to be derived
from the Post Office was not the primary consideration.' [1]

INTRODUCTION: ROWLAND HILL AND THE RAILWAYS

Hidden among its seventy-five miles of shelving and standing high
among the uniformly bound rows of Parliamentary Papers in the State
Paper Room of the British Museum is to be found the evidence to
support the suggestion made in the previous chapter that had Rowland
Hill's proposed reforms been carried out with regard to the railways as
they had with such success in the case of the Post Office, then a postal
Giro system would very possibly have come into being in the United
Kingdom somewhere around the 1870s. State ownership of the railways
is by no means a prerequisite for the establishment of a postal Giro
system, but the experience of other countries would indicate that it
helped in bringing together the two essential sides of rapid money
transfer and focusing them as an issue of public policy. However, as we
shall see, Rowland Hill's drive faltered when it came to pressing the case
for state purchase of the railways. Before looking at the reasons for his
lack of success in this field, closely related as it was with reforms in
postal communications in which he had been pre-eminently successful,
it is necessary for us to turn our attention to the more general picture of
improvements in money transmission in the Victorian age and the
reasons why certain of its inadequacies were largely ignored right up to
the first decade of the twentieth century. The foundations of our modern
financial system, a system that has achieved enduring renown throughout
the world, were laid during the Victorian age and consequently there has

been a pardonable tendency for people to assume that the enviable strength of the British financial system at the end of the Victorian era extended back into the earlier generations in the mid-nineteenth century, even though that was, in point of fact, a time when the failure of banks was accepted as an almost inevitable accompaniment to the periodic financial crises that interrupted the surging progress of those eventful years. Obviously, the most spectacular single improvement in money transmission was the speeding up of the process through the development of a network of railways. It took time to appreciate the wide-ranging benefits which such a rapid transit system could provide, but the Post Office as well as the banks and other financial institutions gradually learned to take fuller advantage of this new rapid method of communication, without however going so far as to advocate, let alone to establish, a Giro system.

ADEQUACY OF MONEY TRANSMISSION SERVICES IN THE NINETEENTH CENTURY

The national attitude in the mid-Victorian era with regard to the bases of our monetary system was complacent and self-satisfied in the extreme. Frank Whitson Fetter in his careful examination of the development of British monetary orthodoxy, quotes an anonymous publication of 1869 which eminently sums up this attitude: 'If a committee of twelve or twenty good business men (I don't mean philosophers or professors) could be selected, and were to study the subject closely for a twelve-month, and could find a plan that could compare with our British coinage and currency (or, in comparison, to come within a hundred miles of it), the writer would be willing to submit to any forefeiture of penalty or liberty.' [2] Despite such optimism, the fact remained that the means of payment and their transmission lagged behind a rapidly rising demand throughout the nineteenth century. Overdue reforms, when they eventually appeared, seemed to meet the situation for a time, usually long enough to take the wind out of the sails of the reformers, but the solutions were often revealed in retrospect as temporary palliatives, and so were soon overtaken in their turn by the growing pressures for new developments, particularly with regard to the millions of very small payments made by the rapidly growing working class, whose ineffective demand provided no *profitable* urge for free enterprise to develop improved money transfer services. Ever since the severe financial crisis of 1826 right up to 1914 the smallest bank notes, whether local or Bank of England, were for £5—vastly beyond the average weekly wages throughout the country. Thus cash wages for adult male agricultural workers averaged only about 14s a week as late as the 1870s [3] and official inquiries showed that this average was barely exceeded in the first decade of the twentieth century, being only 14s 9d in 1907. [4] Similarly, Sidney Pollard's researches indicate that in 1911, including their families, some 8 million, out of a total population for Great Britain of 40·8 million, were dependent on the heads of the families receiving less than 25s a week. [5] It was not, therefore, until money wages and real wages rose substantially in the twentieth century that the chronic inadequacy of money transmission services for a large section of the community became thoroughly exposed.

It has been a generally accepted thesis of our monetary history that only the development of the inland bill of exchange in the first half of the century and the growth in popularity of the cheque in the second part of the century, dependent as they were on the rise of country banking in the first instance and joint-stock and deposit banking in the latter, prevented Britain from being crucified on a cross of gold. The restrictions of the famed banking legislation of 1844 may well have helped to prevent inflation, a view that was authoritatively confirmed by the Radcliffe Committee's Report on the Working of the Monetary System, who considered the 1844 Act 'One of the pillars of the English monetary system' which 'remained on the Statute Book because the ceiling it fixed for the Fiduciary Issue had become to be regarded as an assurance against any collapse of the value of the pound'. [6] Yet it is clear that the 1844 legislation leaned too far in a deflationary direction and by gravely restricting the expanded note issues, whether by the Bank of England or by the joint-stock banks, that the growing economy required, acted as a general brake on progress, which, however, only became obvious to all during the recurring monetary crises. In the peripheral industrial regions, in glaring contrast to the generally complacent attitude of the City of London, the baneful restrictions of the full gold standard were a more constant target for criticism. Thus George Anderson, Member of Parliament for Glasgow, in the course of a parliamentary debate on money and banking in 1873 [7] complained that: 'We have set up gold for our idol—we worship it with a senseless superstition. . . . More poverty, more misery, more broken hearts and more desolated homes, are due to this one cause than to all the others put together.' The sovereign and half-sovereign were undoubtedly some of the finest examples of the art of minting in numismatic history, but where money is concerned quantity is normally of greater importance than quality. From time to time there was a shortage of these excellent gold coins in relation to demand and Goschen, Chancellor of the Exchequer from 1887 to 1892, had to make heroic attempts to popularise silver coins in their place, but with only limited success. Thus as late as 1889 'despite a somewhat unsatisfactory issue of large silver coins ostensibly in celebration of the 1887 Golden Jubilee, Goschen was (still) encouraging the greater use of silver' [8], since it would have been too costly to recoin the estimated 50% of gold circulation that was below the legal weight.

Gold coinage was an expensive luxury which reflected and intensified the limitations on the issue of bank notes and made it all the more necessary for the banks and the Post Office to invent new methods of money transmission, even though these were to remain inadequate for a large section of the population, at least until the postal order system became popular during the last few decades of the nineteenth century. Pressnell, the historian of the country banks, has clearly demonstrated how the desperate need for remittance facilities (together with industrialists' needs for coins to pay wages and the legal profession's need to find safe homes for surplus funds) was one of the three main forces leading to the rapid rise of country banking, especially the remittance of funds between the surplus agricultural counties and the growing industrial centres via the City of London, whether by drovers, traders or collectors of government revenue. [9] The weaknesses and the uneven geographic spread of country banking have been so frequently stressed, both by contemporaries and by later authoritative researchers, that there exists clear and ample evidence of a dire need for a more reliable and efficient means of money transmission during much of the century. Admittedly, in some respects the failures of the country banks have probably been overemphasised, for given the connection with the private banks and agents in London, the country banks, most of which became absorbed with the joint-stock banks in the later part of the nineteenth century, formed an integral working system in which inland bills formed at first the main instrument for money transmission, followed gradually by the cheque. However—and this is the main point of relevance to any history of Giro—the banks' customers were the business, middle and upper classes: they hardly touched the working classes, who were dependent on the patchy facilities of the Friendly Societies and the Trustee Savings Banks for their savings deposits (until Gladstone's Post Office Savings Act of 1861), and on the Post Office for transmitting their monies. In so far as the majority of the poorer people were concerned, the improvements of the main monetary media on which the increasing trade of the Victorian era depended—bank notes, bills of exchange, bank deposits subject to cheque—were beyond their purses and largely beyond their ken.

CURRENT-ACCOUNT DEPOSITS AND CHEQUES

The joint-stock banks, as they grew and amalgamated, almost literally in line with the railways, were a considerable improvement on most of the country banks and to a very large extent they met the demands of the rapidly growing middle class, supplementing rather than supplanting the older private banks. It is indeed of some importance to note that the very fact that these new banks catered very successfully for the growing demands of the lower middle classes, prevented the working classes from having powerful allies in demanding a money transmission service geared for universal use. The expert evidence given before the Select Committee of the House of Commons on the Bank Act, 1858, not only emphasised the growth of these new joint-stock banks, but also stressed the fact that they were extending the bank habit to the lower middle classes. For example, Mr Edward Cardwell, a Director of the London and Westminster Bank, in reply to a question as to whether his bank had received deposits from small depositors, answered 'A very large amount'. [10] His answer to the next question was also illuminating in this respect: 'Do you consider that these deposits have been withdrawn by you from other bankers, or that the institution of joint-stock banks has given rise to a new class of deposits?—I should say that almost the whole of our business describes new business, persons probably who had not banked before; and new connexions, persons who have gone into business within the last twenty-four years. A very inconsiderable portion, indeed, is the transfer of accounts from private bankers to the joint-stock banks.' [11] Thus, when the prosperous Victorian middle classes were so well catered for by the cheque system, why should they bother about new means of money transmission such as a postal Giro system? In Britain, therefore, it was not merely the vested interest of the bankers, but also the satisfied and substantially growing body of their customers who saw little reason for a new money transmission service such as the Giro, at least until well on into the twentieth century. Because the money transmission service was so thoroughly improved during the latter part of the nineteenth century so far as the most affluent section of the community was concerned, then any inadequacies of the system as a whole for most of the people tended to be overlooked.

In Britain much more than on the Continent there was a division between the various classes of society with regard to the adequacy of transmission services. The excellence of the money transmission service provided by British banks for their customers was of course a direct result of their decision to act as *banks of deposit*, rather than as *industrial bankers* as was the case with continental banks, particularly those in Austria, Germany and France. The higher liquidity of British banks meant less direct involvement in industry and much more concentration on meeting the short-term needs of their customers, including the provision of a swift and efficient payment system. It has been insufficiently recognised that the inevitable counterpart of the long history of complaints by academics and industrialists that British banks failed to do all that they should to assist the development of British industry was this counter-emphasis on an efficient transfer payment system. Long-term lending to industry, as on the Continent, needed to be safe-guarded by longer-term, fixed and savings deposits: conversely, short-term lending and the keeping of adequate liquidity to support a large cheque payment business inevitably meant less participation by British banks in the competition for savings deposits, but more competition for demand deposits. One of the few authors to recognise the plain fact of the necessary interdependence of the two sides of the balance sheet was Geoffrey Crowther, who while rather reluctantly conceding that British banks might do more to help industry, nevertheless believed that: 'If a choice must be made between the different functions of a bank, the most important is that it should provide a stable and convenient means of making payments. There are other ways of providing industry with capital; but the modern world knows no more efficient form of money than is provided by the bank deposit.' [12] (Evidently, he appeared ignorant of the advantages of a Giro system, which receives no mention in the work quoted.)

Because the continental banks were much more directly concerned with the development of industry then, again as an inevitable consequence, they gave much less priority to the development of deposit banking and the cheque payment system. The interesting result of this was, of course, that on the Continent all classes of the community tended to be much more united in demanding improvements in their money transmission services, so that they came to welcome much more widely the idea of a postal Giro system and also to make much more use of it when it was established, precisely because their banks were as inadequate in this direction in continental eyes as British banks were inadequate with regard to industrial development in British eyes. However, large numbers of people in Britain, including the vast majority of the working class, were unable to use the excellent transmission service that the banks had built up, and they had to campaign almost alone for a postal Giro system anything like that which had been common on the Continent for two or three generations. Thus the way in which the British banking system developed during the second half of the nineteenth century helps to explain why the case for a Giro system in Britain was, to an extent unusual when compared with continental Giro systems, mainly the result of pressure from the political left. This incipient polarisation along political party lines of support for a state sponsored money transmission service was to become, as we shall see, a recurrent theme in the history of National Giro. It helps to explain the narrow base within Britain of the movement in its favour and accounts for the almost incredible delay in setting up such a system, which had to wait upon the gradual support coming from wider sections of the community before it could ever hope to become an accomplished fact. It also meant that any developments in such payment transfer systems, when and if the state stepped in to fill the gaps, would in Britain be at first narrowly conceived as a charitable or welfare provision for the poorest section of the community rather than in the form of an efficient economic provision for universal use.

Finally, it meant that a postal Giro system was bound to be faced with a much more united opposition from the British joint-stock banks than was generally the case on the Continent, for a postal Giro in the United Kingdom would inevitably compete to a much greater extent than on the Continent with one of the joint-stock banks' main services. In view of this long-standing and united strength of the opposition by British banks, it may be difficult for us to envisage the early and strong support even from bankers and Chambers of Trade on the Continent for setting up a postal Giro system, yet there is clear evidence on this point. For instance, Mr G Hammerby, in a recent book on the Danish Giro, writes that: 'The (commercial) banks were in favour of the idea' and that 'Among the firm supporters of the Giro concept was L A Grundtvig, Professor of Law at Copenhagen, who encouraged a lively agitation in the provinces among the Chambers of Trade, of which he himself was the General Secretary.' [13] In Britain the case for Giro did not become explicit until after the emergence of the big monopolistic joint-stock banks around the turn of the century. If Rowland Hill had managed to achieve his ambition of seeing the railways purchased by the state, as he had attempted to do in a period when local unit banking had not yet been amalgamated into London-based deposit banking, some form of Giro system might well have come about in Britain in the 1870s or shortly thereafter. His failure to do so left the Post Office heavily burdened with railway charges that seriously impeded its development in certain key respects when compared with the situation on the Continent.

LAISSER-FAIRE, THE POST OFFICE AND THE RAILWAYS

One of the more surprising paradoxes of the nineteenth century was that this classical age of laisser-faire saw in fact a tremendous strengthening of monopolies in certain directions, including in particular the Post Office, in contrast to the general dismantling of monopolies in other directions. Thus the monopoly granted by Charles II to the Post Office was greatly intensified during the heyday of laisser-faire because the coming of the railways coupled with Rowland Hill's brilliant concept of uniform and cheap postal facilities made the operation of an almost complete monopoly economically feasible for the first time. Two years before the coming of the Penny Post in 1840, a House of Commons Committee had shown that: 'On certain routes the majority of correspondence was illicit; e.g. five-sixths of the correspondence between London and Manchester was transmitted through private agents.' [14] Lord Robbins has clearly demonstrated, in his trenchant analysis of the economic functions of the state, that it is the result of a popular but nevertheless mistaken mythology to jump to the conclusion that belief in laisser-faire automatically ruled out consideration of state ownership or control, whether of the railways or any other economic activity, in the nineteenth century. On the contrary there was a tendency to examine each case on its merits rather than to indulge in a blanket condemnation of state ownership. [15] However, even if laisser-faire was never the simple concept to its contemporaries that it appears so frequently in retrospect, there can be little doubt that its general philosophy of minimum government played its part in ruling out any early form of postal Giro in Britain.

Perhaps one of the clearest and fairest contemporary pictures of the Victorian attitude towards laisser-faire is that given by John Stuart Mill in his *Principles of Political Economy* in which he attempts to explain the reason for the Victorian ambiguity towards government control: 'We must set out by distinguishing two kinds of intervention by the Government'. First 'authoritative interference' and second 'there is another kind of intervention which is not authoritative, for example, when leaving individuals free to use their own means of pursuing any object of general interest, the government establishes an agency of its own for a like purpose. There might be a national bank, without any monopoly against private banks. There might be a post office without penalties against the conveyance of letters by other means. . . . The only cases in which government agency involves nothing of a compulsory nature are the rare cases in which, without any artificial monopoly, it pays its own expenses, for example, the government railways in Belgium and Germany. The Post Office, if its monopoly were abolished and it still paid its expenses, would be another.' [16] However, when every allowance has been made for the complexity of the concept of laisser-faire there is no doubt in which direction the general bias lay. To Mill, as to many of his contemporaries, state ownership was presumed guilty and the onus of proof of its beneficence or innocence rested squarely on the state department or institution itself: 'Laisser-faire, in short, should be the general practice. Every departure from it, unless required by some great good, is a certain evil'. [17]

Rowland Hill, justly famed all over the world as the founder of the national Penny Post, had become convinced not only by his unrivalled experience in postal matters (which as we have seen was based on an intensification of its original monopoly powers), but also by his twenty-five years as Chairman of the Brighton Railway Company, that competition between the hundreds of railway companies in Great Britain constituted an intolerable waste of resources, was inimical to efficient management and disadvantageous to the profitability and usefulness of the modern postal service that he loved and that he had done more than anyone else to establish. He saw a vital need for state purchase and control of the railways, which would dovetail perfectly with his plans for still further improvements in postal services. Given the complexity of contemporary views regarding the role of the state, Hill's suggestion that the railways should be nationalised was therefore not quite as unthinkable, nor quite as rare, as modern readers might imagine. Hill seized with his customary alacrity the opportunity which presented itself when he was chosen in 1865 as a member of the Royal Commission to look into the matter of the relationship between the railways and the state, a subject ripe for decision since the Railway Act of 1844 had stipulated such a review after twenty-one years. The Commission issued its voluminous Report and Minutes of Evidence, including as might have been expected Rowland Hill's strongly worded minority report, in 1867. 'Finding that, amongst the recommendations contained in the Report there are several in which I cannot concur, and being further of the opinion that measures of a more decided character are required to effect a radical cure of existing ills, I have felt it my duty to present my opinions on such points in a separate Report.' [18] He went on to claim that 'Experience has now shown that railways are essentially monopolies; consequently they are in my opinion, not suitable objects for ordinary commercial enterprise. It seems to follow that they should be in the hands of those who will control the management of them with a view to the interests of the country at large, that is to say, in the hands of the government.' [19] Among the benefits would be a large reduction in the fares of passengers and in the freight of goods, increased postal revenue and a considerable improvement in postal facilities. Rowland Hill had arranged to get his brother, Mr Frederic Hill, Assistant Secretary to the Post Office, Mr Edward Page, Inspector General of Mails and Mr Gregory, the Arbitrator for the Post Office, to present strong evidence to the Commission as to the deleterious effect of railway competition on the revenues and on the facilities provided by the Post Office.

The Royal Commission gave full and careful consideration both to the major question of the transfer of the railways to the state (they certainly did not prejudge the issue because of any doctrinaire attachment to laisser-faire) and to the need for improvements in postal services and revenues. Regarding the former they came to the firm conclusion that: 'It is inexpedient at present to subvert the policy which has hitherto been adopted, of leaving the construction and management of railways to the free enterprise of the people, under such conditions as Parliament may think fit to impose for the general welfare of the public.' [20] With regard to better and cheaper postal communications, although they observed that 'on the continental railways the government has conceded the lines to the railways on the condition that the mails are to be carried free' they could not bring themselves to advocate such a drastic step, contenting themselves rather with mildly recommending that 'a general Act of Parliament be passed to define all those points which have given rise to difficulties between the Postmaster General and the railway companies'. [21] The baneful effect of railway pricing policy on postal development is clearly illustrated with regard to Hill's long-standing suggestion for a uniform parcel post. Despite the strong advocacy of the Royal Commission, who fully supported Hill's proposed scheme for the carriage of parcels, it was to take sixteen long years to carry out their recommendation and even then it was done in so grudging and costly a way that not only were the Post Office finances adversely affected, but the service grew at a much slower pace than Hill had hoped for decades previously. Rowland Hill had always maintained that 'the excessive cost of the railway carriage of mails' was 'one of the reasons for the great drop in the net revenue' when the Penny Post was first introduced. [22]

History was repeating itself with regard to the Parcel Post. The Post Office, prompted by the International Postal Union Conference in 1880, renewed its negotiations with the railways regarding a parcel post, but 'the railways held out for better terms. When an agreement was reached in 1882, the arrangements were embodied in an Act that gave the railways 55% of the postage collected on parcels. It was a hard bargain, and the government had again to pay too high a price for the expansion of its services.' [23] So Britain belatedly adopted a uniform inland parcel post in 1883, the same year that Austria introduced postal Giro to the modern world. Hill's main ambition, therefore, failed with regard to state railways, since with one partial exception, members of the Commission were all strongly opposed to such a revolutionary change. (The partial exception was Mr Monsell, MP, who somewhat illogically wished the state to purchase the Irish railways, but not necessarily those of Great Britain.) However, even had the Committee thought otherwise the strong representation of the railway interest in Parliament would almost certainly have thrown out any Bill proposing such a scheme of state purchase. Henry Parris in his detailed examination of the relationship between the state and the railways (although he surprisingly deals only cursorily with the 1867 Report) reminds us that 'Among the most important facts of Parliamentary life was the strength of the interests represented there . . . especially the railway interest. The conflicting aims of the companies prevented it achieving very much positively to promote the welfare of the railways in general: but as a negative force, united in opposition to measures of regulation, it was to be reckoned with.' [24]

Perhaps another factor which worked against the acceptance of Rowland Hill's advocacy was his very success in revolutionising the Post Office over the heads and against the advice of its own officials. Anthony Trollope, the celebrated Victorian novelist, who gave thirty-three of the best years of his life to the Post Office and who made his mark in postal history by introducing the pillar box to Britain, was, according to his autobiography, 'always an anti-Hillite'. He gave a character sketch of the Hill brothers that might help to explain why these prophets had less honour in their own country than abroad: 'With him (Rowland Hill) I never had any sympathy, nor he with me. In figures and facts he was most accurate, but I never came across anyone who so little understood the ways of men—unless it was his brother Frederic. To the two brothers the servants of the Post Office—men numerous enough to have formed a large army in old days—were so many machines who could be counted on for their exact work without deviation as wheels may be counted on, which are kept going always at the same pace and always by the same power. Rowland Hill was an industrious public servant, anxious for the good of his country; but he was a hard taskmaster, and one who would, I think, have put the great department with which he was concerned altogether out of gear by his hardness, had he not been at last controlled.' [25]

Rowland Hill had always been extremely sensitive to the charge frequently made by his detractors that he had grossly underestimated the cost of introducing his postal reforms: indeed, he himself later admitted that he had been 'over sanguine' in this regard, but blamed the railways more than his own optimism. There were many petty attacks on him over this that would have done justice to the most unadventurous of modern civil servants reaching for a dismal cost-benefit analysis to support his proverbial caution. Hill, however, regarded the estimates of loss in the early years of penny postage to have been exaggerated and the profits of the later years to have been underestimated. He tried to explain the reasons for these differences in a *Memorandum on the Net Revenue of the Post Office* in 1862: 'Much difference of opinion has arisen as to the amount of net revenue or profit of the Post Office department, that is the excess of receipt over expenditure; some estimating it at upwards of £1 500 000 per annum, others affirming that it is really less than £400 000.' [26] The net revenue of 1839, the year before the start of the Penny Post, was not in fact exceeded until 1875. But to base one's judgement of the greatest revolution in the history of postal communications on this narrow financial level would be to ignore its enormous economic and social contributions as indicated by the round figure of 1000 million letters carried in the latter year.

RAILWAY PRICING POLICY IN RETROSPECT

Recent detailed research by P S Bagwell into the history of the railways' pricing policy lends strong confirmation to Hill's statement that 'the ill-judged opposition of the railway companies remained a constant obstacle to any improvement which required Parliamentary sanction'. [27] Bagwell shows that Hill was not an eccentric extremist in blaming the railways for inhibiting postal development, but that he was supported by a wide range of opinion. Edwin Chadwick, the Royal Society of Arts, and the Association of British Chambers of Commerce, had long campaigned for improved postal services, including Hill's idea of a uniform parcel delivery. Hill did manage to get a cheap book post started in 1853 and a 'samples' post ten years later—both of which were blatantly used for general parcels purposes. A Post Office memo of 1871 proved that fully half of the 'samples' were falsely so described. The International Postal Conference held at Paris in 1878 showed that in a number of key sections Britain's lead in postal developments had been overtaken. 'The Postmaster General was under strong pressure.

. . . The Association of Chambers of Commerce was again on the war-path demanding that the British Post Office should provide at least as good a service as that provided in Germany where parcels of up to 140 lb were accepted . . . and where the railways were under the legal obligation to carry parcels under 20 lb weight free of charge.' [28] Far from being carried free of charge, the British private railways, through their clearing house, demanded fully 60% of the postage rate but eventually, with great reluctance, settled, as we have seen, for 55%, thus forcing the Postmaster General to 'give the railways a much larger proportion than was warranted by the service they rendered', higher than anything on the Continent, despite their lower postage rates. [29] The considered opinion of the historian on the Railway Clearing House is that 'There are sound reasons for claiming that had it not been for the existence of the Railway Clearing House the British public would have been provided with a satisfactory and inexpensive parcels delivery service some twenty or thirty years earlier than was in fact the case.' [30]

In the face of the private railways' united monopoly power the arbitration machinery was little more than a legal facade. Another relevant and carefully-researched recent work, by Mr G R Hawke, concludes that 'The pricing policy of railways in England and Wales before 1881 was basically that of discriminating monopoly with company profit as the major aim'. [31] Hawke shows that the argument between the Post Office on the one hand, and the railways, the Royal Commissioners and the arbitrators on the other hand, was, in modern terminology, a conflict as to whether *marginal* or *average* costs should form the basis of the charges. If, in contrast to the case on many continental railways, the British Post Office had to pay for the railways' services, Hill argued that such payment should be based only on the incremental or marginal costs resulting from adding a mail coach to an existing, scheduled train service, or, in the case of a mail train, merely the additional, direct operating costs which its provision necessarily entailed. However, even after arbitration, the actual payments extorted from the Post Office were, according to Hawke, often of the order of three times as much, being based not only on the direct operating costs but also on securing substantial contributions towards the indirect costs. In retrospect, Sir Rowland Hill's position is seen in fairer light to possess a theoretical underpinning which went largely unnoticed at the time. 'This is interest-

50

ing as an early argument about marginal cost pricing, and the Post Office seems to have been the only advocate of marginal cost pricing in the mid-nineteenth century. Its argument was not, of course, based on the premises used in modern welfare economics, but was merely the interpretation given by the Post Office to the concept of a "fair price".' [32] Hill had tried hard to achieve a closer alignment of the postal and railway monopoly as a means of so increasing custom that the finances of both would benefit, and consistently claimed that it was the onerous charges exacted by the private railways which was largely responsible for retarding the expansion of the postal services. As a result, the Post Office was in Hill's view over-conscious of its financial position and so was inhibited from experimenting with a number of new measures including new money transmission services of the kind that would have been likely to lead to a British postal Giro system. Thus, though one half of Rowland Hill's reforms was eminently successful, the other half of the combination, the nationalisation of the railways, had to wait until 1946: and putting the two halves together until 1968. The main chance for a British Giro was missed for nearly a century, but since the pressures for improved forms of money transmission services continued to grow relentlessly, they had to be met, at least as far as a large section of the less affluent members of society were concerned, by a series of improvised and second best alternatives.

POST OFFICE AS A GAP-FILLING BANK

The Post Office has carried out one or other of the functions of a bank almost from its inception, whether as the agent of the Bank of England for Bank Post Bills, of traders and country bankers as transmitters of their notes and Bills of Exchange, as a general carrier of cash for the public, whether registered or unregistered, as transmitter of its own forms of paper money such as money orders, money warrants, postal drafts or postal orders and perhaps most important of all as a savings bank since 1861. Despite this long and varied history of close attachment to money and banking matters, there was a marked tendency among members of the Post Office itself, as well as among outsiders, to regard such affairs as not quite the proper kind of activity for a Post Office to be carrying out. Any reform or extension of monetary or banking facilities by the Post Office had, therefore, to overcome internal domestic opposition as well as that naturally to be expected from those outside who objected either from vested interest or principle. It was partly for this reason that the carriage of money by post officials was at first performed without authority and completely unofficially and was then carried on for forty years in a semi-official manner, before becoming fully accepted as part of its official duties. The money order service is, in fact, except for the letter carrying, the oldest of all the services performed for the public by the Post Office. The Bank of England's Post Bills, first introduced in 1728, grew rapidly in popularity during the latter part of the century, as did other less official kinds of money transmission for smaller amounts. These latter forms had reached such a stage of development by 1792 that it was decided to countenance them in a semi-official manner by setting up a system of money letters under six 'Clerks of the Road' under the direct sanction of the Postmaster General 'for the purpose of affording to the public the means of safely and economically transmitting small sums of money from one part of the United Kingdom to any other'. Its position was still anomalous, being more of a private venture than an official part of the Post Office itself, and it remained as 'a sort of step-child' from 1792 to 1838. [33] It was not until the latter year that the Postmaster General decided to take over this money order business directly, compensating the private investors who had previously run the scheme for profit. The introduction of the Penny Post in 1840 was responsible for a rapid increase in the number of money orders issued which rose from 55 000 in 1836 to 1 500 000 in 1841. Despite this success 'Anthony Trollope in his downright way held that it could not be regarded as a part of the Post Office'. [34] Sir Rowland Hill, was, however, so pleased with the developments that even as early as 1843 he suggested extending the service to the colonies, though this was only done piecemeal, following the outbreak of the Crimean War, for the Army Post Office in the Crimea and at the intermediate staging posts of Gibraltar and Malta. Before tracing its transformation into a much more popular postal order system, it may be helpful to look briefly at the most successful of all the Post Office's monetary functions, namely the establishment of the Post Office Savings Bank, especially since these two aspects of postal banking services were in the overdue course of time to become the aged, respected and slightly frightened parents of National Giro.

PRE-EMINENCE OF THRIFT

A recurring conceptual difficulty which has had, still has, and probably will continue to have, a strong effect on the development of financial institutions and on monetary theory, springs from the essential ambiguity of the term 'money'. It is perhaps only too well known that the many wide-ranging functions of money may be brought together into two main and apparently disparate groups—those concerned with *expenditure* on the one hand and with *saving* on the other. What is equally important, but unfortunately much less widely appreciated, is that there is always a considerable degree of overlap, varying a little according to societies' particular institutions and customs, between these two important functions. The fact that money plays an essentially ambiguous, dual role comes up against man's repeated insistence on dividing and separating these roles by artificial means, even to the extent of frequently assuming that there is a great gulf between them, which is in fact hardly ever the case. In order to appreciate the evolution of thought and practice regarding the scope of the interrelated yet artificially divided financial functions of the Post Office as a money transmitter and as a savings bank, it is essential to realise the fundamental nature of the linkage or overlap between them. This overlap between the currency and savings aspects of money is much more than being either merely an interesting theoretical nicety, or just an example of the accidental and untidy way in which financial institutions actually develop. It is far more than that. A great deal of the powerful novelty of Keynesian theory has sprung from just this emphasis that 'the importance of money essentially flows from its being a link between the present and the future'. [35] This factor helps to explain why urgent problems regarding postal money transmission would at one time force the authorities towards setting up or improving postal savings facilities and why at other times practical difficulties arising out of the day-to-day working of the savings banks would lead to major developments in its money transmission services. This pattern, displaying the repercussions of improvements of one side of the Post Office's banking services on the other, recurs in other countries as well as our own.

Thus it is neither singular nor surprising to find in the confused history of the Money Order Department and of the Post Office Savings Bank, as in contemporary problems with regard to the relationship between both parents and the new Giro, that difficulties recur through trying to find practical solutions to the perennial problems as to the proper extent of the facilities which should be provided for 'money-to-spend' on the one hand, as opposed to 'money-to-save' on the other. However, although this tendency to drive a wedge between savings and currency is a permanent and widespread monetary feature, there can be little doubt that it was particularly noticeable in Britain during the Victorian age. To most Victorians saving was such an unqualified virtue that even the state through the Post Office might very properly be allowed to encourage it. Spending, on the other hand, when not actually sinful, was at any rate hardly better than a regrettable necessity which needed little if any encouragement through improved postal facilities. When these were allowed they were commonly hedged around by awkward penalties or onerous conditions which considerably reduced their effectiveness. This helps further to explain why Britain was the first country in the world to set up a postal savings bank aimed especially at attracting the savings of the working classes, and yet has been the last of the major European nations to provide these same classes with an adequate money transmission service. And our present age, which readily subsidises almost anything from abortion to cremation, ship-building to aviation, opera to hill-farming, still regards the subsidisation of Giro as the unforgivable sin.

The religious zeal surrounding the act of saving money is typified in the works of Samuel Smiles, particularly in his *Self-Help* and *Thrift*. According to no less an authority on the Victorian period than Professor Asa Briggs, 'there are few books in history which have reflected the spirit of their age more faithfully and successfully than Smiles' *Self-Help*. . . . To Smiles as to Mill the Englishman was renowned for his willingness to postpone present pleasures for future good.' [36] Smiles himself, in his chapter on 'Money: its Use and Abuse' leaves one in no doubt as to the general superiority of saving over spending: 'Economy may be styled the daughter of Prudence, the sister of Temperance and the mother of Liberty. It is evidently conservative—conservative of character, of domestic happiness and social well-being. It is, in short, an exhibition of self-help in one of its best forms.' [37] Samuel Smiles's enormously influential *Self-Help* was published in 1859, the same year that a Mr C W Sikes, a Huddersfield banker, despairing of ever getting his novel 'Postal Savings Bank' idea officially accepted, determined to cut through the red tape by writing directly to the Chancellor of the Exchequer, Mr Gladstone, explaining the moral significance as well as the mechanics of his scheme. The time was ripe and Sikes' letter acted as a stimulus for changes which had long been carefully prepared.

SAVINGS BANK SUCCESS

Apart from the basic motivation for encouraging thrift, there were two other principal reasons for engrafting the savings bank concept on to the Post Office's money order system. First was the fact that many of the 638 Trustee Savings Banks in existence in 1861 were small, insecure and incompetently managed, while their geographic coverage was very patchy. Some 300 of them only managed to open for business on one single day each week. In contrast, Sikes planned a secure and nationwide network, for, as he stated in his letter to Gladstone: 'Wherever a Money Order Office is planted let the Savings Bank be under its roof . . . and you virtually bring the Bank within less than *an hour's walk of the fireside* of every working man in the Kingdom.' [38] Second, the huge sums which could thus be placed at the disposal of the government at the very cheap rate of interest of only $2\frac{1}{2}\%$ appealed strongly to two sides of Gladstone's character—his love of economy and his dislike of the big banking interests in the City. 'It was only by the establishment of the Post Office Savings Banks and their progressive development that the finance minister has been provided with an instrument sufficiently powerful to make him independent of the Bank and City power when he has occasion for sums in seven figures.' [39] Little wonder that Gladstone opposed Sikes' original plan to set up an independent Commission for investing the proceeds of the savings banks. The unquestioned security offered by the government had to be paid for by giving the Treasury complete control over investment, although such control, today as then, is not an automatic guarantee of the most efficient or profitable way to run the Post Office's banking services. It was in part for similar reasons of economy that Chetwynd, the Post Office's first Controller of Savings Banks, rejected Sikes' accounting scheme based on slips and vouchers, in some ways similar to subsequent Giro styles, and proposed the Deposit Book system which still remains. The success of the new bank was immediately apparent and *The Bankers' Magazine* of 1862 was moved to pay this tribute: 'The working classes owe a great debt of gratitude to Mr C W Sikes and to Mr Gladstone, as through their instrumentality the savings bank is now brought within a few minutes walk of every working man in the Kingdom; and with facilities for transacting business, and security for the money invested that are not afforded by any existing bank, even to our greatest merchants.' [40] Fifty years later, by which time the bank boasted 8 million accounts totalling £169 million of deposits, its praise for its security was tempered by a hint that its maximum permitted deposit was too low: it quoted a letter from a depositor who wished to invest £500 or £600, and since this exceeded the Post Office Savings Bank limit of £200 he asked 'if the Department would recommend him to any bank that cannot break; and whether the Bank of England is safe like the Post Office Savings Bank'. [41]

POSTAL ORDER—PALE FORE-RUNNER OF GIRO

It soon became apparent that the very success of the savings bank idea, grafted as it had been on to the money order system, made it all the more necessary to improve the Post Office's money transmission services in their turn, so as to cater for working-class transfer payments as efficiently as the savings banks had done for their surplus funds. However, there was no genius like Sikes to step in from outside and to provide the required stimulus for revolutionising postal transfer payments. During the prolonged and confused discussions which preceded the inauguration of postal orders in January 1881, some wanted the Post Office to issue notes just like so many other banks had been in the habit of doing (there were at least 280 banks still issuing their own notes as late as 1844)—but to do so simply by filling the notorious currency gap by issuing circulating or negotiable notes for amounts below £5. Others, stressing the security aspect wished drastically to narrow the negotiability of any such 'notes' by stipulating that they should be payable only to *order* rather than to bearer. The latter group were divided as to whether such 'order-notes' should be for fixed amounts only, for example, 5s, 10s, £1, etc, or whether they should more flexibly provide for any amounts and so be more suitable for paying tradesmen's bills and the like. Thus, though it was not apparent at the time, the argument was in effect between those who wanted the Post Office to issue notes like a bank and those who wished for a postal cheque or

Giro transfer system, but the arguments on both sides stopped short of their ultimate logic and resulted in the end in the cumbersome postal order system which was to continue basically unchanged right up until the coming of Giro in 1968.

The attempt to increase the popularity of the money order system in 1871 by reducing the poundage charged for the service was partially successful so far as the public was concerned, but unprofitable for the Post Office, since the cost of issue and payment of each order was estimated at 3d, while the poundage charged on the orders under £1 was 2d and orders under 10s, 1d. This loss increased the desire of the Post Office to co-operate with the Treasury, the Bank of England and the general public in instituting a simpler, cheaper scheme; and so a Committee comprising representatives from these organisations was set up in 1876 and published its findings in the same year, under the resounding title: *Report from the Committee of Inquiry into the Money Order System of the Post Office into the Proposed Scheme of Post Office Notes.* It examined in considerable detail a scheme submitted by the same Chetwynd—the Post Office's Accountant and Auditor General—that had produced the successful Savings Bank Bill; it also considered (rather cavalierly) and dismissed two other schemes, one by the Post Master of Manchester, Mr J St L Beaufort, for a postal draft scheme intended to be of especial, but not exclusive, use for the payment of tradesmen's bills, and another by Mr Bradfield of the Money Order Office, for a less ambitious, but otherwise similar scheme. Although Chetwynd's scheme for postal notes printed for small, fixed amounts made a strong appeal to the Committee, they felt it could only be accepted if its negotiability were reduced so as to increase its security. All the main witnesses agreed with Chetwynd that 'if the Government had issued £1 notes you never would have had occasion for the money order system at all'. [42]

In view of the awkwardness later commonly attributed to the postal order, it is important to realise that the authorities were seeking an incompatible compromise between the wide circulation that a negotiable bearer note would give—just like a Bank of England note—on the one hand, and a secure form of money transfer, non-negotiable, to a named person at a named office, on the other hand. Chetwynd aimed eventually at a bearer note with wide circulation, but would accept some limitation on its currency until the scheme had proved itself: 'My idea is that the transition from the present money order system would

57

be too great if we adopted a system of open cheques payable to bearer. . . . We may ultimately arrive at such a state as to justify us in adopting an open cheque system, but we must first adopt something giving greater security'. [43] Yet the Committee appeared to accept the view that because 'the Postal Notes are printed (they) are in point of fact notes. You give them out like so many sovereigns'. [44] In rejecting the schemes suggested by Beaufort and Bradfield in favour of a modified version of Chetwynd's, the transfer function became de-emphasised through attempting to maintain the currency function. Some interesting similarities and differences between a modern Giro slip, a bank note and a postal order can be seen if the copy of the proforma of the 1876 Committee's suggested, but abortive, 'Postal Note' as shown in Figure 2.1, is examined.

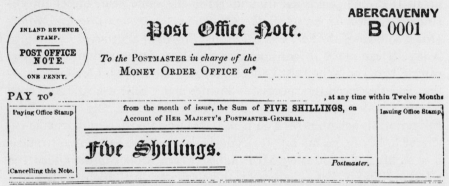

Figure 2.1   First official suggestion for a Postal Order or Post Office Note 1876

In the event, the suggestions of the Committee on Postal Notes proved rather too bold for the authorities, who, in the scheme which was eventually adopted five years later, gave still more attention to security and still less to transferability. The change in emphasis from bearer to order and from currency to draft is shown in the change in title from postal *note* to postal *order* and in the reduction of the term of validity from twelve to three months, a trend which was reinforced some ten years later by the addition of the words 'not negotiable' across the face of the order. In the evolution of the Post Office the postal order became something of a mule: capable of mundanely and morosely carrying out year after year, a useful, routine service, but incapable of generating really new functions either as a currency note or as Giro transfer. Yet it bore such superficial resemblances to both that the attempt to create such offspring was, as we shall see, repeatedly made only as repeatedly to fail. To help in achieving the efficient postal money transfer mechanism the country was silently demanding, the authorities had to look abroad for inspiration, rather than being able to derive such a scheme naturally from within itself by a sensible modification of the postal and money order office. In the meantime, however, since the postal order was a much simpler and cheaper transfer instrument for small sums of money than the money order, and because it was commonly used as a bank note for hand-to-hand currency until 1892, it quickly achieved popularity especially among the lower income groups. Nearly $4\frac{1}{2}$ million orders to the value of over £2 million were issued during 1881, its first year of operation. By 1907, the last year before a 'postal cheque' system like that which had become increasingly common on the Continent, was first cursorily examined within the Post Office, and of course summarily dismissed, the annual number of postal orders issued had passed the 100 million mark and represented a value of £43 million.

CONCLUSION: GIRO FINDS ITS VOICE

The history of the two previous generations has demonstrated that in so many ways we nearly achieved the Giro system we deserved, but not quite. The main reasons which prevented the case for some form of Giro being consciously, thoroughly and explicitly considered during the second half of the nineteenth century, when so many developments pointed towards it, were first, the failure to nationalise or at least to control the fare structure of the railways in such a way as to relieve the Post Office of the heavy burden of charges it bore when compared with railways on the Continent; second, the popularity of the bank cheque which derived from the particular form of our amalgamated, deposit-banking system which catered so well for the richer section of the community, including the growing middle class; and third, the enormous and early reputation of the world's first Postal Savings Bank, coupled with the continually expanding use of the postal order system.

Contemporary opinion on the whole considered that the authorities had done their fair share in providing for the savings and transfer requirements of the working classes. There seemed on the surface to be no obvious reason to differ from the Post Office's view in rejecting a postal cheque system.

However, the battle for Giro, hitherto undeclared and implicit, far from being over, was in fact just about to enter its open, declared and explicit state. For deeper down, particularly among the trade unions, whose power was growing apace in the period from 1906 to 1914, there was such a strong disillusionment, based on their own practical experience with regard to the quality of service provided by the Post Office, whether for savings or for transfer, that, at long last, an explicit demand for a postal cheque service on the continental model, began to force itself upon the attention of the general public and hence impelled the authorities to reconsider their position. Finally, in view of our earlier insistence on the inevitable and natural linkage between the spending and lending functions of money, it may be worth reminding ourselves that the case for Giro sprang not only from the inadequacies of the expenditure functions of current account banks, but also originated to a significant degree from the failure of the savings banks to carry out in an adequate manner their pretended functions, by failing to accept the substantial deposits made up of millions of very small contributions that the trade unions were keen to place in the care of the Post Office. But the reason for this unusual, if not unique, spectacle of a bank voluntarily declining to accept millions of pounds of normally stable deposits and the relationship of such a phenomenon to the case for a postal Giro, is better reserved for the next chapter, for it was from these frustrations that the vague, incoherent needs of the previous years became transformed into an explicit and vociferous demand for Giro.

REFERENCES

1 HILL, ROWLAND, *Post Office Reform: its Importance and Practicability* (London, 1837). The statement was printed by Hill on the title page of his epoch-making book and was in turn taken from a Report on the Reform of the Post Office by Lord Lowther, Earl of Lonsdale, a Tory much interested in postal reform and a keen supporter of Rowland Hill. Lord Lowther was made President of the Board of Trade in 1834 and fittingly enough was Postmaster General from 1841–46.

2 FETTER, F W, *Development of British Monetary Orthodoxy* (Harvard University Press, 1965), p. 220.

3   JONES, G P and POOL, A G, *A Hundred Years of Economic Development in Great Britain* (London, 1948), p. 223.
4   *Report of Inquiry by the Board of Trade into the Earnings and Hours of Work of Work-people in the United Kingdom* (Cd. 5460, 1910), Vol. V, p. 23.
5   POLLARD, S, *Development of the British Economy 1914–1950* (London, 1962), p. 27.
6   *Radcliffe Report on the Working of the Monetary System* (Cmnd. 827, 1959), para. 522.
7   *Hansard*, 25 March 1873, col. 117.
8   PRESSNELL, L S, 'Gold Reserves, Banking Reserves and the Baring Crisis of 1890', p. 178, in *Essays in Money and Banking in Honour of R. S. Sayers*, edited by C R Whittlesey and J S G Wilson (Oxford, 1968).
9   PRESSNELL, L S, *Country Banking in the Industrial Revolution* (Oxford, 1966), Ch. 3, p. 12–74.
10 GREGORY, T E, *Statutes, Documents and Reports Relating to British Banking 1832–1928* (London, 1964), Vol. 2, p. 88, 1137.
11 GREGORY, T E, *ibid.*, p. 88.
12 CROWTHER, G, *An Outline of Money* (London, 1940), p. 85.
13 HAMMERBY, G, *Postgiro i 50 Aar* (Copenhagen, 1970), p. 7.
14 FAY, C R, *Great Britain from Adam Smith to the Present Day* (London, 1937), p. 212.
15 ROBBINS, LORD, *Theory of Economic Policy* (London, 1952), Ch. 2, p. 37.
16 MILL, J S, *Principles of Political Economy* (London, 1862), Vol. 2, p. 546–9.
17 MILL, J S, *ibid.*, p. 556.
18 HILL, SIR ROWLAND, *Report of Matters Connected with the Railways of Great Britain and Ireland* 1867, Minority Report, para. 1.
19 HILL, SIR ROWLAND, *ibid.*, para. 9.
20 *Report of Matters Connected with the Railways of Great Britain and Ireland* 1867, para. 74.
21 *Ibid.*, para. 135.
22 ROBINSON, H, *Britain's Post Office: History of Development from its Beginnings to the Present Day* (London, 1953), p. 170.
23 ROBINSON, H, *ibid.*, p. 206.
24 PARRIS, HENRY, *Government and the Railways in Nineteenth Century Britain* (London, 1965), p. viii.
25 TROLLOPE, ANTHONY, *An Autobiography* (London, 1950), p. 133.
26 HILL, SIR ROWLAND, *Memorandum on the Net Revenue of the Post Office* (London, 1862).
27 BAGWELL, P S, *The Railway Clearing House in the British Economy* (London, 1968), p. 93.
28 BAGWELL, P S, *ibid.*, p. 108.
29 BAGWELL, P S, *ibid.*, p. 112.
30 BAGWELL, P S, *ibid.*, p. 118.
31 HAWKE, G R, 'Pricing Policy of Railways in England and Wales before 1881', in *Railways in the Victorian Economy: Studies in Finance and Economic Growth*, edited by M. C. Reed (Newton Abbot, 1969), p. 110.
32 HAWKE, G R, *ibid.*, p. 94.
33 ROBINSON, H, *op. cit.*, p. 194.
34 ROBINSON, H, *ibid.*, p. 195.

35 KEYNES, J M, *General Theory of Employment, Interest and Money* (London, 1936), p. 293, italics in original.
36 SMILES, SAMUEL, *Self-Help*, Introduction by Professor Asa Briggs to Centenary Edition (London, 1958), pp. 7 and 27.
37 SMILES, SAMUEL, *ibid.*, p. 286.
38 SIKES, C W, Quoted in Horne, H O, *A History of Savings Banks* (London, 1947), p. 176.
39 MORLEY, J, *The Life of W E Gladstone* (London, 1911), Vol. iii, p. 431.
40 *The Bankers' Magazine* (London, 1862), p. 721.
41 *The Banker's Magazine* (London, 1911), p. 360.
42 *Report from the Committee of Enquiry into the Money Order System* (H.M.S.O.: London, 1876), Minutes of Evidence, Question 89(*a*).
43 *Ibid.*, Question 89(*a*).
44 *Ibid.*, Question 252(*g*).

Chapter 3

TUC versus PMG

'Projectors see no difficulties and critics see nothing else.' [1]

INTRODUCTION: STAGES IN THE CAMPAIGN

Support for the establishment of a British Giro ebbed and flowed to a remarkable degree over the course of the sixty years 1908–68, beginning with a sudden surge from 1908 to the end of 1916, followed by a slackening of interest until a renewed flow of support showed itself in the three or four years preceding the General Strike of 1926. The reaction of the public at large to that year of strikes was hardly calculated to provide an atmosphere conducive to union-inspired reforms. The consequent ebb in support of Giro was confirmed by the publication of the Post Office's Advisory Council's Report on the Postal Cheque System in August 1928, which marked a severe reverse for those whose efforts a few years earlier had seemed to be gaining a wider measure of support than ever before. As a result of that Committee's ill-considered condemnation, interest in Giro fell to such a low ebb in Britain that hardly any progress could be registered by its remaining supporters throughout the 1930s, a decade which was in any case dominated by economic problems which dwarfed the arguments concerning the merits or demerits of Giro. The outbreak of the war in 1939 seemed to render irrelevant the whole of the case for Giro (though both Finland and Norway, as we shall see later, began their Giros during the war years), while the post-war Government, wrestling with the problems of reconstruction, could afford no very high priority for the concept.

Nevertheless, the longest and darkest hour is, proverbially, that which precedes the dawn. The attempt to revive monetary policy during the 1950s led to a gradual but general recognition among Ministers, financial journalists, academics and the bankers themselves—and roughly in that order—that the monetary system no longer worked in the conventionally accepted manner. So baffling were the financial problems of the fifties that only a comprehensive and thorough review of the working of the monetary system as a whole could be expected to reveal its hidden complexities. The wide terms of reference given to the Radcliffe Committee when it was set up in 1957 obviously embraced a review of the adequacy of the existing systems of money transfer in the United Kingdom, and this naturally required a comparison with that of our European neighbours, where postal Giros had long proved themselves. It was therefore chiefly due to the findings of the Radcliffe Committee—a much higher-powered and wider-ranging affair than the myopic and pessimistic three-man Post Office Advisory Committee of 1928—that the tide turned at last so strongly in Giro's favour that the Conservative Government's decision in 1963 not to establish a Giro at that time was brushed aside by the Labour Government's policy declaration given in the White Paper of 1965 to establish a National Giro as soon as possible. And so the long struggle to set up a modern postal money transfer system along continental lines was eventually crowned with success.

There are, therefore, four natural stages in this development which will be traced out in this and in the following chapters. The first stage covers the years from around 1908–26, during which the case for Giro was first consciously spelled out and pressed forward strongly, almost exclusively by the trade unions, but eventually gaining a wider measure of support, even if still confined mainly to the political left. The second stage covers the three decades from 1927–56: a virtual doldrums, at least when compared either with what went before or what was to come afterwards. The third stage spans the period from 1957–65, beginning with the Radcliffe-inspired revival of interest in the case for and against Giro and culminating with its official acceptance in 1965. The fourth stage covers the frantic preparation involved in getting the world's first fully computerised postal Giro conceived, planned, constructed and manned during the three years from the date of the publication of the White Paper in August 1965 until 18 October 1968, the day National Giro began its business.

TRADE UNIONS' OPENING BARRAGE 1908–14

There were two separate sources which led to the first public demand for a postal cheque and transfer system in the five years or so preceding the outbreak of the First World War, a demand which grew so quickly in strength that not only was the idea adopted by the Trades Union Congress as part of its official policy, but also caused the Postmaster General, in a move that was then as exceptional as it is common today, to agree to receive on two succeeding years a deputation on the subject from the Parliamentary Committee of the TUC. The second of these sources was the lively awareness among some of the more junior-ranking staff of the Post Office itself of the benefits which were being gained through the extension of the Giro system from Austria to its neighbours Switzerland and Germany in 1906 and 1908, respectively, and even to far-away and apparently primitive Japan in 1906.

There had long existed a rather imprecise, but massive and growing unease among the larger trade unions concerning the facilities provided by the Post Office for the deposit and transfer of their funds. Such facilities they considered to be woefully inadequate, so much so that they were driven much against their will to make use of the commercial banks whose services they grudgingly admitted were in certain vital respects far superior to those of the Post Office. What made the matter worse was that the trade unions considered that since the Post Office Savings Bank, the Postal and Money Order Departments had all originated especially to satisfy the needs of the working classes then the views of the trade unions should have received a much better response. The Post Office had however, in their view, failed lamentably to adapt their activities to the changing requirements of the working man and of his union. The Post Office was obviously backsliding from its original virtuous relationship with the trade unions for right at the beginning Mr Gladstone had, at the request of the union leaders, expressly conceded to them and to the Friendly Societies, the privilege of opening accounts with the bank. That this was not a minor matter is clearly shown by the Webbs who in their famous *History of Trade Unionism*, were at pains to describe how the contemporary trade union leaders, rather prematurely as it happened, took this singular privilege to mean their acceptance as legal entities, a move which would henceforward give some legal protection for their funds, which at that time totalled around a quarter of a million pounds. [2] The phenomenal growth in the size, political power and financial strength of the trade union movement and the fundamental changes in its structure combined to render those postal monetary facilities which had at one time looked so beneficent, later seem so paltry as to become a source of continued attack. In 1890 there were about $1\frac{1}{2}$ million trade union members; by 1900 about 2 million; by 1914 about 4 million and by 1920 the vast inter-war peak figure of over 8 million was recorded. [3]

The process of amalgamation changed the structure of unionism from countless local, independent and relatively small units, into a formidable mass of really large and powerful Unions, some fifty of which had by 1920 over 50 000 members each, while some dozen of the largest each registered a quarter of a million members. Belying their humble origins they were now big businesses, handling vast amounts of money daily, and needing not only deposit and transfer facilities throughout the country for a variety of small individual benefits and contributions in connection with the local branches, but also needing deposit facilities for the hundreds of thousands of pounds at the disposal of union headquarters. There were thus two interrelated disadvantages pertaining to postal facilities which the union leaders wished to remove: the maximum limit on deposits was ridiculously small and the transfer facilities were hopelessly inadequate. The efforts which were made by the Post Office to meet these criticisms were so pathetically limited in scope as to reveal a total lack of understanding of the scale of the problem. The amalgamated commercial banks were well aware as we have seen, of the deposit and transfer needs of big business—whether capitalistic or trade unionist: the Post Office remained atomistic, chained by its constitution and unable to adapt its thinking to the enlarged scale of activity of its biggest and potentially its most enthusiastic customers.

It was not that the Post Office adopted a purely negative stance, but rather that it was mainly a case of a huge increase in demand coming up against a supply situation that could not be expected to expand at anything like the same pace, so that relatively the Post Office's monetary services seemed to the unions actually to be deteriorating. In certain other respects, however, the Post Office's attitude towards the unions changed dramatically in their favour in the first decade of the twentieth century, when the previous total refusal to condone trade union activities within its own organisation gave way to a somewhat grudging acceptance of their existence by the Duke of Norfolk when he was Postmaster General in 1899. This first hesitant step soon led to a resounding victory for union recognition for 'Mr Sydney Buxton, on becoming Postmaster General in 1906, opened the door considerably wider and announced that he would "frankly recognise any duly constituted association or federation of postal servants".' [4] According to the Webbs, this official recognition of the postal unions gave 'a tremendous fillip' to the growth of trade unionism throughout the public sector. [5] It certainly helped to educate the bigger craft unions into a greater appreciation of the kinds of financial services which the Post Office could reasonably be expected to offer, based on the postal unions' knowledge of the operation of foreign postal savings and money transfer systems. In this way the three biggest of the fifty or so postal unions—the Postal Clerks Association, the Postmen's Federation and the Fawcett Association, which were to amalgamate in 1919 to form the present Union of Post Office Workers—formed a bridge between the big, powerful and wealthy unions who wished to reform the Post Office Savings Bank, but did not quite know exactly what to suggest, and the postal authorities who plainly failed to appreciate the scale of the changes demanded of them.

FIRST BLUE PRINT FOR GIRO

The credit for being the first person in this country to draw up a detailed coherent, clear and simple case for the establishment of Giro belongs of right to an obscure and hitherto almost totally ignored Yorkshireman, a Mr W Crossley of Leeds. This rather self-effacing member of the United Kingdom Postal Clerks' Association drew up and published on behalf of his Association, a thirteen page pamphlet which with typical modesty was unsigned and which with a disregard of trifles was also undated. (There can be little doubt that this was in fact largely the work of Mr William Crossley himself, who with the active co-operation of Mr Albert Varley of Manchester, the union's General Secretary, prepared and published the pamphlet shortly after their Union's Annual Meeting held in Leicester in 1911. In view of the importance of this document as the first published record of the case for a British Giro, a summary of it is given in Appendix A.) Crossley had already been compaigning to some

67

effect for some time previous to this, for having persuaded his own branch at Leeds as to the rightness of his cause, he was sent as their delegate to the Bradford Conference of the UKPCA in 1910, where he moved a resolution instructing the executive to take active steps to educate public opinion in favour of the reform and extension of the work of the Post Office Savings Bank to bring it up to the standard of foreign banks. In his Bradford speech, he stressed the need for postal cheque facilities for holders of current accounts and urged the holding of public meetings, the issue of leaflets, the badgering of Members of Parliament, and, of course, pressure and propaganda among other trade unions—all methods which were in fact subsequently adopted—in order to forward the cause to which he was such an enthusiastic convert.

The main craft unions—the Boilermakers, Shipbuilders, Steam Engine Makers, Carpenters and Joiners, etc—had their own reasons for wishing to bring about radical changes in the operations of the Post Office Savings Bank: the influence of the postal unions was however an important factor in instructing them how best to set about this task. It was in this way that the wide and still rather vague, if vociferous, pressures of the large unions and of the TUC itself, were channelled by the educative procedures of the United Kingdom Postal Clerks' Association into a drive for Giro in conjunction with other reforms of the Post Office Savings Bank and postal order system.

Union pressure exposed the dilemma of the Post Office, which wished to justify the *savings* part of its bank's title by stressing the longer period of deposit as opposed to the use of bank current accounts, while it also felt it still to be essential to limit the use of the bank to the *small* savings for which it was originally established. The original maximum of £30 in any one year and £150 in all had, it is true, been gradually increased first to £50 and £200 and then to £100 and £250 respectively. Following the growing pressure from the Parliamentary Committee of the Trade Union Council in 1907, the Post Office made what was for it a significant jump, raising the annual limit for individual deposits to £250 and the total to £1000. However, far from satisfying the unions, this was merely a sop to whet their appetites. At the 1909 Annual Conference of the TUC, Mr J Hill, General Secretary of the Boilermakers and Shipbuilders' Union, moved ... 'That the Parliamentary Committee be instructed to interview the Postmaster General with a view to granting further banking facilities to Trade Unions'. While admitting that the enlarged deposit facilities went some way to meet the needs of the branches, nevertheless he argued strongly that 'the difficulty they still laboured under was that they had not sufficient scope in connection with their head office. They wanted to be able to bank £100 000, which was the minimum required by his society per annum. Every week they were in the habit of transmitting to the branches an average of £2000; and while the branches banked with the Post Office, the headquarters had to deal with the commercial banks.' [6] Mr Hill was supported by the representatives of the Steam Engine Makers and by the delegate of the Postal Clerks' Association, Mr R R Millard. The Postmaster General, however, refused to receive a delegation that year, so precisely the same resolution was moved, again by the Boilermakers, at the 1910 Annual Meeting of the Congress, though in his supporting speech, Mr J Baird changed the emphasis from deposits to cheques: 'He pointed out the great trouble involved in the payment of benefits, especially in the case of the larger unions with branches all over the country. . . . Instead of having first to go to the bank for the money . . . they were desirous of being able to make payments from the Post Office direct by cheque . . . it ought to be possible to provide this post office banking accommodation for those societies that wanted it.' [7]

TUC VERSUS PMG

As a result of this barrage, the new Postmaster General, Mr Herbert Samuel, who took up his office in January 1910, agreed to receive a deputation from the Parliamentary Committee of the TUC on 16 March 1910, and since the results of the discussions were inconclusive, both sides remaining as far apart after the meeting as they were before, a further meeting was arranged about a year later on 7 February 1911. Both meetings were held at the Postal Headquarters in St Martins le Grand, the two sides consisting of the Postmaster General, the Secretary of the Post Office and other senior officials on the one hand, and the representatives of the TUC, whose chief spokesman was Mr Hill of the Boilermakers, and of the Postal Clerks' Association on the other. The full shorthand transcripts which were taken of both confrontations enable us to follow the course of the discussions blow by verbal blow, but in what follows only the main points required for analysing the reasons why the two sides remained so far apart are examined. 'What we are asking for', declared Mr Hill of the Boilermakers in opening his case in the 1910 interview, 'is not only increased facilities for deposits but (also) for the transmission of money.' He showed the Postmaster General the promised land: 'We have £8 million and the Government might hold at a very small rate of interest the whole of the money of the Trade Unions.' He threatened: 'We must get an extension of facilities or we shall have to withdraw the accounts and deal exclusively with the commercial banks.' Since, however, 'as Trade Unionists we believe in the nationalisation of the banking system' he emphasised that 'we prefer that this business should be wholly, exclusively and entirely through the Post Office'. [8] Hill's threat was no bluff. Around this time the Co-operative Bank carried out a successful drive for trade union funds so that eventually the majority of trade unions banked with the Co-operative.

In his reply Mr Herbert Samuel stated that 'it is of course the desire of the Post Office that the Savings Bank should as far as possible be of the greatest possible service to the industrial classes, but . . . the difficulty that stands in the way of having unlimited accounts and enabling sums to be transferred by cheque is that many of the smaller offices would not have the money at their disposal to cash the cheques when presented.' He finally pleaded that any decisions to alter the rules governing the Savings Bank were not his alone: 'I cannot give any decision on my own authority, for all matters relating to Savings Bank deposits are under the control of the Treasury—by Statute the ultimate control is vested in the National Debt Commissioners—and it would be essential therefore that I should consult with them.' [9]

Clearly very little to please the unions came from such consultation, either with the Treasury or with that almost mythical body the Commissioners for the Reduction of the National Debt (the *full* body of National Commissioners has not met since 1860) [10], so that in the second deputation in February 1911, the unions' leaders were still more blunt and outspoken in presenting their case. Hill again led off and was soon into his stride: 'I found the facilities given by the Post Office absolutely valueless. . . . We ask you for facilities for the transmission of money. I would like to say boldly that the Department is not as good for our class as is the ordinary commercial bank. . . . You said that the granting of facilities for the transmission of money was not the proper function of the Post Office. It is for you to say what the proper functions of the

Post Office are, but I am satisfied that it is in your power to modify the functions of your Department as you go along. For instance, at the present time you are making a very large departure for the advantage of the middle and upper classes. I refer to the telephones. These are not working men's facilities or luxuries. . . . I do ask when you are making for the commercial and upper classes a great extension of work in the matter of telephones you should also at the same time make some little departure on behalf of the classes we represent. It should be your care to extend the cheque facilities which you have been good enough to grant in certain instances with considerable advantage. We are anxious to make full use of the Post Office Savings Bank wherever possible. It is part of our policy to encourage these transactions between the Unions and the Government and we do ask that you should make some further extension: if you cannot give us all we are appealing for, will you give us at least a moiety?' [11] Mr Hill was again supported by Mr Millard of the Postal Clerks' Association, who thought that 'It may fairly be said that the Post Office Savings Bank does not attempt seriously to cater for modern needs. We of the Post Office Staff join strongly with the Trades Union Congress in begging you to do something to grant those facilities to outside Trade Unions for the transmission of their funds.' [12] It appears that the Post Office officials' siding with the TUC was not very popular with the Postmaster General, particularly when, at the Annual General Meetings for instance, it became hardly distinguishable from party political propaganda, so that official directives were issued to try and prevent the postal unions from presenting their case at political rallies.

The opposing side of the case was given in a much milder manner by the Postmaster General, who nevertheless held his ground and refused to give a mite, let alone the moiety which Mr Hill demanded, at least until the outbreak of war in 1914 forced his hand. Once again he promised to look into the TUC resolutions and in particular Mr Hill's suggestion regarding the postal cheques: 'As I understand Mr Hill, his point would be largely met if he were able to transfer sums of money —I think it is transmission he has mainly in mind—in such a way that the Branch Secretary in the Provinces, would be able to receive the sums which are due to him through the Post Office. . . . I will look into it and see whether there are any drawbacks. Frequently, there are hidden difficulties which do not at first sight present themselves.' [13] The difficulties and drawbacks did not take too long to reveal themselves to the postal officials. They had in fact already been foreshadowed in the course of the Postmaster General's own replies to the two deputations, and these replies formed substantially the core of the case against Giro as the Post Office saw it, not only at the time, but for the whole of the period from 1911 right up to the period of the Johnston Report of 1928, which merely took the arguments a stage or two further. In view of the obstructive and delaying power of these views it is necessary to give them an airing.

The official attitude was firmly fixed against any radical changes simply because the Postmaster General and his officials did not see that one of the main and proper purposes of the Post Office was to facilitate the transfer of monies, even where this might be thought to impinge on the preserves of the banks in operating current accounts. Furthermore, it was the firm conviction of the postal officials that any reform of the existing postal order and Savings Bank in the manner suggested would result in greatly increased costs. Such additional costs would spring directly from having to man the Post Office with staff possessing or capable of acquiring some elements of banking expertise. Much more important as a cost raising feature was that the proposed scheme would necessitate the holding of much higher reserves of 'till money' in all the many thousands of money order offices throughout the Kingdom, so as to meet the more frequent withdrawals implicit in the current account as opposed to savings deposits. If the ceiling of deposits were raised as high as the unions wished, this would naturally entail a risk of very much higher levels of withdrawal. There was a danger springing from the corporate nature of unionism, particularly in view of the current wave of syndicalism, which might lead to withdrawals becoming very heavily concentrated in time and place because of strikes and lock-outs. The Postmaster General raised this bogey and certainly scared himself with it. Hill refuted the danger to the Post Office Savings Bank from strikes by replying: 'Surely a National Bank would be quite as able as any commercial bank to stand the strain from a strike or lock-out'. [14] There might however have been a noticeable difference between the impact on the twenty or so commercial banks who carried on a wide variety of other business and had major deposits from commerce and industry as well as other smaller deposits, compared with the likely impact on the one Post Office Savings Bank wherein the largest single element by far would be the deposits of the trade unions.

In so far as the fear of strikes was an issue, the statistics for the years in question were not reassuring, for these were years when the growth of syndicalism, the growth of wide-spread militancy and the growth of strikes went together. The number of days lost by strike action jumped from 2 150 000 in 1907, a figure around the average of the previous seven years, to 10 790 000 in 1908, and after declining to 2 690 000 in 1909 rose again to 10 160 000 in 1911 and shot up to what was then easily the record figure of 40 890 000 in 1912. [15] To some extent, therefore, what the unions had been hoping to gain from tempting the Postmaster General with large deposits for the postal bank from union funds, seemed to suffer from the possibility as shown by these figures of a fairly high degree of volatility and instability. But there existed a still more important reason as to why the Post Office Savings Bank did not seem keen, to say the least, to accept the £8 million of deposits which John Hill had been dangling before the Postmaster General, which was that quite apart from the question of their volatility such deposits might not have been all that profitable given the cheap money which had typically prevailed during much of the decade before the war. On the one hand, the comparatively generous and fixed interest rate granted on postal deposits meant relatively high costs, while the inflexible and limited avenues available to the Post Office for the investment of the proceeds meant, on the other hand, low returns. Turning to the latter point, it was quite relevant and true, as the Postmaster General stated during the interview with the Unions 'that since the commercial banks take risks which a government bank could not take, and (since) the field of investment for us is far more limited' the earning power of the deposits was lower than that of the private banks. [16] Furthermore, the Post Office was faced with the traditionally irreducible $2\frac{1}{2}\%$ cost of deposits, unlike the more variable rates paid by other banks. Sir Herbert Samuel also expressed the view that with a fluctuating money market the Post Office might be called upon to accept deposits when money was cheap, only to find them withdrawn when money was dear, thus involving the Post Office Bank in considerable loss. That the officials of the Post Office were in fact seriously worried by this matter subsequently became clear from comments made by Sir Evelyn Murray, Secretary to the Post Office for the long period from 1914–34, in his authoritative history of the Post Office which was published in 1927. After referring to the great financial success which the Savings Bank had achieved in accumulating nearly £25 million of surpluses over the years, he noted that 'The deficits which fell upon the Exchequer have aggregated less than £900 000 since the institution was established.' However he added very significantly that 'the bulk of them occurred in the years 1903–10 following the reduction to $2\frac{1}{2}\%$ in the rate of interest on Consols under the Goschen conversion scheme'. [17]

For an institution the bulk of whose investments were bound to be in Government Bonds, the fall in the price of Consols, from 113 in 1897 to 75 in 1912, was of course a matter of considerable concern. A recent researcher into bank statistics and practices of the period, Mr C A E Goodhart, refers to a contemporary suggestion by Sir Samuel Montague, that the rate of interest allowed on Post Office Savings Bank deposits ought to be reduced, though this was not so much to recoup the losses which the bank was then suffering, but rather as a device to enable the Treasury to build up the country's gold reserves which almost everyone then, as subsequently, considered to be too low. [18] All in all, therefore, it would appear that given the constitutional antipathy of the postal authorities to any substantial reforms of their well-tried, but old-fashioned and inefficient methods of banking and money transfer, there was no shortage of plausible reasons to justify their negative reactions to the continuous promptings of the unions, who nevertheless refused to take 'No' for an answer. At the TUC Annual General Meeting at Newport in 1912 their previous resolutions, which in 1909 and 1910 referred rather vaguely, as we have seen, to 'granting further banking facilities for Trade Unions' became translated into a much more specific request for a Giro system for the sake of the widespread advantages which it would confer upon the public in general. Mr Lynes of the Postal Clerks moved that 'This Congress is of the opinion that the establishment of a postal cheque system in this country would be a public benefit, and would particularly be of advantage to Trade Unions and working-class organisations; and requests the Government to consider the question of introducing the system.' [19] And whereas the resolutions of the earlier years had been 'agreed to', it is a further indication of the growing popularity of the case for Giro that this resolution was 'carried unanimously'. In view of the Postmaster General's attempts to quash what he felt to be the over-enthusiastic promotion of Giro by postal workers, it is interesting to read that Mr E C Gates (Postal Telegraph Clerks) in seconding the resolution 'did so all the more readily because he had been given to understand since his arrival in Newport that the Postal Clerks' Association had been forbidden to continue their propaganda on its behalf'. [20]

POST OFFICE AS A NOTE-ISSUING BANK

If the unions, despite their growing power, failed to budge the Post Office from their entrenched position, the outbreak of the war led to two significant changes relating to money transfer and deposits which gave them for a time part of what they had been demanding over the previous four or five years. First came the freeing of the postal order from poundage, so that it became for a short while what the Committee of 1876 had recommended as a permanent solution, a postal note just like a bank note; and second, there followed the removal of the ceilings on Savings Bank deposits, a welcome provision which lasted until 1923. Lloyd George in explaining 'How we Saved the City', describes how the humble postal order found itself as part of an express financial package high on the Cabinet's agenda. [21] The expected financial crisis following the outbreak of war on 4 August was met with a series of emergency measures such as raising the bank rate to 10%, suspending the 1844 Bank Charter Act, declaring a four-day Bank Holiday, and by rushing through Parliament a Currency and Bank Notes Bill which authorised the issue of small notes of £1 and 10s by the Treasury—the 'Bradburys' as they became known from the Secretary to the Treasury, whose signature they carried. In addition, in order to deal with the rapidly increasing demand for currency, the need to conserve gold, and to hold the stage until the Bradburys were printed and issued, postal orders were declared to be legal tender. [22] The declaration was made by Royal Proclamation on 7 August 1914 and orders were used as official currency until a further such proclamation withdrawing the legal tender privilege and re-instating poundage and commission for new orders was issued on 4 February 1915.

The eagerness with which the postal order was used as currency during the first six months of the war provided a conclusive demonstration of the case which had long been expounded of the need for small notes and of the part the Post Office could play in supplying a current account banking system had it so wished. Clearly an effective demand was already in existence, and when after six months the postal order resumed

75

its previous awkward limitations, the complaints, despite the crackle of the Bradburys, were loud and long. The Post Office had become both in fact and in law, what it had long resisted, a note-issuing bank. Yet it remained probably the only such bank in history which refused to offer a proper current account banking service. What it had been forced by events to supply was a form of bank currency without the accounting methods which would support a transfer system—one half of Giro without its essential complement. The postal order thus achieved for a time a most remarkable, indeed a unique position as a monetary instrument, being the only form of unlimited legal tender currency in common use throughout the United Kingdom, given the fact that the otherwise similar but more prestigious forms of money were each suffering from some disability or other. Thus golden sovereigns were being withdrawn for a war reserve, the minimum Bank of England note remained at £5 and in any case it was still not very popular in Scotland or Ireland where although the indigenous bank notes had also been granted legal tender, this was confined to their country of issue only. Finally, the new Bradburys spread relatively slowly over the country and postal records reveal that one of the reasons for demonetising the postal order was precisely in order to force people towards making greater use of the Treasury notes. [23] The popularity of the postal order was not in the least hindered by its rather peculiar legal situation, a subject which formed the substance of the First Gilbart Lecture of 1915 given at the Institute of Bankers and duly reported in *The Bankers' Magazine* of that year. The Lecture made great play with the introduction of 'a new species of negotiable instrument' and went on: 'These words mean nothing if not that postal orders are and shall be absolutely negotiable; but the words "not negotiable" are already there. We have the incongruous result that an instrument which denies its position of negotiability has the greatness of negotiability thrust upon it, and we obtain temporarily a unique specimen of a negotiable instrument.' [24]

It was all too much for the Post Office who, with a sigh of relief, welcomed the premature return of 'normalcy' by reverting to the old system in February 1915. Postal records, however, give ample evidence of the acute distress occasioned by this move so far as certain underprivileged groups were concerned, particularly the families of soldiers and sailors whose bread-winners had joined the forces. Letters of complaint were sent to the Postmaster General from the Hearts of Oak

Society; from the manager of an electric light bulb company with head-quarters in Carnaby Street not very far from Postal Headquarters; from a colliery manager at Rotherham; from a large and patriotic manufacturing firm in Bristol with 250 of its employees having already joined the Army; and from the Chairman of the Manchester Soldiers' and Sailors' Families Relief Subcommittee whose urgent telegram protesting against the demonetisation of the postal order was followed by a letter of support from the Town Clerk of Manchester, a Mr Thomas Hudson. The burden of all these complaints may be illustrated by an extract from Mr Hudson's letter which illustrates how useful the new paper money was for transmitting large amounts of small and varying individual sums of money through the post, in his case to make welfare grants to the poorer families of servicemen:

To the Postmaster General   9th February, 1915.

The work of the Local Committee involves the employment of a large staff of assistants and it has been found desirable that all payments of dependants of soldiers and sailors shall be made by paper money. The imposition of a charge of about £70 per month (in poundage) is a most serious problem and will give rise to much comment amongst members of the Local Relief Committee when the issue becomes known. I am desired to make a strong representation to you that if no exception can be made with regard to the payment of poundage, the Government should remit the amounts paid to the dependents of soldiers and sailors . . . or suggest some other arrangement which will allow the dependents to be paid in paper money without inflicting a charge upon the funds of the Society.

Rarely could the labour-saving potentialities of even a partial Giro system have been more clearly demonstrated, but instead of extending its obvious advantages more widely the Postmaster General in his reply used the excuse that 'any special arrangements could not be limited in scope but would have to be extended generally throughout the Country' as a reason for refusing the Manchester request, and replied in similar vein to the other protestations and pleadings. [25]

The continuance of even half a Giro was beyond the vision of the

77

authorities, though they remained aware of the pressing needs for paper currency. According to an internal memorandum sent on 15 October 1915 to Sir Evelyn Murray, Secretary of the Post Office: 'The Treasury at inconveniently short notice are contemplating the conversion of two values of Postal Orders, 2s 6d and 5s, into currency'. [26] But nothing came of this, nor of a similar plan to issue Treasury Notes for 5s. (A very small number of these '5s Bradburys' were actually printed, and are still in existence, but in view of their scarcity value it may be as well not to disclose their whereabouts.) The two main lessons to be drawn from the Post Office's experience as a Bank of Issue—an experience which was repeated as a sort of reflex action at the beginning of the Second World War when postal orders were again made legal tender from 3 September to 20 December 1939—were first, that the Post Office had not the remotest intention of backing up its currency issuing powers with the kind of accounting framework which would have provided a much needed, if elementary Giro system; and second, as an obvious corollary, this meant that any form of Giro in the United Kingdom, rather than evolving gradually and naturally in a series of realistic, step by step adjustments within the Post Office itself, could come about, if at all, only as an enforced result of outside political pressures.

GROWTH OF SUPPORT FOR GIRO 1916–26

Easily the most readable of any of the propaganda material in favour of Giro that has appeared in Britain was the fifty page pamphlet issued by the Fabian Society in 1916 which was incorporated under Sidney Webb's editorship in a more general work entitled *How to Pay for the War*. It began roundly by saying that 'The British Post Office is far and away the biggest business undertaking in the British Empire . . . which could be sold any day on the basis of annual profits to an American or other capitalist syndicate for £100 million. . . . The British Postmaster General is the biggest banker in the world, but he is also the most cramped in his operations. This banking business has become extremely profitable to the Government, but owing to the jealousy of the capitalist banks, which do not like this Government competition, the Postmaster General is checked at every turn in expanding his business.' [27] As well as being the common carrier of the nation, the Post Office should also be its 'common banker, its common debt collector, its common investment agent and the common remittance market for the whole world'. It pointed to the profitable twenty year experience of Austria, of Germany and even of Japan—'more up to date than our own country'. In a special section dealing with its proposals for the development of banking and remittance business it pleaded for a change in the public's attitude: 'What is wanted is to get rid of the notion that there is something special and exceptional in the kind of bank which we call a Savings Bank: or that the Government is doing any favour to "the poorer classes" in running this extremely profitable business. In the United Kingdom the Post Office Savings Bank like the public elementary school was originally started, not as a proper and essential function of Government, but as a work of philanthropy . . . and is still regarded by persons of the "Upper Class" as in the nature of "charity", akin to Poor Relief. This conception has to be got rid of. In other countries every class, the richest as well as the poorest, uses the Post Office Savings Bank.' [28] The Fabians finished with an appeal especially 'to the bankers and the Stock Exchange . . . do not rashly be induced to back up those who have obstructed every Post Office reform'. [29]

Despite its military title neither the bankers nor the Stock Exchange, nor indeed many among the upper classes heard this clarion call above the tumult of war. Nevertheless, the Fabian pamphlet had its effect, especially just after the war, in inducing the main body of the political left, including the Labour Party as a whole, to adopt the cause of Giro, so that the support which before 1916 had been almost entirely confined to the trade unions, starting with only the postal unions, then the big craft unions followed by the TUC, had by the end of the war grown to embrace not only the unions as a whole, but also a rather wider spectrum of academic and political opinion, though still with a pronounced socialistic bias. Thus although yet another union deputation was sent away empty-handed by Lord Illingworth, Postmaster General, in November 1917, the postal unions, the TUC and a growing number of Labour MPs, nothing daunted stepped up the pressure in the first half of the 1920s. Consequently, the tide of socialist propaganda rose during 1924 and 1925 to reach its high water mark in 1926, a point from which it subsequently fell away, failing to reach such a high level again until the 1960s.

The establishment of the first Labour Government under Ramsay

MacDonald in January 1924, with a cabinet in which seven of its twenty members came from the trade unions, and with the Union of Postal Workers having their own chief spokesman, Mr Charles G Ammon elected to Parliament, seemed too good an opportunity to be lost. Mr Vernon Hartshorn, Labour's first Postmaster General, who might be expected to be more sympathetic than the previous nine holders of the post in the last decade—the appropriate badge of office would have been a baton—agreed to receive the inevitable deputation, which took place on 15 July 1924. This deputation as well as emphasising the benefits which would flow from a postal cheque system were so confident of their cause that they pressed for the appointment of a Committee of Enquiry to settle the matter once and for all. Before the end of the year the sympathetic Hartshorn had departed, handing his baton on to Sir William Mitchell-Thomson (later Lord Selsdon). The new Postmaster General arranged that the more permanent Secretary of the Post Office, the durable Sir Evelyn Murray, should receive the 1925 visitation, a slight but noticeable demotion for the deputation. At the same time (July 1925) Mr Charles Ammon, who luckily for the Union of Postal Workers had kept his seat at Camberwell North, took advantage of the debate on the Post Office estimates to ask the Chancellor of the Exchequer (Winston Churchill) if he would look into the matter. Having done so Churchill wrote to Mr Ammon on 7 September as follows: 'I find that the Post Office have investigated this system from 1908 onwards, but have never felt able to recommend its adoption. It is true that certain Continental countries have made a success of it . . . the main reason is that their banking systems are relatively undeveloped and the postal cheque system has the field more or less to itself. I am advised that it would be impossible for us to adopt the system without serious financial loss.' [30] Mr Ammon did not accept Churchill's argument (which carried of course the intonation if not the voice of Sir Evelyn Murray). He wrote an article explaining Giro in *The Times* and replied in some detail to Churchill's points in a further article in the *Labour Magazine* for December 1925: 'The British Postmaster General is the biggest banker in the world, although the most cramped in his operations'—proof at least of the lasting influence of the Fabian pamphlet of 1916. [31] Ammon also seconded the TUC's motion 'urging the adoption of the Postal Cheque System in conjunction with adequate expansion of the Post Office Savings Bank', at its Annual Meeting held in Bournemouth just four days after Churchill's letter of refusal. The resolution was of course carried, but already, partly as an indirect result of the General Strike, the tide in favour of Giro had begun to recede. [32]

DOLDRUMS 1927–56

As a result of the intense pressure of the previous three years Sir William Mitchell-Thomson finally agreed in December 1926 to set up the enquiry which had been demanded. The review was conducted by a three-man Committee consisting of George Lawson Johnston, John Cairns and Robert Holland-Martin (names not calculated to set the houses on fire). Their investigations, including a questionnaire addressed to the heads of continental postal Giros, were carried out during the course of 1926 and their findings, entitled *Postal Cheque System: Report of a Committee of the Post Office Advisory Council*, were published in March 1928. [33] The long awaited report comprised only ten pages in all, including the title page and three pages of rather skimpy statistics. The positive contribution of Mr Bowen of the Union of Post Office Workers, who had painstakingly presented the evidence for Giro—and who had taken a prominent part in all the deputations on the subject during the previous four years—had been almost summarised out of existence in three brief sentences. Apart from the questionnaire which proved, even to the satisfaction of the Committee, the widespread nature and general profitability of continental Giros, they went wearily over ground already well trampled. As to their conclusions, after managing to agree unanimously 'That a Postal Cheque System on the continental model should not be embarked on at the present stage'—chiefly because our commercial banking system would confine postal current accounts to unprofitably low values—they fell to quibbling about which particular form of completely useless substitute should be suggested instead. [34] Two went one way in proposing an unworkable scheme of limited cheques, while Mr John Cairns appended a one-page *Reservation* advocating a restricted system of 'unlimited' as well as limited cheques.

The publication of this thin, divisive and gloomy document symbolised the funeral rites of a movement which had shown such marked vigour and promise over the previous four years. So effectively was the campaign killed off that it took a generation to revive any real interest. It would however be paying the Johnston Committee an undeserved tribute to ascribe such lethal power to their adumbrations. The real causes of Giro's defeat lay mainly elsewhere, in the suicidal tendancies among the trade union movement as a whole associated with the disastrous General Strike of 1926. For the next twenty years the unions were to be too concerned with bigger things, including the long and painful attempt to regain the power, the numbers, the prestige and the legality that they lost as a result of the strike, to be able to afford to continue to espouse to any effect the cause of Giro, to which, as we have seen, they had devoted unstinted attention for twenty years before 1928. Trade Union membership fell by over $2\frac{1}{2}$ million in the two years following the strike, 'the heaviest loss of members that ever occurred in so short a time'. [35] The decline continued until 1933 when union membership fell to just over 4 million, compared with over 8 million in 1920.

We have seen that successive Postmasters General had always felt uncomfortable about the closeness of the links which the postal trade unions enjoyed with the TUC and the Labour Party and also had repeatedly expressed fears concerning the vulnerability of any reformed postal bank to the huge synchronised withdrawals which they felt would accompany strikes or lock-outs. Despite the fact that the postal trade unions were specifically excused by the TUC from joining in the General Strike, the punitive Trades Dispute and Trade Union Act of 1927 indirectly struck a severe blow at a strategic point by severing that close and fruitful connection which had done so much to channel the wider political and unionist powers behind the movement of Giro. Although civil servants could still remain members of their union, each union of civil servants had to leave both the Trades Union Congress and the Labour Party and dissociate itself from any similar relationships with other unions. In this connection it is worth noticing that one of the first measures taken by the Labour Government after the 1945 election was to repeal the 1927 Act, and that one of the first unions to seek immediate re-affiliation with the TUC as a result was the Union of Post Office Workers. In the intervening years, however, this severance goes far to explain the collapse of the campaign for Giro.

With regard to the actual as opposed to the anticipated effects of strikes on the safety of banks because of withdrawals of working-class deposits, it is instructive to consider the statistics during the three-year period spanning the General Strike. Some 162 230 000 working days were lost by strikes during 1926, an unprecedented situation which might have been expected to lead, both directly and indirectly, to what in the nineteenth century would have been called a 'run' on the banks. Since, however, a major part of the case for Giro lay in the fact that the working class as a whole did not have accounts with the joint-stock banks, then the direct effects on these banks were bound to be somewhat limited. By the same token, however, the effects on those institutions which did cater for working-class deposits, might be expected to be all the greater. An examination of the relevant figures as given in the tables, however, explodes the myth of the inevitable weakness of working-class financial institutions because of strikes. The figures for the Post Office Savings Bank, the Trustee Savings Bank and the Co-operative Bank for the mid-1920s show results very different from those which might have been expected. The Post Office Savings Bank statistics show relatively minor variations in deposits and withdrawals over the three years 1925–27 and are so reassuring that even the strongest opponents of Giro would find it difficult to interpret these figures as offering any confirmation of the fears expressed by Sir Herbert Samuel and others. The statistics for the second type of working-class bank, the Trustee Savings Banks, show that although deposits fell this was more than compensated for by the increase in other deposits, so that the total balances due to depositors rose by about £3 million in 1926 and £5 million in 1927. The number of depositors also increased by 70 000 during this period. There was not the slightest sign of a 'run' on either of these banks.

Furthermore, the experience of the only other widespread 'working-class' bank, and one which moreover combined a current account with deposit and savings accounts, the Co-operative Bank, would indicate that even in those exceptionally adverse conditions, such a bank could not only survive but within a remarkably short while begin to flourish again. Indeed, far from looking at their experiences as a defeat the Co-operative Bank proudly singles out this period for mention in its Centenary Report: 'Considerable demands were made upon the Bank for strike pay. Postal communications were dislocated and thousands of instructions to co-operative societies to cash pay cheques had to be telephoned and telegraphed to virtually every town and village in the country. The great flexibility of the Bank's Retail Society Agency System was clearly demonstrated in that period of national crisis.' [36] The

83

	ORDINARY DEPOSITS			NATIONAL SAVINGS CERTIFICATES			GOVERNMENT STOCK		
	DEPOSITS £M	WITHDRAWALS £M	OUTSTANDING DEPOSITS £M	DEPOSITS £M	WITHDRAWALS £M	OUTSTANDING £M	PURCHASES £M	SALES £M	OUTSTANDING £M
1925	83	85	285·5	37	35	374	6·5	20·8	183·7
1926	74	83	283·7	32	42	374	5·9	6·0	184·6
1927	76	81	284·6	36	58	368	10·8	11·2	188·6

Table 3.1 Post Office Savings Bank Accounts 1925–27

	NUMBER OF DEPOSITORS '000s	ORDINARY DEPARTMENT £M	STOCK DEPARTMENT £M	SPECIAL INVESTMENT DEPARTMENT £M	TOTAL BALANCES DUE TO DEPOSITORS £M
1925	2341	83·4	31·8	27·0	142·2
1926	2355	82·0	34·0	28·8	144·9
1927	2413	81·4	36·2	32·5	150·1

Table 3.2 Trustee Saving Bank Accounts 1925–27

growth of the bank hardly faltered. The number of current accounts, which was only 5300 in 1919 rose to 21 600 in 1926, to 23 250 in 1927 and to 26 000 by the end of 1929. Its assets similarly grew from only £10 million in 1919 to £29 million in 1925, fell slightly to £28·5 million in 1926, bounded up again to nearly £33 million in 1927 and reached £43 million in 1929. What is being argued is *not* that the huge Post Office Savings Bank could have grown at anything like the pace of the comparatively small Co-operative Bank, for clearly it could not; but the point, which is a valid one, is that if a small bank without government backing could survive the storm with hardly a tremor, then this destroyed the argument that a large government-backed bank would inevitably fail. Therefore, it did not follow that a strike would be bound to ruin a Post Office Bank which combined both current and deposit accounts— but the argument had been sufficiently plausible to carry conviction.

CONCLUSION: DEATH OF THE FIRST CAMPAIGN

The events outlined above help to explain the reverse suffered by Giro supporters in the years following the General Strike. Yet in retrospect, the extent of the collapse and its duration remain astonishing. It was not that the subject of the Post Office or of its reform was neglected: far from it, for this period was most prolific in producing a series of official and private publications assailing the Post Office from inside and out-side, not only from the Labour left, but also from the Liberal centre and the Conservative right. The Secretary of the Post Office, a former Under-Secretary and Assistant Postmaster General, a former Post-master General, as well as the Postal Unions themselves, all published detailed criticisms of the Post Office. It was not as if the Post Office were making a loss. At a time of deep business depression when so many private firms were failing, the Post Office was if anything increasing its profits and raking in something between £10 million and £13 million per annum. Thus it is still the more remarkable that these critical publica-tions all managed to prod and probe the Post Office without once sug-gesting that the postal cheque and Giro system was ever a live issue. Sir Evelyn Murray, who as Secretary had been at the centre of the Giro controversy, had taken the refuge customary to the cautious public servant: 'A civil servant must walk warily in writing of the affairs of his own Department . . . I have endeavoured to avoid questions of current controversy'. [37] This remark, taken from the Preface of his book on *The Post Office* is a masterpiece of understatement. Lord Wolmer, Assistant Postmaster General for five years, was not quite so circumspect, for he purposely, and no doubt a little pretentiously, chose the title of Rowland Hill's explosive book *Post Office Reform: Its Importance and Practicability* as his own: yet not a word of Giro. When the new Parliament of the National Government met at the end of 1931, no fewer than 320 supporters of the Government, comprising more than half of the House of Commons, signed the following Memorial to the Prime Minister: 'We the undersigned Members of Parliament are of the opinion that at a time of National Reconstruction, and when the greatest economy and efficiency are necessary in all the Services of the State, a thorough and impartial examination should be made into the status and organisation of the Post Office with a view to effecting such changes in its constitution as will tend to improve the efficiency of the services for which it is responsible.' [38] The resulting Bridgeman Committee on Post Office Reform might sadly be excused for sticking so supinely to its restrictive terms of reference that it, too, completely ignored what so recently had been such a burning topic. Major Clement Attlee, however, a former Postmaster General and future Labour leader, could have had no such alibi; and yet in writing on the subject of Post Office reform in the not usually very conservative *New Statesman*, he too signally failed to breathe a word about Giro. [39] Still more surprising is the fact that in presenting its case for postal reform before the Bridgeman Committee, the Secretary of the Union of Post Office Workers was similarly completely silent on the subject of Giro. [40]

Thus the first campaign which had been promising, active and growing for the twenty years from 1908–28 had suddenly became moribund and eventually died away so completely that no effective progress was made either in the 1930s or 1940s. It required the growing disenchantment with the working of the monetary system which began to show itself in the 1950s and the resulting outside stimulus in the shape of the Radcliffe Committee to bring about a new, shorter and this time successful campaign for a British Giro.

REFERENCES

1   BURKE, EDWARD, Quoted by Lord Wolmer in *Post Office Reform* (London, 1932), p. 32.

2   WEBB, B and WEBB, S, *History of Trade Unionism* (London, 1920), pp. 261–2.
3   PELLING, H, *A History of British Trade Unionism* (London, 1963), pp. 261–2.
4   MURRAY, SIR EVELYN, *The Post Office* (London, 1927), p. 197.
5   WEBB, B and WEBB, S, *op. cit.*, p. 508.
6   *Trades Union Congress Report, 1909.*
7   *Trades Union Congress Report, 1910.*
8   *Post Office Records File, England, 6637/1911.*
9   *Ibid.*
10 COFFIELD, J, *A Popular History of Taxation* (London, 1970), p. 171.
11 *Post Office Records File, 6637/1911*, Notes on second deputation, pp. 7–8.
12 *Ibid.*
13 *Ibid.*, pp. 42–3.
14 *Post Office Records File, 6636/1911*, p. 8.
15 PELLING, H, *op. cit.*, pp. 136–8, 261–2.
16 *Post Office Records File, 6636/1911*, Evidence of the Postmaster General, p. 42.
17 MURRAY, SIR EVELYN, *op. cit.*, pp. 154–5.
18 GOODHART, C A E, *The Business of Banking 1891–1914* (London, 1972), p. 107.
19 *Trades Union Congress Report, 1912.*
20 *Ibid.*
21 LLOYD GEORGE, D, *War Memoirs* (London, 1938), Vol. 1, pp. 64–5.
22 *Currency and Bank Notes Act 1914*, Section 1(6).
23 *Post Office Records File, 4455/1915, September.*
24 'Additional Legal Tender', Gilbart Lectures No. 1, *The Bankers' Magazine* (February, 1915).
25 *Post Office Records File, 4455/1915 October.*
26 *Ibid.*, 'Postal Orders as Currency: 5s and 2s 6d Orders as Legal Tender'.
27 WEBB, S, *The Fabian Society: The Development of the Post Office: A Study prepared in the Research Department* (London, 1916) pp. 1 and 14 (also occurs as Chapter 1 of *How to Pay for the War* (London, 1916)).
28 WEBB, S, *ibid.*, pp. 20–1.
29 WEBB, S, *ibid.*, p. 48.
30 CHURCHILL, W S, Quoted by Charles G Ammon in 'Banking Reform and the Postal Cheque System', *The Labour Magazine* (London, December 1925), p. 346.
31 CHURCHILL, W S, *ibid.*, p. 347.
32 *Trades Union Congress Report (1926)*, p. 481.
33 *Postal Cheque System: Report of a Committee of the Post Office Advisory Council*, Cmd. 3151 (H.M.S.O., 1928).
34 *Ibid.*, p. 6.
35 PELLING, H, *op. cit.*, p. 178.
36 PARRY, B T, *A Brief History of the Co-operative Bank* (1972)—published by the Bank to mark its 100 Anniversary.
37 MURRAY, SIR EVELYN, *op. cit.*, Preface.
38 *Report of the Committee of Enquiry on The Post Office*, Cmd. 4149.
39 ATTLEE, C R, *New Statesman* (London, 7 November 1931), p. 565.
40 *The Post*, 4 April 1932.

Chapter 4

The Tide of Success: 1957–65

'The question is so wide and complicated that it takes a long time to resolve.'
J R Bevins, Postmaster General, 1962. [1]

RUMBLINGS PRE-RADCLIFFE

The 1940s showed only the merest trickle of interest in the cause of a
British Giro, a trickle which grew into a stream in the 1950s and which in
turn, after the publication of the Radcliffe Report in 1959, grew into a
flood that by the mid 1960s swept all opposition before it. Although the
general public hardly became aware of the renewal of the movement in
favour of postal current-account banking until the Radcliffe Committee
began its historic enquiry into the working of the monetary system—
the first such examination since the Macmillan Report of 1931, and so
far as Giro was concerned, the first since the ill-starred Johnston Report
of 1928—there had already been a few signs of renewed interest, in the
shape of published papers by academics, financial journalists and practical bankers, so that the subject was already being warmed up by the
time the members of the 1957 Committee recaptured the wider attention of the general public. However, if one particular date was to be
chosen to mark the effective start of the final campaign, a campaign
which was to lead with hardly an interruption to the opening of National
Giro just over a decade later, it is the 3 May 1957, when the Radcliffe
Committee was appointed with the following vague, brief but gloriously
wide terms of reference: 'To enquire into the working of the monetary
and credit system and to make recommendations'. [2] Without the
powerful, neutral, but on balance distinctly favourable light cast by
this Committee, it is doubtful whether Britain would ever have come

88

round to setting up a postal Giro system, or even its pale reflection the so-called 'bank-Giro' which the clearing banks themselves developed.

In order to restrain current consumption during the Second World War, a system of 'post-war credits' was inaugurated along the lines suggested in J M Keynes' *How to Pay for the War*. Whereas Sidney Webb's 1916 book of the same title was directly and powerfully concerned with proposing a Giro system, Keynes' 1940 publication was only very indirectly responsible for reviving an ephemeral interest in the concept, in that it prompted Dr A Fischer, a graduate of Prague University and a former representative of the Federation of British Industries in Czechoslovakia, to contribute an article to the *Accountant* in December 1941, suggesting that here was an admirable practical opportunity for the British Post Office to benefit from the example of those continental post offices with which the author was familiar. His article had just one purpose: 'It only intends to show, as briefly as possible, the means of effecting payments provided by the Postal Cheque Institutes established in the Central European Countries, and it may be that the Postmaster General will find that similar facilities would permanently benefit the millions of prospective holders of savings tax accounts.' [3] Fischer's faith in the superiority of a Giro system was obvious, and he felt confident that if only the Post Office could bring itself to experiment with this one simple arrangement for recording and transferring tax credits then the benefits would be so widely welcomed that a permanent Giro system would inevitably result.

Needless to say the authorities were deaf to this advice. The Post Office Savings Bank—as its later testimony to the Radcliffe Committee was to make crystal clear—remained obdurately hostile to the concept of current account banking. The war gratuities and other release benefits paid to ex-service men helped to boost annual deposits in the Post Office Savings Bank from the 1939 figure of £149 million to £558 million in 1945 and to £754 million in 1946 and much of these, had Fischer's idea been adopted, might have remained inside the postal banking system. As it was however, withdrawals from the POSB exceeded deposits in each of the following eleven years from 1947 to 1957 inclusive. [4] What an opportunity was lost through ignoring Fischer's advice. The millions of ex-service men and women, as well as the millions of civilians with post-war credits, who might so easily have become a captive market for a postal Giro service, reverted by and large to the old-fashioned and inconvenient awkwardness of a cash-bound society.

The campaign which apart from Fischer's fleeting contribution had remained dormant if not dead ever since 1928, was raised to new life in March 1954 when the Manchester Statistical Society invited Professor R S Sayers of the London School of Economics to deliver a lecture on 'Twentieth Century Banking'. The distinguished Professor—who was shortly afterward to be chosen as a member of the Radcliffe Committee—declared that: 'It seems likely enough that we could get most of our banking accounting work done for us at lower real cost if it were hived off from the banks and handed over to a single highly-centralised and mechanised branch of the Post Office . . . The banks, historically more concerned with their function in the capital market, have equipped themselves with offices and personnel which though appropriate to their earlier functions, are rather extravagant for a purely accounting machine. In short, are so many fine and well-staffed offices necessary when so much of the business is of a routine accounting nature?' [5] Although he claimed to be sitting on the fence—for his stated purpose was 'to raise the questions rather than to suggest final answers'—nevertheless, he conceded that 'If this argument were accepted, the logical consequence would be for the State to establish forthwith a State postal cheque system of the Continental kind. I am indeed always wondering why such a plan has never been seriously discussed.' [6] Regarding the latter point, even if the long series of discussions during the twenty years preceding the Johnston Report were nothing like as penetrating or effective as those which Professor Sayers and his fellow committee members were soon to undertake, they had as we have demonstrated been carried out with considerable patience and much gravity! Yet it is a telling indication of how dead the issue of postal Giro had become since 1928 that Sayers could consider himself with at least some justification as a pioneer in resurrecting the subject in this controversial manner.

His Manchester Lecture prompted Professor G Clayton, then a lecturer in Economics at Liverpool, who was perturbed by the 'widespread ignorance in this country about the operation of postal cheque systems' to contribute to our enlightenment by publishing a brief analysis of the Swedish postal Giro in *The Bankers' Magazine* of September 1956. He justified 'the value of studying the monetary systems of

90

other countries' by 'the stimulus it may give to a critical examination of the practices of one's own'. He concluded with a clear warning to the banks, coupled with a rather left-handed invitation to the Post Office: 'It would be a complacent man who, after studying the efficient operation of the Swedish post Giro and the Swedish banks' customer transfer service, would argue that the British methods and costs of handling payment by cheque could not be improved. It is clear that many small account-holders are dissatisfied with the present level of bank charges and the anomalies in the methods of calculating them. The more vigorously the commercial banks tackle the problem of reducing them, the less likely that there will be a demand for taking the extreme step of establishing a postal cheque system under the GPO.' [7]

BANKS BECOME INVOLVED

So far the protagonists of a British Giro had included few, if any, practising bankers, but in the course of the following two years first the industrial bankers and directors of the hire purchase finance companies and secondly the joint-stock bankers themselves began to join in the fray. The tremendous growth of hire purchase in the post-war period meant that an increasing number of customers, including a high proportion without bank accounts, were having to make periodic repayments for the cars and other consumer durables which they had purchased. Many were finding the process more awkward and costly than seemed necessary. Consequently, the Industrial Bankers' Association first approached the Postmaster General in July 1957 to advocate 'a new transfer system on the lines of the Giro'. [8] In September 1958 the subject exploded inside the joint-stock banking world itself when Mr C F Karsten, Managing Director of the Rotterdamsche Bank, delivered a paper entitled *Banking without Cheques* at the Eleventh International Banking Summer School, which was being held that year at St Andrews, and which had taken as its general theme the future organisation of banking. Drawing from his detailed knowledge of the Dutch scene, Mr Karsten unequivocally claimed that: 'Apart from being cheap, the postal transfer service has an enormous advantage over the banks in that it has a practically unlimited number of branches . . . It is clear that it is impossible for the banks to compete with this service for the same

91

price.' [9] No longer could the case for Giro be dismissed as a left-wing fantasy or as a flight of theorising suitable for academics without the responsibility for translating thought into action.

Karsten's practical approach immediately struck a sympathetic cord in the mind of Sir Oscar Hobson, the doyen of financial journalists, who expanded and Anglicised Karsten's ideas so as to present a formidable challenge to British Bankers—a challenge which they could no longer afford to ignore. Sir Oscar presented his views in *The Banker* of November 1958 under the heading 'Towards a Banking Democracy'. After pointing to the overdue need to modify the old Truck Acts so as to allow the payment of wages by cheque or transfer—otherwise the democratisation of banking would remain an empty dream—he went on to contrast the cumbersome and awkward method of the typical payment by cheque, 'requiring as it does some six physical journeys before the cheque finally returns to its originator', with the simplicity and directness of a Giro order: 'There is no doubt that the Giro method of payment is simpler and more straightforward, and therefore cheaper to operate, than the cheque method . . . The extension of the banking habit among the mass of the workers in Britain will hardly be possible unless and until the Giro system is greatly developed. Payment by transfer and not by cheque will have to become the rule and not the exception, and all the resources of modern science—electronics, photography, calculating and record-storing machinery—will have to be invoked to make that possible.' [10] Sir Oscar's prophetic article also correctly foreshadowed the clearing banks' reaction as soon as they became convinced that a postal Giro was inevitable. He agreed with Karsten that 'our banks would be very foolish to allow the Post Office or any other authority to get away with (the profits to be made from) the establishment of an efficient Giro system'. [11] The very next issue of *The Banker* contained a letter from Mr A D Chesterfield, Chief General Manager of the Westminster Bank, replying to Sir Oscar Hobson's challenge. The controversy was now raised to a new level of intensity, and so it was most opportune that at this stage the whole of the argument should be taken up by the Radcliffe Committee which as we have seen, had been in operation for a year, but had been occupied in the main with other matters. It was now ready to take up this ripe, controversial and topical subject with the Committee of the London Clearing Bankers and with the officials of the Post Office Savings Bank.

RADCLIFFE WEIGHS THE EVIDENCE

The Radcliffe Committee (a galaxy of legal, financial, academic, business and trade union talent) achieved a high velocity in leaving no banking tablets unturned, however apparently sacred and fixed they might previously have appeared. They were resolved that all the oral evidence given at 59 of their 88 meetings and all the main written memoranda would be available for publication. Thus, although they were asked in their terms of reference to make recommendations, the report does not conclude with an 'action list' of direct and specific recommendations. The general philosophy inspiring the eminent Committee was rather to give the subjects to be dealt with such a public airing that the reader of the Report and still more of the voluminous Memoranda and Minutes of Evidence would be able to arrive at a much more informed and correct, if perhaps less dogmatic, conclusion than would have been the case if he could simply have turned to a final brief list of recommendations carrying the whiff of authoritative commandments. There were, however, four rather exceptional instances where the Committee made pointed and specific recommendations with regard to the development of monetary institutions—export finance, the finance of industrial innovation, longer-term loans for industry and agriculture and the transfer of payments. Thus although the subject of Giro could not be claimed to have been of paramount concern to the Committee and although it was the penultimate subject dealt with in the Report, yet the various conflicting views were so thoroughly investigated that the public were able to judge the merits of the case in a way that had never been possible previously.

The first of the clearing bankers to be questioned on the subject of Giro were Messrs William Watson, Treasurer of the Bank of Scotland, and A P Anderson, General Manager of the British Linen Bank, representing the Committee of Scottish Bank General Managers. In answer to Professor Sayers' question regarding their attitude if a postal Giro were established they replied simply, 'We should not regard that with favour'. They attempted to explain away the success of continental Giros as arising from their lack of 'a highly developed branch banking system' only to be pulled up by Sayers' rejoinder that Norway, Switzerland, Holland and Sweden all had highly developed branch banking systems and this had not prevented their Giros from being profitable, cheap and efficient. [12] This was but a foretaste of the more substantial discussions which took place nearly a year later with the representatives of the English clearing bankers—Messrs D J Robarts, Chairman of the National Provincial Bank, A W Tuke, Director of Barclays and A D Chesterfield, the Chief General Manager of Westminster Bank. They had been given beforehand a list of eight points as a basis for their discussion, the fourth of these being concerned with 'personal cheques' and 'continental experience with postal Giro' including 'the consequences for the banks'. [13] Not only were the English bankers forewarned in a way the Scots had not been, but in the meantime the subject of Giro had caught the attention of the banking world as shown above. Furthermore, Chesterfield himself had become publicly involved in print. His letter was therefore the obvious starting point for the discussion, particularly since all agreed that it could be taken as representing the views of the banks as a whole.

Mr Chesterfield's letter, though brief, was and probably still remains the best statement of the case made out by those bankers who have consistently opposed the postal Giro system, partly indeed because of the letter's quiet reasonableness and its pervading quality of restraint. Indeed, so restrained were its contents that Professor Sayers, mistakenly as it turned out, 'had the impression from it . . . that if there is a job to be done it is to be done by the Post Office rather than the banks'. [14] This was not at all what the bankers had wished to convey. Chesterfield, however, put his finger on what in retrospect has been seen to be a most vulnerable spot, in questioning whether a Giro system 'would bring in sufficient interest-free deposits to make it a profitable undertaking'. He believed that it would take years to establish a postal Giro and that it might have some effect in reducing the rate of growth of bank current accounts—which he vaguely estimated was then growing at an annual rate of between two and three hundred thousand. Since the banks did not seem very frightened at the prospect of some loss of potential customers, it is perhaps difficult to reconcile this with the strength of their opposition. In reply to Professor Cairncross the banks admitted that they did not know what proportion of the adult population carried current accounts with the banks, but guessed that it was 'at least 50%', which would leave a substantial potential for new competition. Mr Tuke enlivened the proceedings by repeating the point made by the Scottish bankers that on the Continent 'the banking system is not so highly developed as here and people get their money paid to them in cash. We have a highly developed banking system and that is a higher grade of society. It would be a retrograde thing for England to go in for a Giro'. [15] To this Professor Sayers suggested that it was rather the case 'that in England the banking system has had the opportunity to push further down the income structure because the Post Office has been so backward in not providing us with a system of this kind'. [16]

Mr Tuke then pointed to the example of the United States where the cheque was used even more than in Britain and objected to the development of a streamlined personal cheque system as introducing a 'second-class' service into banking. Much of the irrelevance of this traditional banking view—that the use of cheques was a rough index of economic maturity—had already been good humouredly but devastatingly attacked by Karsten at St Andrews the previous summer: 'Though it is often said that this relation has something to do with the state of economic and social development of the country concerned, I can hardly believe that you will be quite satisfied by this explanation. To our Belgian friends this would mean that their highly industrialised country is as yet to be put somewhere on the list of less developed regions. I feel, therefore, more inclined to ascribe this and also other differences in paying habits to the influence of tradition.' [17] The subsequent surge of economic growth in the European Economic Community has encouraged a vast expansion both in the commercial banking and in the postal banking systems of these countries, and in so doing has further eroded the dubious merits of the claim that our 'higher grade of society' rendered a Giro system inappropriate. Be that as it may, it was at last abundantly clear from the evidence of the London and Scottish clearing bankers, that the British banking tradition seemed dead set against any development of a postal current account banking system. It also became painfully clear that this tradition was still being shared by the postal authorities themselves.

The Post Office Savings Bank submitted a long Memorandum to the Committee in which it pointed out that the greater proportion of the banks' total deposits 'is owned by a minority of the depositors and to a considerable degree transactions are in the nature of current account banking or for short-term savings purposes'. [18] It also stated explicitly that 'The Post Office Savings Bank does not encourage current account banking business, nor does it encourage the payment of household bills, such as rates, gas and electricity accounts, through Savings Bank accounts. These activities are contrary to the purpose of the Savings Bank and are costly to the State.' [19] In his evidence Mr G D Frazer, Director of Savings, explained with apparent pride how the Savings Bank did all it could to *prevent* the deposit of wages and salaries: 'We are to some extent able to control the current account aspect of the Savings Bank. The limit on deposits is £500 in any one year. We have held on to that maximum annual investment, and we would not like to see it rise, because if it were higher it would encourage the deposit of salary cheques. . . . By restraining the investment potential to £500 a year, we feel that we are keeping out the deposit of salary cheques to a very large extent'. [20] Since the Post Office Savings Bank was thus obviously worried because the bank was being used for short-term accounts, Professor Sayers asked whether they might not 'offer a current account service (which, obviously from your experience of people using this, is a thing much in demand)? Have you considered hiving off of the current account business?'. To this Mr Frazer replied 'No, we have not. We have thought that it would not be practicable to distinguish between types of accounts within the one organisation. We have always operated as the Post Office Savings Bank and we have always frowned upon the use of the Savings Bank for current account purposes.' [21] When Professor Sayers again pressed the matter and referred to continental postal cheque systems, Mr Frazer repeated the argument which the joint-stock bankers were always using adding that 'if the commercial banks had developed as well in the Continental countries as they are in this country, they probably would not have had a postal cheque system.' Sayers considered this 'a travesty of the facts'. Mr Frazer refused to be drawn into considering a postal cheque system: 'The ramifications of that are rather outside my own responsibility as Director of Savings. . . . I do not feel that I am capable of giving a closer opinion than that the Post Office Savings Bank could not take on a postal cheque system without very grave consideration.' [22] It was obvious that the attitude of the postal authorities was as far removed as it had always been from any eager acceptance of current account banking, a situation which persistently prevented the natural development of Giro as a closely integrated branch of the Post Office Savings Bank, as had been the case in a number of continental countries.

In weighing the conflicting streams of evidence, the Radcliffe Committee came to their considered opinion, a landmark in the history of National Giro, that:

The experience of other countries suggests that some simple mechanism for transferring payments, without the ancillary services provided by the banks, would be an amenity which might be welcomed and used by the public in this country. A new payments mechanism might take the form of a 'giro' system operated by the General Post Office; the Post Office's comprehensive network of branches would clearly be a strong argument in favour of providing the mechanism in this way, and, even though it would mean some additional staff and extension of premises for the Post Office, it must be borne in mind that some of the existing postal and money order business would be transferred to the 'giro' side. It could on the other hand, be provided by the joint-stock banks, or by the Trustee Savings Banks (though this would give rather less satisfactory geographical coverage); or by a combination of all three ... We consider that, in the absence of an early move on the part of existing institutions to provide the services which will cater for the need we have in mind, there would be a case for investigating the possibility of instituting a 'giro' system to be operated by the Post Office. This investigation would have to make some assessment of the demand for, and likely use and growth of, such a system, the technical and practical problems of entrusting the operation of the system to the Post Office, and the possibility of co-operating with the joint-stock banks and savings banks: in all these matters it would be necessary to take full account of continental experience. [23]

RIVAL TRANSFER PAYMENT SCHEMES

The publication of the Radcliffe Report led immediately to two important streams of development: first, it posed an urgent problem for the Post Office, the clearing banks and the Trustee Savings Banks, who would now be clearly expected by the public to make up their minds about whether they wished to set up a Giro system or not; and second, it brought the general public back into the discussion regarding the pros and cons of Giro, which was all the more necessary since any positive decision arrived at by either the Post Office or the Trustee Savings Banks would require new legislation and hence would necessarily involve the political machine. Although the Radcliffe Report did not, as we have seen, make a definite suggestion that the Post Office, or anyone else, should immediately set about establishing a Giro system (what it did was to emphasise the urgent need for a detailed examination of the case), yet it seems equally clear that the Committee's view of the probable order of priority was first the Post Office, second the banks and then some distance behind, the Trustee Savings Banks, which latter they considered, however, to be rather too thin on the ground to have much of a claim if either of the other two main contenders were to press ahead with their own payment transfer scheme. In retrospect it is an ironic commentary on how new financial institutions actually come to be founded that none of those suggested by the Radcliffe Committee as potential parents had themselves proposed such a solution: they had either pointedly ignored or strongly opposed it. A three-way combined Giro operated by the Post Office, the Trustee and the clearing banks together demanded a common will and a degree of mutual confidence that were obviously lacking. Each went its own way so that instead of having a single simple credit-transfer system operated from one centre, we managed to develop a number of different systems operating from at least two centres. The danger that we should find ourselves with too many payment systems chasing too few and too confused customers did not become widely apparent until the beginning of the 1970s, and though this *was* a factor in explaining the Conservative Government's hesitancy, even then it was the stagnation of the economy in general that was largely to blame for the disappointingly slow rate of growth of new accounts for all three institutions taken together, so that the gain of one was at the expense of the other. Inevitably, in these circumstances it was the last of the three to get going that suffered the most. Even before the decision to establish a postal Giro was announced in 1965 the two other rival institutions had already gone some considerable way in developing their competing services and capturing potential postal Giro accounts.

First off the mark were the clearing banks. The Midland Bank had already introduced its 'personal cheque' service for those customers who wanted a simple payments mechanism with a fixed charge known beforehand without requiring any ancillary services. Barclays Bank, which as

we have seen, did not particularly like this 'second-class' form of banking, launched its credit card, while the other banks developed their
cheque-guarantee cards and similar devices to improve the usefulness
and attractiveness of the cheque or debit-transfer system for those customers with current accounts. Much more directly competitive with any
potential postal Giro was the clearing banks' credit transfer or 'bank
Giro' service which they agreed upon and developed quickly in a number of stages so that by 1 October 1961, just over two years after Radcliffe had reported on the need for them to make 'early moves' in this
direction, their initial credit transfer scheme became fully operative,
while from 1967 their more comprehensive 'bank-Giro' began to be
vigorously advertised. The banks' credit clearing, involving accounts of
non-bank customers as well as for the banks' own customers, was performed by their London Clearing House which had long carried out the
vastly more important debit or cheque clearing system. To call this
bank credit-transfer scheme a 'Giro' might have been technically correct, but it was a somewhat unfortunate use of terminology. As we saw
in the first chapter with over fifty countries using different varieties of
Giro, the term has a range and elasticity of meaning which could at a
stretch encompass even the British clearing banks' new scheme. But
neither in geographical range of coverage nor in its charges did the so-
called bank Giro compare with the typical continental Giro with its
single centralised accounting system and its completely free current
accounts. Eventually the clearing banks did develop a joint purpose-
built central computing centre, at Edgware, London; but this was not
opened until November 1972. Thus as well as running off with some
of the belated National Giro's potential customers, the clearing banks
made off also with the core of its distinctive name, so adding to the
difficulties of the Post Office's infant organisation and to the confusion
of customers faced with two British variants of a novel foreign-sounding
institution.

The high cost of bank money transfer had featured in the evidence
which the Finance Houses Association gave to the Radcliffe Committee:
'In recent years there has been a regrettable tendency for Joint-Stock
Banks to act in concert in fixing terms'. The Finance Houses Association
complained about the 'charge of 1s for each payment received over a
bank counter for the credit of a Hire Purchase Finance Company'. [24]
Consequently, the hire purchase firms were glad that their customers

could benefit from the banks' new credit-transfer facilities, though they clearly saw it as a second best solution. In 1962, two years after the early stages of the so-called bank Giro had been set up, the Industrial Bankers' Association was still complaining about the time taken to clear their credit transfer slips and still demanding a proper postal Giro service: a demand they repeated in the following year. [25] These new credit-transfer payments as well as the cheque facilities offered by non-clearing bankers, such as the Co-operative and Trustee Savings Banks, were completely dependent for their operation on the good will of the joint-stock banks who own and control the London Clearing House. This exclusive and monopolistic position of the London Clearing House has subsequently grown from being a minor irritant into a major target for outside criticism. Thus Brian Griffiths in a timely publication which heralded the new era of more open competition has strongly recommended that: 'The Co-operative Bank, savings banks, building societies and foreign banks should neither be discouraged from entering retail banking nor from becoming members of the clearing house, which should be run as an independent agency of the central bank'. [26]

It is a noteworthy but apparently perverse and permanent feature of the British financial scene that governmental or government-sponsored banks have always been most narrowly and strictly circumscribed by written and inflexible legal constitutions, whereas, in happy contrast, private sector banks, including foreign banks, have enjoyed a far greater degree of freedom from legal constraint. This crucial difference between state and private banking was partly concealed by the recurrent credit squeezes of the post-war period, but became wider and much more obvious after the revolutionary change to the new and freer forms of 'competition and credit control' which were announced in August 1971. It was therefore not surprising that this emerged as a specific issue of complaint to the Page Committee which investigated the various segments of the National Savings Movement during 1972; but the fact that the joint-stock banks reacted much more quickly to the Radcliffe proposals than did either the Postal or Trustee Savings Banks was an earlier example of the inhibiting influence of the constitutions of the latter banks. Before any real advance could be made by either the Trustee Savings Banks or the Post Office towards establishing the current account banking services which their existing constitutions denied them, not only did a series of internal examinations have to be conducted, but also the laborious and time-consuming process had to be followed of carrying new Bills through Parliament.

As for National Giro's other main rival, the Association of the Trustee Savings Banks decided against setting up a Giro system for their own customers, preferring instead to imitate the banks' chequing account system. Among the reasons for this was the fact noted by Radcliffe that their geographic coverage was thin. Their 1300 branches in 1959 compared very unfavourably with the Post Office's 24 000. Their coverage was also very uneven. Whereas as many as nearly one-third of the population of Scotland have Trustee Savings Bank accounts (and in three Scottish counties the proportion rises to over 50%), in England and in Wales the proportion falls to 17% and 9% respectively. Three counties, two in Wales and one in Scotland—Anglesey, Merioneth and Sutherland—had, in 1970, no Trustee Savings Bank account holders, while in London the proportion was less than 4%. [27] Furthermore, the resources of the seventy-five Trustee Savings Banks varied enormously, ranging from the biggest, which since the merger of the London and Brighton banks in November 1971 is the 'London and South Eastern Trustee Savings Bank' with funds of over £250 million, through Glasgow Trustee Savings Bank, now the second in size but previously the largest with around £180 million, down to that of the smallest, Newburgh, with funds of only around £160 000. Thus the strain of launching a new Giro system was considered beyond the power of the numerous smaller Trustee Savings Banks, and without a Central Savings Bank to compensate for these deficiencies, the difficulties, it was felt, could not be surmounted. Thus the 'supply' side of the equation was weak. With regard to creating an effective demand it was also felt that the Trustee Savings Bank did not have the funds available for the kind of advertising required to persuade existing and potential customers to switch to a new system with which they were completely unfamiliar. For these reasons the Trustee Savings Banks decided instead to press for the less radical current account chequing system operated through the London clearing banks, a service which the Trustee Savings Banks considered they could develop gradually in line with their limited advertising budgets. After a difficult series of discussions with the Treasury, the National Debt Office and the joint-stock banks, whose clearing system was essential for their scheme, the official sanction was given.

As a result of a Private Members' Bill introduced by Lord Burden into the Upper House in December 1963, where it was unopposed at the Second Reading, the enabling Act was passed in 1964 and the scheme put into operation in the following year. Of course, four needless and irritating restrictions had to be enacted as the price of conceding to the Trustee Savings Banks their long-standing desire to offer cheque-drawing facilities: (1) the new current accounts were to bear no interest: (2) overdrafts were not to be granted, nor, (3) were the facilities to be used for trade, industrial or business purposes. Fourth, the service was not open to any individual (as were those of the commercial banks) however credit-worthy, but was restricted solely to those Trustee Savings Bank customers who had a certain minimum, usually around £25 to £50, in their ordinary savings account at the time of applying for a current account and who had already maintained such an account for a reasonable period, normally six months. Nevertheless, despite these restrictions so typical of state-sponsored or state-guaranteed institutions, there was such a strong demand for improved transfer payments from persons not normally having accounts with the joint-stock banks that by the time National Giro began its operations in 1968 about 90 000 current accounts were being operated by the Trustee Savings Banks, a figure which rose to 285 000 by July 1972. These new current accounts together with the 'bank Giro', the banks' personal loan, cheque-cards and other such newly evolving schemes, provide some of the main examples of how the delay in setting up the postal Giro system inevitably robbed it of a considerable, if not precisely quantifiable, number of potential customers. Time slipped by during which the dice were being loaded, with official assistance, against the anticipated postal Giro service. Without in any way decrying the positive achievements of the Trustee Savings Banks which had to accept a variety of ridiculous restrictions that they now plainly resent, the final result was that another bitty, marginal, make-shift, half-solution, so beloved of the British at their worst, was preferred to the more fundamental, quicker, cheaper, more logical and much more convenient postal Giro system.

FROM DALLIANCE TO DECISION

The repeated official excuses for the inordinate delay in deciding on whether to set up a postal Giro were becoming worn and threadbare as the 1960s progressed. In August 1960 the Industrial Bankers' Association again pressed the Postmaster General, Mr J R Bevins, for a positive reply to the questions which it had repeatedly asked since 1957. Mr Bevins however 'advised the Association that the result of the Post Office enquiry into the new transfer system and the questions arising were being considered at government level. This consideration had led to the need for further enquiries which were then being pursued.' [28] Inquiry was begetting inquiry and research reproducing further research as if the matter were merely an academic exercise of no practical consequence nor particular urgency. Moreover, the results of these reviews, to judge by the evidence of the conflicting official and semi-official pronouncements of the time were disconcertingly ambiguous. The Conservative Government seemed to be playing hot and cold and even the political heads of the Post Office itself appeared to be talking with two voices. In May 1961 Mr Bevins addressed the Annual Conference of the National Federation of Sub-Postmasters at Clacton, a body which was so vitally concerned with implementing Giro that any pronouncement on the subject would be taken most seriously. The Sub-Postmasters had become rather concerned because of certain features contained in the Report of the Committee on Crown Post Offices (The Taylor Report) which had just been issued and which had recommended that some of the existing Post Office agency business might with advantage be shed. The Sub-Postmasters who manned the smaller Post Offices feared that any decline in agency business would hit them even harder than the larger and more prestigious Crown Offices. Mr Bevins, however, reassured them that any such shrinkages 'were outweighed by other changes in the opposite direction'. Among these he briefly mentioned Giro which was not only 'a fascinating subject' in its own right but that 'speaking as an individual'—a facility which post-war Ministers seem to have acquired to a far greater extent than in previous constitutional history—he felt that 'Giro was a project on which the Post Office could well embark', and he expressed the hope that he 'might have something material to report in the very near future'. [29]

However, when no hint of further progress was given for almost a year after the Clacton speech, Mr W R Williams, the Member of Parliament for the Openshaw division of Manchester, who had had considerable experience in the Post Office and so was appropriately enough the main Opposition spokesman on these matters, raised the question again. In a disappointingly pessimistic reply to Mr Williams in March 1962 the

Postmaster General confirmed Mr Williams' fears by stating that 'the Government are not at present convinced of the long-term need for a Post Office Giro . . . The delay is due to the enormous complications in the consideration of the whole problem . . . the question is so wide and complicated that it takes a long time to resolve'. [30] At the same time the Industrial Bankers' Association again received a similarly nebulous and discouraging answer to its annual request for a postal Giro. The Postmaster General's reply prompted them to comment wryly that 'As it is now nearly five years since the Association first raised the matter with the Post Office one clearly cannot deny that the matter is receiving careful consideration. Perhaps it is not unreasonable to suggest that the time for action is fast approaching'. [31] Early in 1963 Mr Williams was 'utterly amazed' to be informed once more that the Government were not yet convinced of the need for Giro and feared that it would not be wise to duplicate transfer payment systems. It did not require much reading between the lines to conclude that the Conservative Government's views had hardened considerably against Giro. Mr W R Williams managed to raise a brief debate on the subject on the adjournment of Parliament before the Easter recess in 1963, when his powerful plea for Giro was supported by Mr Jeremy Thorpe for the Liberals. Mr Williams expressed dismay that 'after four years, after receiving all the reports and all the information, after all the surveys and inquiries, we are back where we started'. Mr R L Mawby, presiding over his first Parliamentary task since his appointment that same day as Assistant Postmaster General, gave the Government's view that 'the Post Office ought not to launch into what might easily be a losing venture until it is far clearer than it is now that the Clearing Bank system is incapable of developing so as to meet all the country's needs', a procrastinating negative that was repeated with emphasis in December 1963. [32]

WHITE-HOT TECHNOLOGICAL REVOLUTION

Despite official remonstrations that the Conservative administration was not condemning Giro for all time, it was abundantly clear that only in the circumstances of a change of government could the concept find any real chance of acceptance. This is not to say that all Conservative opinion was hostile, for some of the most penetrating and powerful analyses of the case for Giro were, in fact, issued by the Conservative

Political Centre itself, although these were personal contributions to discussion and not official Party pronouncements. Thus Sir Brandon Rhys-Williams, Member of Parliament for South Kensington, proposed an audacious and revolutionary scheme, worthy of the widest publicity, for using the postal Giro as an essential instrument in the modern welfare state. In his fundamental and prophetic scheme for a New Social Contract, national insurance payments and benefits together with positive and negative income taxation would be combined by means of a computerised system requiring an all-embracing National Giro involving every person in the country—a Giro with 55 million or more customers. [33] From the same source and similar in concept came Mrs Hilary Sewill's ingenious yet 'practical concept for bringing together all the individual's cash dealings with the State into a single computer system'. [34] Mrs Sewill's outline sketch of an Automatic Unit for National Taxation and Insurance, especially obvious in its abbreviated title 'Auntie', bore a strong family resemblance to the Post Office's 'Ernie', the electronic random number indicator equipment which had by that time already become a household word, for it had been choosing the lucky numbers for winners of National Savings Premium Bond prizes since shortly after they were first issued in November 1956. Yet when every allowance is made for the spread of a fervent belief among some sections of Conservative opinion in the urgent necessity for a national postal Giro, the old political divisions delineated in the earlier chapters, were still predominantly in evidence and effectively scotched any practical progress in establishing such a Giro until the fall of the Conservative Government in the election of October 1964 brought into power a Party known to be much more favourably disposed to the idea.

Second only therefore to the stimulation of the Radcliffe Report, National Giro owes its existence to the electronic revolution of the 1960s and to the political adaptations which resulted therefrom. Given the virtual certainty that Giro was likely to come into being only under a Labour Government it was a fortunate omen, for his Party and for postal Giro, that Mr Harold Wilson should make the scientific revolution the main theme of the Labour Party Conference held at Scarborough in the Autumn of 1963. In a speech which the *Economist* considered 'a remarkably good inspirational job' which 'dazzled the delegates by science into the right mental attitude' [35], Mr Wilson

105

claimed that 'We are re-defining and re-stating our socialism in terms of the scientific revolution . . . The Britain that is going to be forged in the white heat of this revolution will be no place for restrictive practices or for outdated methods.' [36] He made a special point of praising the achievements of the Post Office as a shining example of what could be done, given the will: 'The Post Office workers and the Post Office engineers have pioneered some of the major developments in automation and, thanks to the combination of our trade union skill and of public ownership in the Post Office, lead the world in these developments.' [37] Within a year, with Harold Wilson as Prime Minister, the Labour Government was in power, and despite having a majority of only five members, after a further nine months National Giro's birth certificate was issued in the form of a Resolution triumphantly and unopposedly passed by the House of Commons on 21 June 1965, following the longest debate ever held on the subject. This positive resolution was followed within a month by the explanatory White Paper entitled *A Post Office Giro*, which together with the Postmaster General's comments during the Debate, clearly indicate the result of the review which the Labour Government had undertaken during the previous nine months. Before examining these historic documents (a task better reserved for the following chapters where the hopes portrayed in the Debate and the White Paper's projections can be compared with the actual achievements) it is necessary to look outside Parliament at some of the wider circles of discussion and to estimate the part played by a few of the more prominent participants in the struggle for and against Giro during this final and successful phase of what had been an almost incredibly long campaign.

Foremost among the popularisers of postal Giro in Britain in this period was Mr F P Thomson, a systems engineer who had become impressed with the efficient simplicity of the postal Giro when working in Scandinavia and had subsequently been seeking for nearly fifteen years to find 'a book publisher in this country willing to risk incurring the displeasure of the banking world'. [38] Mr Thomson's forceful book *Giro Credit Transfer Systems*, supported by a foreword from the then President of the Board of Trade, Mr Douglas Jay, was published in October 1964 and was quickly 'instrumental in building up a body of informed public opinion which urgently looked to Parliament to introduce a giro system'. [39] *The Financial Times* had long been favourably disposed towards a postal Giro, particularly in its 'Lombard' Column, and dealt specifically with the subject at least a dozen times in the first half of the 1960s under such eye-catching and thought-provoking titles as 'Mr Bevins Wants a Post Office Giro', 'Our Poor Old-Fashioned Post Office' and 'The Crime Wave and the Missing Giro'. [40] The trade unions continued to give Giro its strong support with the largest general unions as well as the more highly-paid craft unions now educating their workers in the more practical aspects of a postal Giro. Thus Mr J M Griffiths wrote persuasively in favour of 'The Case for a Post Giro System' in the *Record*, the organ of the Transport and General Workers Union, the country's largest trade union, with around $1\frac{1}{2}$ million members. After mentioning that 'there is a growing request from managements that workers agree to be paid by cheque or bank transfer' he went on to point out the disadvantages of these, particularly the bank charges, contrasted the free services which would be provided by Giro, and emphasised that 'whereas the joint-stock banks operate on the basis of the profit motive, any profit from Giro would be available to the National economy'. [41]

Opponents of postal Giro, particularly and predictably the joint-stock bankers, were stimulated into counter-attack, which took the complementary forms of pointing to the alleged weaknesses of postal Giro and of the arguments used to support it and extolling the extent to which the banks themselves had developed a much wider-ranging money-transfer system as advocated by the Radcliffe Report. Thus Mr John Hunsworth, Secretary of the Banking Information Service, delivered a vitriolic attack on Thomson's book advising any purchaser to return the book to the publisher and ask for his money back. [42] Mr C F Karsten, addressing the Institute of Bankers at their Summer School in 1964, referred in glowing terms to the considerable progress made by the bankers in Britain since his 1958 lecture in developing their credit transfer system which 'as the advertisements of the eleven clearing banks tell us, works extremely well'. [43] In similar vein Sir Ronald Thornton, the Vice Chairman of Barclays Bank and the Chairman of the Banking Information Service did not 'think it sensible to set up a debt settlement machinery to duplicate a system already available through the Banks'. This was 'a job for the banks' rather than for 'a government-controlled body'. [44] The joint-stock bankers' rearguard action availed them little. Already it was being confidently rumoured that the Labour Government had virtually made up its mind, a rumour that soon reached the proportions of a 'leak', and was eventually confirmed by the announcement of the Postmaster General, Mr Wedgwood Benn, on 21 July 1965 that the Government had firmly and finally decided that 'a Post Office Giro, offering the same basic facilities as the European Giro, would be a useful addition to the means of transmitting money'. [45] Despite all the caution, the doubts and the persistent and powerful opposition of vested interests, the Resolution to welcome the establishment of the postal Giro service was, as we have seen, agreed without a division. The long campaign was over, the conceptual battle had been won: but the real test—the struggle for viability—had not yet begun.

REFERENCES

1 BEVINS, J R, *Hansard* (27 March 1962), col. 995.
2 *Committee on the Working of the Monetary System* (H.M.S.O., 1959), comprising the 'Report' (Cmnd. 827), 'Memoranda' and 'Minutes of Evidence'. The terms of reference quoted are from the Report para. 1.
3 FISCHER, A, 'Postal Cheque Institutes', in *The Accountant* (London, 13 December 1941), p. 338.
4 Post Office Savings Bank statistics given in *Radcliffe Memoranda*, Vol. 1, p. 214.
5 SAYERS, R S, 'Twentieth Century Banking' in *Transactions of the Manchester Statistical Society* (1954), pp. 14–15.
6 SAYERS, R S, *ibid.*, p. 16.
7 CLAYTON, G, 'The Swedish Post Giro', *The Bankers' Magazine* (London, September 1956), pp. 229–32.
8 *Industrial Bankers Association, Annual Report* (London, May 1962).
9 KARSTEN C F, 'Banking Without Cheques' in *The Future Organisation of Banking* (Institute of Bankers in Scotland: Edinburgh, 1958), pp. 55–56.
10 HOBSON, SIR OSCAR, 'Towards a Banking Democracy', *The Banker* (London, November 1958), pp. 713–4.
11 HOBSON, SIR OSCAR, *ibid.*, p. 714.
12 *Op. cit., Radcliffe Minutes of Evidence*, Q. 4906–12.
13 *Ibid.*, p. 911.
14 *Ibid.*, Q. 13105.
15 *Ibid.*, Q. 13107.
16 *Ibid.*, Q. 13108.
17 KARSTEN, C F, *op. cit.*, p. 48.
18 *Op. cit., Radcliffe Memoranda*, Vol. 1, p. 210.
19 *Ibid.*, p. 212.
20 *Op. cit., Radcliffe Minutes of Evidence*, Q. 6880.
21 *Ibid.*, Q. 6883, 6884.
22 *Ibid.*, Q. 6887, 6888.

23 *Op. cit., Radcliffe Report*, paras. 963–4.

24 *Radcliffe Memoranda*, Vol. 2, p. 26.

25 *Industrial Bankers Association, Annual Report* (London, May 1962 and May 1963).

26 GRIFFITHS, BRIAN, *Competition in Banking* (London, 1970), Hobart Paper No. 51, p. 37.

27 *Page Committee: Evidence submitted by the Trustee Savings Bank Association*, Appendix 3, p. 68.

28 *Industrial Bankers Association, Annual Report* (London, May 1962), p. 4.

29 BEVINS, J R, Clacton Speech as reported in *The Sub-Postmaster* (Perth, June 1961), pp. 136–7.

30 *Hansard* (27 March 1962), cols. 994–5.

31 *Industrial Bankers Association, Annual Report* (May 1962), p. 4.

32 *Hansard* (4 March 1963), cols. 165–74.

33 RHYS-WILLIAMS, SIR BRANDON, *The New Social Contract* (Conservative Political Centre: London, 1967).

34 SEWILL, H, *Auntie*, Introduction (Conservative Political Centre: London, 1966).

35 *The Economist* (London, 5 October 1963).

36 WILSON, HAROLD, *Annual Report of the Labour Party Conference* (London, 1963), p. 140.

37 WILSON, HAROLD, *ibid.*, p. 134.

38 TUCK, R, *Hansard* (21 July 1965), col. 1606.

39 TUCK, R, *ibid.*, col. 1606.

40 'Lombard', *Financial Times* (10 May 1961, 18 August 1962, and 9 February 1963).

41 GRIFFITHS, J M, *The Record* (Transport and General Workers Union: London, December 1963), pp. 42–3.

42 HUNSWORTH, J, 'No Service to Giro', *Bankers Magazine* (London, December 1964), p. 350.

43 KARSTEN, C F, 'Transfer Systems: Development, Diversification and Automation'; in *Banking Trends in Europe Today* (Institute of Bankers: London 1964), p. 139.

44 THORNTON, SIR R, 'The Banks and a Postal Giro System', *Credit* (London, March 1965), pp. 8–9.

45 WEDGWOOD BENN, A, *Hansard* (21 July 1965), col. 1636.

Chapter 5

Giro 1965–70:
Great Expectations and Hard Times

'What is science? It is a vision with its working clothes on,
nothing more and nothing less.'
Frank Cousins. [1]

AN AMBITIOUS PROGRAMME

The many hundreds of attractive young ladies at the National Giro
Centre in Bootle busily controlling their electronic impulses form but
the latest link in the historical chain of financial accounting that goes
back to the bags of pebbles kept as numerical records by the young
shepherds of pre-historic times. The proud achievement of being the
first bank in the world to be planned and built from its very beginning
as a fully computerised unit belongs to the British Post Office. There
were of course a number of other fully computerised banks already in
existence in 1968, but they were still rather rare and they had all developed from institutions which had already been established as banks
for a considerable period before this. It was therefore a bold and imagi-
native step—science in the form of a vision with its working clothes on—
to set up *ab initio* Europe's largest computer centre to introduce an
entirely new form of current account banking into this country. Despite
the series of investigations which were undertaken at the instigation of
the various Governments, it was just not possible to set up and run an
experimental, scaled-down 'pilot' scheme, either covering just part of
Giro's expected functions, or merely confined to a particular region. It
had to be all or nothing; and though there could be some legitimate
argument about the particular size of the 'all', no logical case could be
made out for either a sectoral or regional Giro.

The Post Office as one of the ten biggest companies in the world en-

110

joys a deep and wide-ranging experience of investment appraisal techniques and procedures and had long been used to testing out its novel ideas on a modest scale before becoming involved in mammoth undertakings. But in the case of Giro this sort of procedure was ruled out by the very nature of the scheme. This was particularly so with regard to the relatively unified and closely centralised financial market that is Britain, and more especially with regard to monetary transfers. Given this situation potential Giro account holders could be expected to become actual customers only if they could be fairly certain that within a short space of time a reasonable number of other customers spread over a number of industrial and commercial sectors comprising most of the country would be included in the scheme. There would hardly be much point in established industrial firms forsaking in whole or in part their own joint-stock banks to take up an account in a competing bank if from the start that bank could be seen to be restricted in time or confined within a particular region or designed exclusively for a restricted type of customer. And without a fair sprinkling of the large accounts which industrial and commercial businesses would bring, it was realised right from the start that Giro would be unlikely to be able to supply the greater number of private individual account holders with the required service at a cost cheap enough to attract and hold them. Anything that looked like an experiment would by that very fact be condemned to failure, for in such circumstances everyone would adopt a wait and see attitude so that such limited experiments or pilot schemes would be bound to underestimate to a substantial but unquantifiable degree the true potential demand for Giro, whatever that figure might be. There was therefore general agreement with the views expressed by Mr David Gibson-Watt, Member of Parliament for Hereford, when in the Debate preceding the Government's declaration of intent to set up Giro he stated that 'It is not easy just to make an experiment. If the system is to be carried out, it is a question of the Postmaster General diving in at the deep end'. [2]

A number of Opposition speakers in this Debate, including Mr Gibson-Watt, did however call for the Government to commission yet more 'market research' before deciding to go ahead. There was still in the mid-1960s a rather touchingly naïve faith among psephologists, econometricians, politicians and the public regarding the virtues of market researchers and in their ability to peer into the future. In any

111

case the subject of Giro had not in the recent past suffered from a dearth of enquiries and surveys and though these remained unpublished, their main results were usually disclosed in fairly detailed official statements. The Opposition call for yet another investigation therefore seemed to be merely a thinly disguised device for further procrastination. Even if another investigation were undertaken and published, its results, given the large penumbra of uncertainty surrounding the question, would be unlikely to be such as to convert the unbelievers or disabuse dedicated enthusiasts, while the time to be used up in conducting and analysing a thorough-going survey would inevitably play into the hands of competing institutions who were, as we have seen, busily engaged in stealing Giro's potential customers.

REVERSAL OF REVIEW CONCLUSIONS

In December 1963 after the latest of a series of reviews the Conservative Government rejected Giro; in July 1965 after yet another review which seems to have refuted the pessimistic finding of the previous survey the Government accepted the case for Giro. It is perhaps a little too cynically obvious to comment that the desired answers of the commissioner seem to have affected the conclusions of the investigators. It is possibly less obvious but certainly more true to say that a number of fundamental trends which had been developing in the economy during the 1950s and early 1960s were given different weights both by the investigators and by the Governments, so that the costs and disadvantages facing a postal Giro seemed to be growing markedly less, while on the other hand the potential with regard to demand and revenues seemed to be growing substantially greater. As a contemporary observer, Mr Anthony Bambridge, commented in *The Banker* of September 1965, the methods of approach adopted by the reviewers were also quite different: 'In 1963 the approach had been one of calculating how much it would cost to set up and run a Giro, and then to work out the level of business necessary to cover that expenditure. On this occasion the Post Office Giro researchers have worked from the other end. They have estimated the minimum business a Giro could reasonably be expected to do, and on that basis have calculated whether it could be made to pay.' [3] The reversal of review conclusions was however much more than a mere change of political mood or postal research methods. There were substantial technical, economic and social changes which, in combination, appeared to constitute quite convincing grounds for reversing the pessimistic conclusions of the Conservative Government's 1963 review, and so to justify Mr Wedgwood Benn's confidence in these 'new factors which led (the Labour Government) to consider the matter in a more favourable light'. [4]

With regard to the supply side the delay in setting up Giro had coincided with dramatic improvements in electronic equipment and, since the Post Office was already the biggest and most experienced user of computers in Britain, it was immediately aware of the practical and financial implications of these developments for Giro. On the very firm basis, therefore, of its own practical experience, the Post Office estimated that a considerable reduction could be achieved in the manpower required to run Giro. The 1963 review figure of 5000 was reduced substantially to 3000. This factor alone 'promised a saving in the salary bill, always the biggest single expense in a Giro operation, of around £1$\frac{1}{2}$ million' per annum. [5] Second, such improvements in the design and speed of operation of the automated equipment seemed likely to increase the through-put of paper at the Giro centre so that the desired one-day clearance seemed to be more easily attainable by the mid 1960s than had appeared to be the case a few years earlier. Since speed was one of the chief factors influencing not only the supply side, but acted also as a considerable attraction for potential customers, then this technological advance as well as leading to savings on the cost side was also responsible for more favourable estimates of potential demand. There were a number of other economic changes which similarly led to legitimate expectations on the part of even the most uncommitted observer that the potential demand for non-cash money transfers was increasing and that Giro might well gain a considerable share of this new banking market. The new review revealed that mail order business had doubled in size in the seven years from 1957-64, while the growth in instalment payments had been even more dramatic doubling in the still shorter space of the four years preceding the review. (This fact helps to explain the impatience which we noted in the previous chapter shown by the finance houses and the industrial bankers, with regard to the delay in improving payment methods.) Similarly, the growing popularity of television led to greatly increased periodic rental payments, a further substantial potential market for Giro standing orders.

The new review team took a fresh look at the progress of European

113

Giros adding visits to Sweden and Switzerland to those made by the 1963 reviewers to France, Germany, Holland, Norway and Denmark: and thus brought their news, views and statistics of continental Giros up to date, so as to form a thoroughly comprehensive combination of subjective and objective analysis. In every case, including those where Giro had been established for generations, demand for Giro's services was growing, so that if continental experience was anything to go by, their example seemed to augur well for National Giro. Table 5.1 illustrates the growth in five-year periods between 1950 and 1965 of the number of account holders in France, West Germany, Sweden and Denmark. In the decade-and-a-half the French postal cheque service, the world's largest, increased the number of its accounts by the vast total of nearly $3\frac{1}{2}$ million, a proportionate increase of 133%. West Germany's postal Giro similarly attracted almost $1\frac{1}{2}$ million additional accounts, an increase of 152%. Much smaller absolute and somewhat smaller percentage increases were shown by Sweden and Denmark, but even in these countries there was obviously a steady and sustained growth in new accounts and similar trends were discernible in all the other main Giro-using countries examined. There is no doubt that this continued and substantial growth of European Giros during the latter part of the 1950s and early 1960s, in demonstrating that this was not merely a temporary post-war surge of recovery but rather part of a long, sustained trend, helped to strengthen the resolve and weaken the doubts of those concerned with a postal Giro for Britain.

CRIME, CASH AND CREDIT

One of the more unfortunate paradoxes of the affluent society has been the increase in crime which has accompanied the rise in living standards. Unless this growth in the standard of living was itself associated with a widespread change in social patterns of behaviour so as rapidly to reduce dependence on cash and increase the use of credit for payment purposes, either in the form of cheques, credit transfers or credit cards, then the opportunities for the criminal would grow year by year; which latter is precisely what happened. It was not simply the fact that crime in general was increasing at a disturbing pace, but in addition that crimes of theft, and still more disturbing, crimes involving personal violence were increasing faster still. There is no doubt that the general public

114

	FRANCE		WEST GERMANY		SWEDEN		DENMARK	
	NUMBER OF ACCOUNTS '000s	INDEX OF GROWTH	NUMBER OF ACCOUNTS '000s	INDEX OF GROWTH	NUMBER OF ACCOUNTS '000s	INDEX OF GROWTH	NUMBER OF ACCOUNTS '000s	INDEX OF GROWTH
1950	2603	100·0	929	100·0	283	100·0	85	100·0
1955	3974	152·7	1475	158·8	360	127·2	97	114·1
1960	4709	180·9	1980	213·1	431	152·3	112	131·8
1965	6067	233·1	2337	251·6	515	182·0	150	176·5
Increase 1965 over 1950:								
(a) Numbers	3464		1408		232		65	
(b) Percentage	133·1		151·6		82·0		76·5	

Table 5.1 Growth of continental Giros 1950–65. (Growth since 1965 is examined in Chapter 8)

Source: Annual Reports 1950–70

115

	1958	1964		1970	
		NO.	% INCREASE OVER 1958	NO.	% INCREASE OVER 1958
All offences	993 445	1 327 649	33·6	1 674 056	68·5
Larceny and theft	87 966	119 264	35·5	176 502	100·6
Violence against the person	7 895	14 141	79·1	23 443	296·9

Table 5.2   Increased trend of offences in England and Wales 1958–70

Source: Annual Abstract of Statistics, 1968 and 1970

were becoming much more aware and much more troubled about this dangerous and frightening state of affairs than they had been just a few years earlier. It was becoming clear that to rely simply on the growth of the bank habit, as most of the joint stock banks seemed to wish, was far too tardy a process. Giro could obviously step in and introduce schemes of credit transfer which would greatly reduce the use of cash, particularly for sections of the community not yet accustomed to using joint-stock banks. The dismal statistics given in Table 5.2 provide merely a rough summary of the increased trend of offences in England and Wales during the two six-year periods from 1958 to 1964 and from 1964 to 1970. Crime is of course always a very newsworthy subject, so that these flat and impersonal statistics were accompanied by a more vivid treatment by the Press and television. The statistics will help to indicate the basic reasons for the change in public awareness and hence in the more ready acceptance of the case put forward by the proponents of Giro that here was a tailor-made method of overcoming the bandit. In the first six-year period 'All Offences' and 'Larceny and Theft' both increased by about a third, but 'Violence against the Person' increased by almost 80%. Since this subject of the relationship between crime and non-cash payments is so vital to the story of Giro we shall return to it in later chapters, but it may be convenient to notice here that the trends shown in the first six-year period became even more pronounced in the second six-year period, for whereas 'All Offences' increased by just about another third, the increase in 'Larceny and Theft' was about double that rate, while the crimes of 'Violence against the Person' rose

116

at an alarming rate, so as to be nearly treble in 1970 what they were in 1958. The statistics for Scotland tell a similar tale, but because of the differences in the legal systems offences in Scotland are categorised in a different fashion and so cannot be simply aggregated with those for England and Wales. There could therefore be no disagreement with the general sentiments expressed by the Postmaster General during the Debate: 'Anything we can do to make the transmission of money more secure will be of advantage to the community as a whole'. [6] The increase in crime was an ill wind that blew the cause of Giro some good.

Information regarding the extent to which the public already made use of the banks for current account purposes had always been unclear and imprecise, chiefly because, although each bank did from time to time carry out market surveys for its own institution, the results even when published were released only in part, were made up of different times with differing coverages and for different purposes, and so could not possibly be aggregated to give a satisfactorily comprehensive picture. We saw in Chapter 4 that Mr Chesterfield, Chief Managing Director of the Westminster Bank, had been forced to reply in a somewhat unsatisfactory fashion during the Radcliffe Enquiry to Sir Alexander Cairncross's question on this subject. When asked: 'About what proportion of the adult population have bank accounts in this country?' Mr Chesterfield had to admit 'I do not know: I should think at least 50%'. Mr Robarts, then Chairman of National Provincial, replied that 'collectively the banks had never carried out any market research on this matter'. [7] It would appear that neither the promptings of the professors, nor the pull of the purse strings could cause the banks to co-operate in such research in the 1960's, so it was both fortuitous and fortunate for them and for Giro that Thomas de la Rue, the cheque and security printers, themselves engaged the services of the National Opinion Poll to carry out just such a survey in July 1965 of a representative sample of some 2000 adults aged sixteen and over throughout Great Britain. The main results of this survey were made known just about the same time that the Government's White Paper on Giro was published, a most convenient coincidence. The survey found that only just a little over a quarter (26·7%) of all the population over sixteen years of age, numbering about 10·7 million persons, had a current account and made use of a cheque book. This national average embraced considerable and somewhat intriguing regional differences, ratios

117

varying from 16% for Scotland, 22% for Northern England, 19% for the Midlands, up to as high as 35% for the South East and, surprisingly, 35% for Wales and the South West. Slightly more than three-quarters (76%) of those in the higher and intermediate professional and management categories kept bank current accounts, while only some 17% of the skilled manual workers had such accounts, As for the unskilled and other workers earning less than £14 per week not surprisingly only about 7% kept a cheque book. 'The sharpest division however'— according to *The Banker*—was 'not so much that between classes as between those paid weekly and those paid fortnightly or monthly. Of the former only 3% were shown by the survey to be paid by cheque or credit transfer, compared with 88% of the latter.' [8] The NOP's July survey was used as the basis for a more selective survey which was carried out in November 1965 on behalf of Thomas de la Rue and Barclays Bank to assess the potential demand for automatic cash dispensers. This more selective survey concluded that 22% of those with a bank account 'were very likely' and a further 16% were 'likely' to use such a machine instead of going to a cashier and furthermore that such a facility would be 'likely to be attractive to people who have not got an account'. [9]

These pioneering and comprehensive market researches by the National Opinion Poll demonstrated that the banking habit, despite the extensive efforts which had been made by the banks between 1959 and 1965, and despite the optimistic, but inevitably partial views of the banks' own surveys, was far less developed than the banks' spokesmen had estimated during the Radcliffe Enquiry. Another interesting example of one of the joint-stock banks' own researches regarding new market potential was that carried out by the Midland Bank in 1963, and very briefly summarised in the Annual Report and Chairman's Statement published in January 1965. The survey 'showed a rapid rate of growth in the number of new customers, an average net gain of well over 600 on each working day'. Second, it revealed that 'more than one-third of the new customers were paid weekly . . . the annual incomes of over half of the new customers were £750 or less . . . and nearly three-quarters of the new accounts were opened with balances of less than £100'. [10] As might have been expected, the banks used the figures of their own experience in an attempt to justify their opposition to a postal Giro and indeed even to a Giro of any sort. Thus Sir Archibald Forbes considered the Midland's figures convincing proof, (1) that there was no need for a postal Giro, and (2) that if such a need were eventually to arise the best way of meeting it 'would be for the banks to graft such a system on to existing clearing arrangements'. However, he still remained convinced that 'there is as yet no evidence of either the need nor the economic justification for doing so'. [11] Similar views were given in the Westminster Bank Statement of the same year and in an article in *The Times* of 31 December 1965, by Sir Ronald Thornton, Chairman of the Banking Information Service.

The NOP statistics however showed that far from Chesterfield's 'at least 50%' or even that 'most-quoted statistic of one in three of Britain's adult population holding a bank current account' the true figure was much lower. [12] Despite all the ballyhoo the plain fact remained that over 25 million of the country's adult population, in the NOP sense of being over sixteen years of age, were still without bank current accounts. If the Midland Bank's 'rapid' net recruitment figure of about 600 every working day could be taken as a rough guide to the future growth of the 'Big Four', this would mean a combined net addition of around 600 000 per annum. At that rate it would take roughly forty years before every adult carried a bank current account. However, one could hardly expect that initial rate to be maintained as ever lower income groups were tapped; so that the time scale in question would inevitably extend considerably beyond two generations. When this rather modest rate of increase in bank custom was being bandied about with apparent pride and moreover used as if it were unanswerable evidence against the need for a postal Giro, then clearly the banking monopoly could hardly avoid charges of being complacently self-satisfied with their own achievements and of adopting a dog-in-the-manger attitude towards National Giro. In a most fair and interesting admission given in an interview in mid-1965, with Mr Anthony Bambridge, then on the staff of *The Economist*, one of the more liberal-minded of the Big Five General Managers conceded that 'it does look as if there is a need for "Giro"' and that 'it would be churlish for the banks to say there is no demand'. For good measure he went on to say that for the banks to introduce their own Giro system would simply be 'vindictive'. [13] Thus at that time there certainly appeared to be plenty of room for the banks, and still more for a Giro specially tailored for the task, to capture customers from among the currently large non-banking population. Of course, it was

119

realised that this potential market could only be translated into an effective demand if the inertia of ingrained habits could be overcome, a process which was likely to be more easily realised thenceforth because certain age-long legal hindrances which had acted up until then to inhibit current account banking among the working classes were just in the process of being removed.

REPEAL OF THE TRUCK ACTS

The Truck Acts of 1831 to 1940 had been designed to protect the worker from exploitation by his employer by stipulating that payment of wages had to be made in cash, that is in current coin of the realm, or very exceptionally in other agreed and generally acceptable forms of money and not in such items as blankets or yards of cloth, or credit slips exchangeable in the company's 'tommy-shop'; nor under similar legislation passed in 1883, could wages be paid out, in any form, in a public house. In course of time developments in economic patterns of trade and in particular in the structure of banking had turned this sensible and protective framework of legislation, despite its being in many respects commendably forward-looking, into a strait-jacket impeding the acceptance of modern systems of payment, especially as regards the lower income groups. It is interesting to note that the Act of 1831, contrary to common belief, did in fact permit the payment of wages by cheque—but only if the workman agreed and if 'the cheque was a bearer cheque drawn on a bank licensed to issue notes and situated within 15 miles of the place of payment'. 'Changes in the banking structure since 1831 had turned that provision into a virtual prohibition on the payment of wages by cheque in England and Wales, as the Bank of England had since become the only note-issuing bank in these areas.' [14] Not only did the Truck Acts effectively prevent payment of wages by cheque or credit transfer, but also the blanket prohibition of payment in kind hindered employers from paying 'fringe benefits' over and above the nominal wage. Legislation designed to bring wages up to the agreed minima was now in many instances preventing payments from rising above such minima—and this at a time of over-full employment when 'fringe benefits' were becoming of vital concern to employers seeking scarce labour. 'The desirability of amending the Truck Acts first became a matter of public concern when publicity was given to the fact that the

Pye Radio Company had reluctantly discontinued the practice of paying their workers' wages by cheque following legal advice that this might be considered an infringement of the provisions of the Truck Act 1831.' [15]

The growth of public demand for an enquiry led Mr Iain Macleod, then Minister of Labour, to appoint a committee in July 1959—just a week or so before the Radcliffe Report was published—under the chairmanship of Mr David Karmel, QC, with the following terms of reference: 'To consider in the light of present day conditions the opera-tion of the Truck Acts 1831–1940 and related legislation and to make recommendations'. [16] The views put to the Committee by a wide variety of organisations—the Gas Council, the National Coal Board, the National Savings Committee, Courtaulds—were summed up in this quotation from the memorandum submitted by the British Employers' Confederation: 'In modern conditions there are many instances where the Truck Acts have in fact prevented employers from providing ameni-ties which would be of value to their employees.' [17] Surprisingly, and inexcusably, the Post Office, despite the fact that at this very time the Radcliffe Report was urging it to consider setting up a Giro, and despite its close interest in the increased use of postal orders and money orders for the payment of wages, failed to send in any memorandum or to pre-sent its views to the Committee. Nevertheless, so urgent was a reform of the method of paying wages considered, that while the Committee was still sitting the Government pushed through the Payment of Wages Act 1960 which enabled the wages of workmen to be paid into a bank account or by postal or money order as from 1 December 1960, and by cheque as from 1 March 1963. It was in this way that Sir Oscar Hobson's plea for the removal of obstructions to the 'democratisation of banking' was enacted. Although, judged by the experience of the first half of the 1960s, workers were slow to avail themselves of these new provisions this was thought to be largely because of the inappropriate hours kept by the banks, plus the fact that the banks chose this time to make a substantial increase in their charges for running current accounts. These disadvantages were made still worse when the banks began to suggest that they would close on Saturdays—a suggestion which they carried on as from 1 July 1969. Mr Wedgwood Benn, the Postmaster General, was careful to hammer this point home in his address in the Debate: 'Post Offices are open all day and every day, including Saturdays, which

121

is intensely important to those people who would be the likely users of the Giro service, including, of course, the Post Office Savings Bank, with its 22 million people with live accounts.' [18] It was therefore confidently expected that it would be Giro rather than the banks which would reap the main advantage of the permitted reforms in wage payment systems.

DEAR MONEY—A BOON TO GIRO

One aspect which was brought out explicitly in the Debate by Mr Mawby, but not mentioned at all by the Government side, though it was of such importance that it could hardly have escaped emphasis by the Treasury, was the change, after twenty years of cheap money, to very much higher levels of interest rates from the later 1950s onwards and the implications of this for Giro's finances. Compared with the 2% Bank Rate which prevailed from 1932 to 1951 with only insignificant rises above that rate, Bank Rate remained above 4% from early 1955 on, reaching 7% for three periods between September 1957 and June 1965, with the average of roughly between 5% and 6% affording clear evidence to all of a long-term change of gear. In fact this increase in Bank Rate considerably understates the general rise in interest rates for instead of a large section of lending rates being fairly closely in touch with Bank Rate, there occurred during this period a much wider spread of rates above Bank Rate. There were also a number of other developments which improved the investment opportunities for any institution with large sums of money to lend; for example, this was the period when local authorities had increasing recourse to the market for their borrowings and when the Eurocurrency market began its meteoric rise. Therefore for this and a number of other reasons which will be looked into in greater detail later, the existence of dear money improved the outlook for Giro. Since Giro paid no interest on its balances, the higher level of interest rates meant a much higher net revenue than Giro could previously have expected, so that the break-even point could be achieved with a considerably smaller number of customers (or more strictly of customer-balances) than had been thought necessary previously. Mr Mawby was afraid of the effects of a return to cheap money on Giro's finances. His solicitude turned out to be unnecessary for Giro was to operate in an economic environment of unprecedentedly high rates of interest. Thus whereas Mr Mawby had in 1963, on the advice of his particular reviewers, based his calculations on the need for average balances of around £200, Mr Wedgwood Benn was satisfied that an average balance of 'only between £100 and £150 would be ample', and went on to suggest that since France with over 5 million accounts managed to reach an average balance of £400 'then assumptions of this kind really are more than reasonable'. [19]

It should be clear from the foregoing that an analysis of the technological economic, social and financial evidence available in the mid-1960s provided a reasonable justification for the Labour Governments renewed confidence in the viability, of a postal Giro system. Indeed apart from the opposition which came almost as a reflex action from the joint-stock banks (and even they did not present an unbroken front) there was at that time very nearly unanimous support for the concept. In view both of the marked political polarisation on which we have commented above and of subsequent developments, it is important to be quite clear on this point: National Giro was not the result of a doctrinaire attachment to socialist principles backed by a government which was determined to go ahead no matter what the evidence revealed. On the contrary there appeared to be so convincing a case for a viable Giro and expectations rose to so high a pitch that justifiable confidence began to enlarge itself into a heady euphoria. The higher the expectation, the greater, of course, was the disappointment which inevitably supervened. However before turning to examine the reasons for the subsequent hard times, it is necessary first to consider the practical steps taken to set up the world's first fully computerised postal Giro; a formidable task successfully achieved in the short space of three years against a background of growing confidence which encouraged the general acceptance of the belief that a high degree of utilisation of the large-scale capacity being installed in the new Giro Centre would quickly be achieved.

WHITE PAPER AND THE PLANNING PROGRAMME

By mid-1965 the Government had already decided that Giro Centre would most probably be sited somewhere in Merseyside, this area obviously offering strategic advantages (which will be examined more closely in Chapter 7) as a centre for nationwide collection and distribution of the millions of documents to be handled each week. By the time the White Paper was published in August of the same year the sense of purpose and urgency then permeating the authorities on this issue was shown in the announcement that a Director had already been appointed. It was hoped that the whole scheme would begin operation in 1968–69. In the days when failure to meet target dates even when building traditional constructions or conventional ships was not unknown, the postal authorities successfully completed the building, equipping and staffing of Giro Centre, and the staffing of its London headquarters, all entirely new ventures, well within the target date. It is significant, indeed one might also say symptomatic, that for the vital position of Director of Giro the Post Office did not seek an outsider, either from banking or from the world of private business, but rather chose someone who had spent his entire career within the Post Office and was therefore very much an insider, a civil servant, a successful product of the Post Office's own selection and promotion procedure. John William Grady joined the Post Office in 1935 as an Executive Officer and after serving in a number of different branches, including five years' in Organisation and Methods (which was later to be of direct usefulness in streamlining the Giro administration), he then moved up and over into the fields of finance and accountancy in 1955, becoming in turn Assistant Accountant General and then Finance Adviser in 1962. In 1964 he was made Deputy Director of Finance from which position he was as a natural progression chosen to head the National Giro system: almost a classic case of self-selection along the well-trodden paths of merit in the civil service.

Immediately following the appointment of the Director to head not only the build up of the new Giro but also the consequent run down of the Post Office's traditional Remittance Services to a slimmer size, a number of other key staff appointments were made so as to form the Giro planning team which quickly set to work from their London headquarters, almost all such appointments coming about as a result of transfers and promotions from within the civil service and in the main from within the existing staff of the Post Office itself. Inevitably the question arose as to whether what amounted to the establishment of a major new bank did not by its very nature call for more direct experience from among its staff with the private sector in general and the financial market-place in particular. It was only a year or so later however that such questioning acquired a sharper edge and so the matter will be deferred for consideration below. At the time in question, just when the plans for Giro were being translated into concrete achievement with commendable smoothness by Mr John Grady and his new Post Office team, the mood of confidence was, if anything, increasing in strength, so that any such doubts were either overlooked or overruled.

The Post Office's acknowledged skills in the new science of 'computerisation' and in the not-so-new managerial techniques of 'organisation and methods studies' and in 'systems analyses' were stretched to the full in carrying out its plans to scale up Giro to such a size that it could within a short time be capable of processing the 'million documents a day' that had been confidently forecast. By April 1967 contracts had been placed for £4 million worth of equipment comprising computers, high speed optical character reading and sorting equipment and document encoding machines. [20] The Post Office Report for the year ending 31 March 1968 spoke of the satisfactory progress that had been made in constructing the National Giro Centre at Bootle and was confident that most of the building complex would be ready for occupation by the middle of 1968. As a matter of fact the managerial and planning staff moved from London to Bootle in March 1968 and large-scale recruitment of operational staff quickly followed. The detailed testing and re-testing of all this new and expensive equipment was dovetailed in admirable fashion with the training of the operational staff, a process which occupied most of the seven-month period between mid-March and 18 October 1968, so that by the opening date some 2000 of the first-stage complement of 3000 employees were already trained. On the basis of such solid achievement, the Post Office Annual Reports for the years in question continued to predict the brightest of futures for Giro: for example, the Report for 1966–67 concluded its brief section on Giro as follows: 'An exhaustive market research and test advertising programme is being carried out, the results from which suggest that Giro should quickly reach a viable level of business'. The Report for the subsequent year repeated this confident conclusion in almost the same terms: 'The response to Giro from the business community has been favourable and an increasing number of organisations have been reserving account numbers since early in 1968. . . . Market surveys have indicated that Giro will also be widely used by the general public and it is expected that the service will quickly attract the level of business required to make it commercially viable.' [21] The marked success with which the physical and administrative problems of setting up Giro were being overcome tended to feed this feeling of euphoria and seemed to confirm the belief that the modest targets suggested in the official documents would clearly be exceeded.

Some indication of the importance attached to the new venture is given by the fact that the official opening ceremony on Friday 18 October 1968 was carried out by the Prime Minister, Mr Harold Wilson, whose constituency, Huyton, bordered on that of Bootle. The impressively functional yet aesthetically attractive operational centre, comprising 566 000 square feet and housing the largest complex of computers that had, up to then, ever been assembled together anywhere in Europe, was now ready for the expected rush of customers. In a booklet produced by National Giro to celebrate the occasion it was confidently predicted that '*Within one or two years* the National Giro Centre will be handling the accounts of some 1 200 000 customers including many large firms and organisations'. [22] A Press release issued at the same time repeated the target for the first-stage capacity of the National Giro Centre as 1 million private accounts and 200 000 business accounts and went on yet more euphorically to state that 'Giro has carried out research into the ultimate potential size of the market among private account holders; this might grow in time to 3 million or more'. [23]

WHAT WENT WRONG?

It was therefore with shocked surprise and considerable heart-burning that Giro's actual performance over the first two years turned out to be dismally disappointing, for although the White Paper itself had indicated that the total of 1 200 000 customers was to be achieved within five years, it needs to be emphasised that repeated official statements in Parliament and by the postal authorities themselves insisted, as we have seen, that these targets were thought to be rather conservative estimates which might easily be exceeded. The glaring difference between hopeful plan and heart-breaking performance is clearly demonstrated in the Tables and graphs given in Chapter 7 below, where the slow growth of Giro's accounts and balances are recorded, quarter by quarter from its opening until the most recent date available. After a short-lived initial boom in the last quarter of 1968 the number of accounts levelled out alarmingly in 1969, and though they rose again somewhat promisingly during the next six months, by mid-1970 the total number of accounts had only just topped the 300 000 mark, while balances remaining within Giro had not quite reached £50 million. Far from the break-even point being reached, or even being noticeably approached, losses at a rate of around £6 million per annum were being built up without much sign of viability on the horizon.

Some of the factors which led to this disappointing outcome have already been dealt with, including the strong and vociferous build up of competition by the joint-stock banks and the more silent development of competitive current accounts by the Trustee Savings Banks. Giro had been held back just when its competitors had been busily preparing their ground in the long period between 1959 and 1968. On the basis of such careful planning the joint-stock banks could now quickly enlarge their improved credit transfer system into the more comprehensive and more competitive 'bank giro'. Bank credit cards were also beginning to make their impact during this time—although this again was a rather slow process. Such competition from the rival organisations on the supply side was felt all the more keenly not because it was particularly successful—for as we have seen it was not—but precisely because the surprisingly inelastic demand meant that there was not enough actual custom around to satisfy the supply now eagerly being offered. Giro supporters had not reckoned on the innate conservatism and the deeply rooted habits of the cash-loving working classes who by and large rejected the world's most modern purpose-built workers' current account bank despite the fact that it was offering them cheaper, safer and quicker facilities for pay and money transfer than had ever been possible before.

The gap between potential and actual demand was much wider and much more difficult to fill than had been appreciated by Giro, or for that matter than had been feared by the banks. The National Opinion Poll Survey of June 1965 had revealed as we have seen that only 3% of those paid weekly were paid other than in cash. This seemed to indicate a vast potential market of the kind which the optimistic market surveys by the postal authorities confidently predicted. However, it was also pointed out by the NOP survey that 'Of those at present paid in cash 46% stated that they would not be pleased if their employers suggested payment by cheque or credit transfer' and 'a further 41% were indifferent'. [24] Inertia and indifference, these then were the enemies and they could only have been overcome by a massive marketing campaign which, alas, had not been provided for. In fact the postal authorities had been so convinced by the euphoria of the market surveys carried out for them that the customers would be queuing impatiently all over the country's 24 000 Post Offices that the main concern appeared to be how they would ever be able to cope with the flood of new business. They plainly feared that they would be swamped by the demand if it were artificially—and as their own surveys suggested, unnecessarily— boosted by a massive marketing campaign. By the time a really success-ful campaign was under way it coincided, most unfortunately for Giro, with a change of government and the subsequent ordeal by review which will be examined in greater detail later.

There was obviously something also in the argument put forward by bankers in general and Karsten and Hunsworth in particular that 'A much larger proportion of the money supply is held in the form of cash in (continental) Giro countries than in Britain or the United States' and this therefore allowed room for easier penetration by non-cash media as the continental economies expanded. Currency as a percentage of money supply was only 21 and 22%, respectively, for Britain and the USA compared with 51, 46 and 43%, respectively, for Sweden, Holland and Germany. [25] Furthermore, the prevalence of piece-work and, above all, overtime working in Britain increased the difficulties associ-ated with any massive switching to Giro. The detailed researches carried out during 1965 for the Royal Commission on Trade Unions and Employers' Associations clearly demonstrated that such disabilities were more pronounced in Britain than on the continent and were if anything growing stronger in this period: 'The persistence of high levels of regularly worked overtime making many firms and individuals dependent on it is something which has developed in Britain only since the Second World War. Moreover, it has developed to a greater extent than in most other countries. . . . Average overtime in excess of five hours per man per week was perfectly normal throughout the 1950s and early 1960s. Since then the national statistics show that it has increased further.' [26] The baneful effect of piece-work and overtime as hin-drances to wage payments through Giro will be referred to again in Chapter 9 but here it is important to notice that these singularly British disabilities were growing stronger just at the very time when Giro was hoping to capture a large part of this particular market.

It is well known and yet insufficiently appreciated that an expanding economy can absorb new developments impossible in a stagnant or slowly growing one: and compared with the European economic miracle our pedestrian progress looked like stagnation. [27] Although the British economy had long escaped the danger of being 'crucified on a cross of gold' we were still painfully stretched over the balance of payments barrel and this meant that economic controls, intermittently of some severity, were almost continuous and that the joint-stock banks in particular, as the traditional springs of the inflationary money supply, were singled out for stern measures of constraint. Since the joint-stock banks could not at that time compete for deposits by raising their interest rates, their expansion such as was allowed, was all the more dependent upon maintaining or increasing their total of current accounts. This then is a further clue to the ferocity of their opposition to National Giro, a paper tiger enlarged by their own fears.

Just when the Post Office was launching Giro it was also attempting to carry out a number of other fundamental changes any one of which would normally have been considered of sufficient importance to engage its undivided attention, but coming together as they did then it meant plainly that the Post Office was over-reaching itself. As its Annual Report claimed 'The Financial Year of 1968–69 was the most significant in the history of the Post Office since the Rowland Hill reforms of 1840. In 1968 the new letter service was introduced in September, the Giro was opened in October by the Prime Minister and the Bill to transform the GPO into a Public Corporation received its Commons Second Reading in November.' [28] All this activity inevitably led to a certain amount of indigestion. The two-tier post was not accepted by the public with unalloyed enthusiasm and however much the inflation of costs had necessitated increased charges for postal services, publicity resulting from the National Board for Prices and Incomes' enquiry into Post Office business [29] inevitably added to the general public's none-too-friendly mood: and some of this rubbed off on Giro. In trying to carry out so many basic changes at the same time the Post Office could hardly give its infant current-account bank the individual attention which it obviously required. Giro was ill-equipped to suffer such a spartan nativity. Also at this time the old Post Office Savings Bank (now the National Savings Bank) was being more widely separated administratively and geographically from National Giro, a move which hardly made it easier to attract large numbers of the 22 million savings customers over to the Post Office's new current-account bank.

SOLID WORTH ECLIPSED

There were therefore so many hard economic reasons why Giro fell far short of expectations, that the argument that such failure was due to an insufficiency of bankers among its staff can be seen to be largely irrelevant. Only if such recruitment had led to the more ready acceptance by the postal authorities of the need for a massive marketing drive to coincide with the opening of Giro could some reliance be placed on the not very plausible argument that Giro failed because it failed to employ enough bankers: it might have helped a little, but hardly in any fundamental manner. Given Giro's real difficulties such fancied disabilities should not receive undue emphasis. Although the ultimate responsibility rested inescapably with the government and still more directly with the postal authorities, the misleading market researches and surveys, which—like those of the Ford Edsel and some of the electoral polls of the period—turned out to be miles off the mark, helped to encourage exaggerated claims by proponents of Giro to an extent which denied the necessity of providing the really vigorous and sustained marketing campaign which might have gone far towards justifying such confidence. At the same time the surveys generated such exaggerated fears among the other current-account banking institutions that competition was unnecessarily stimulated. Finally, both these extremes of hope and of fear combined to detract from what otherwise would be seen as a considerable achievement by National Giro in providing a safe, satisfactory, speedy and convenient service, completely free or at very cheap rates, to hundreds of thousands of customers, both business and private, over all parts of the country. It is now time to turn to an assessment of the value of the many services provided unspectacularly by Giro for its varied customers to help them along in the course of their day to day work: scientific banking with its working clothes on.

REFERENCES

1   COUSINS, FRANK, In a speech made at the 62nd Annual Conference of the Labour Party, Scarborough, *Report* (London, 1963), p. 145.

2   GIBSON-WATT, D, *Hansard* (21 July 1965), col. 1632.
3   BAMBRIDGE, A, Living with the Giro, *The Banker* (London, September 1965), p. 581.
4   WEDGWOOD BENN, A, *Hansard* (21 July 1965), col. 1634.
5   BAMBRIDGE, A, *op. cit.*, p. 580.
6   WEDGWOOD BENN A, *op. cit.*, col. 1638.
7   *Radcliffe Committee on the Working of the Monetary System* (H.M.S.O.: London, 1959), Minutes of Evidence, Q.Q. 13123, 13124.
8   *The Banker* (London, September 1965), pp. 572–3.
9   *National Opinion Poll, Bank Habits Survey* (London, November 1965), Conclusions p. 4. The Clearers have since realised the importance of a collective approach and have employed NOP to carry out a continuous survey on this and related matters.
10 *Midland Bank Annual Report and Chairman's Statement for the year* 1964 (London, January 1965).
11 FORBES, SIR ARCHIBALD, *ibid.*
12 BAMBRIDGE, A, *op. cit.*, p. 582.
13 BAMBRIDGE, A, *ibid.*, p. 580.
14 Department of Employment, *Report on Methods of Payment of Wages* (H.M.S.O.: London, 1972), p. 4.
15 *Ibid.*, pp. 3–4.
16 Ministry of Labour, *Report of the Committee on the Truck Acts* (H.M.S.O.: London, 1961), p. 2.
17 *Ibid.*, p. 8, para. 12.
18 WEDGWOOD BENN, A, *op. cit.*, col. 1637.
19 WEDGWOOD BENN, A, *ibid.*, col. 1635.
20 *Post Office Report and Accounts 1966–67*, para. 73.
21 *Post Office Report and Accounts 1966–67*, para. 75; 1967–68, paras. 81 and 82.
22 National Giro, *The Opening of the National Giro* (Bootle, 18 October 1968), Italics added.
23 National Giro Centre, Bootle, *Launching the National Giro*, Press and Broadcast Notice (October 1968), p. 1.
24 National Opinion Poll Survey (London, June 1965), quoted by *The Banker* (September 1965), p. 573.
25 HUNSWORTH J. *The Bankers Magazine* (London, December 1964), pp. 348–9.
26 WHYBREW, E G, *Overtime Working in Britain*, Research Paper No. 9, Royal Commission on Trade Unions and Employers' Associations (H.M.S.O.: London, 1965), paras. 66 and 54.
27 Among the numerous books and articles dealing with the post-war European miracle and Anglo-saxon pedestrianism mention might be made of (*a*) MADDISON, A, *Economic Growth in the West, New York* (1964) Ch. 1, and (*b*) *The Economist*, 'Falling Behind Again' (London, 14 August 1971), pp. 54–5.
28 *Post Office Report and Accounts, 1968–69*, p. 5.
29 National Board for Prices and Incomes, Report No. 58, *Post Office Charges* (London, March 1968).

Chapter 6

Giro at Work: Customer Case Studies

'The trivial round, the common task
Would furnish all we ought to ask.'
John Keble. [1]

CREATURES OF HABIT

To be taken for granted, that is the essence of good money and of a good money and credit transfer system: one that with little fuss or formality enables payments or transfers of any sums of money, from the widow's mite to the institutions' millions, with a feeling that one can rest assured that what has been simply ordered will as a matter of 100% certainty be carried out so quickly and conveniently that neither the initiator of the process of monetary exchange or transfer, nor any intermediary nor the final contacts are bothered by the mechanics of the system. To perform such a task the system must operate with well-oiled and silent automaticity, providing with unfailing regularity to all its customers the highest possible degree of certainty, security, speed and convenience. In this sense money and monetary institutions are at their best when they are least obtrusive: at their most impressive when they leave no impression, when in fact they are of so little account that one hardly bothers to notice them. (In other respects of course the monetary institutions vie with one another to be as conspicuous as possible, but in the simple mechanics of monetary transfer this need not be so: Giro can well operate without prestigious marble halls.) It was this aspect of the many-sided nature of money that was supremely well captured by J S Mill in his chapter on Money in his classical work on *The Principles of Political Economy*. 'There cannot, in short, be intrinsically a more insignificant thing, in the economy of society, than money;

132

except in the character of a contrivance for sparing time and labour. It is a machine for doing quickly and commodiously, what would be done, though less quickly and commodiously, without it.' [2]

Since payment is thus largely, and rightly so, a matter of habit, this helps to explain why most people are very conservative when it comes to the question of adopting new methods of making payment. Were it not so then innovations in payment techniques would be more easily accomplished and Giro would no doubt have grown much more quickly than it has. If before making every payment or even if at regular short intervals one had to pause to consider the various alternative ways it was possible to make such payments—in other words if most payments were not a matter of almost reflex action—then an enormous amount of social energy would be wasted. But the importance of 'habit' or inertia is largely overlooked in modern economics, except perhaps to concentrate on its disadvantages, even though it is largely because this human trait has certain positive advantages to offset its shortcomings that it stubbornly persists. For a rare and well-balanced treatment of the importance of habit one may refer to Wicksteed's rather old-fashioned but perennially apposite *Common Sense of Political Economy*: 'A vast amount of the work of the world is probably done, to the great advantage of all concerned, and to the saving of much fretting upon the higher strings of motive and efforts of will, by the mere drift and momentum of acquired habit. The thought once put into the formation of habit carries life forward with an economy of thought in future.' Thus although 'from one point of view the whole weight of custom and tradition may be regarded as a drag upon wise living; from another point of view it may be regarded as a fly-wheel, storing energy to carry us over dead points'. [3] Since the majority of payments are repetitive, previous patterns, based on old-fashioned ways of living, tend to be continually reaffirmed. This may be a partial explanation of the fact that a general aura of custom and conservatism is particularly noticeable in monetary matters. Manual workers have notoriously been very reluctant to relinquish cash payments, while in a similar fashion the typical individual among the higher income groups has generally hesitated a long while before daring to change his bank. We have already seen how the leaders of the Trustee Savings Bank movement when faced by the challenge thrown down by the Radcliffe Committee decided as a matter of deliberate policy not to opt for what they considered to be the more revolutionary and novel form of Giro, but chose instead to bring the more familiar middle-class instrument of the cheque down to meet the needs of the rising expenditures of the increasingly affluent from among their working-class customers. Thus, it is touching the heart of the matter to say that the old, well-tried, well-established and familiar means of payment are much more easily taken for granted and un-questionably accepted than newer forms, even when the latter are demonstrably superior. In contrast, as a new institution, Giro, by a series of major steps and in a short space of time, has had to try to create a stream-lined, simple and convenient means of payment that could compete effectively not only with older and more firmly established methods, but also with newer methods which though improvements on the older types were less revolutionary and more easily adopted since they were mainly modifications of already firmly accepted payment instruments offered by traditional banking institutions. This was and still remains a mammoth task, which no-one would claim to have been achieved with complete success: but the wonder is, given the nature of the problem, not that complete success was not achieved, but rather that such a fair degree of progress has in fact been achieved in this aim. [4]

The proof of the pudding is however in the eating. As a result of a series of personal interviews the author allows the experience and comments of actual customers, whether critical or appreciative to speak for themselves so as to complement the more abstract and objective statistical tables and figures by which the progress of Giro must in the main, but certainly not exclusively, be judged. In the first section of our analysis of Giro at work, therefore, major policy matters will be avoided and attention will be concentrated on the ordinary day-to-day work of Giro, seeing how the system is used in a variety of ways by a number of different but specific users, drawn from the whole range of socio-economic groups, purposely to bring out the customary everyday monetary tasks that Giro carries out for its ordinary everyday customers, with on the whole, a commendably high degree of satisfaction.

The customers stand, as we have seen, at the periphery of the Giro system: from anywhere in the country (and to a limited, but growing extent, also from abroad) they initiate express money flows via the postal system which are received, verified and processed at the Giro Centre at Bootle, following which the notification of the results of the transaction are sent back again by post to the peripheral customers to complete the cycle. As a necessary by-product of this process a pool of money of fluctuating size remains at the Centre and is available to Giro for investing according to its own discretion within certain fairly well-defined statutory limitations. This latter is one of the main tasks of the London Office. Consequently, after dealing with Giro as seen from the point of view of a number of different kinds of customer, we shall then look closely at the operations of the National Giro Centre at Bootle and finally deal with the important investment services provided by the money desk at the London Office.

GOWER AND RURAL RENTS

The Gower Peninsula, which (together with the Quantocks) was the first region in Britain to be declared 'an area of outstanding natural beauty' [5] lies next door to one of the most heavily industrialised regions in South Wales; though the contrast is such that it might well be a hundred miles away. The Gower shares also another distinction: its Local Authority was certainly among the very first to avail itself of one of the special privileges of Giro membership, namely the great convenience which it affords to its tenants for making their rate and rent payments by post. The Treasurer and Rating Officer to the Gower Rural District Council, Mr C L Jones, a Fellow of the Institute of Municipal Treasurers and Accountants, had, like a number of his colleagues in other Local Authorities, long been working towards just such a system. Mr Jones had already successfully developed a system whereby rates were collected through the medium of the local Post Offices. This postal rate payment scheme had been running since 1961 and had yielded valuable experience which was put to good use in devising a Giro rent system tailored to the special needs of the Gower Local Authority and its council tenants. In a Paper presented to a joint meeting of the Carmarthenshire, Pembrokeshire and Glamorgan Financial Officers' Associations at Neath on 6 November 1970, the Gower Treasurer described the reasons why Giro was chosen as the preferred method of payment and traces the steps by which a 100% transfer to Giro was achieved: 'The compelling force behind the adoption of this early system was five-fold:

1   Distance of certain parishes from Council offices.
2   High cost of transport where ratepayers paid in the Council offices.

135

3   High cost of poundage on postal and money orders where rate-payers had no bank accounts.
4   Not sufficient staff to man sub-offices.
5   Avoidance of queues on or about Discount periods.

The adoption of rate collection was a real break-through and all five reasons were completely fulfilled.' [6] The collection of rates through Giro coincided with the opening of the National Giro system on 18 October 1968, and immediately afterwards certain tenants of Council houses situated furthest from the Council offices, in villages like Llanrhidian and Llangennith, were also encouraged to pay their rent by Giro. Within just a few months almost 30% of the Council tenants were taking advantage of this scheme and in March 1969 a further opportunity presented itself to bring about a 100% collection as shown in the following letter:

Dear Sir/Madam,

One of the Council's Rent Collectors has been promoted to another post in the Engineer's Department, and in consequence it is necessary to review the rent collection service. At present approximately 30% of the Council's tenants pay their rent through the Post Office Giro system and in view of this high percentage it would be uneconomical to employ another full time Collector as it would only add to the cost of the rent. I would strongly recommend the Giro system of rent payment to you for the reasons stated below and if you can agree to this method of collection it would greatly assist the Council to keep down costs.

The Giro system enables a person:

(a)   To pay his rent weekly.
(b)   To pay his rent at any Post Office, and not only at your local Post Office.
(c)   Payment is free of cost to the Tenant.
(d)   Payment of Rent can be done on any day convenient to you; it could coincide with your visit to the Post Office to draw your Family Allowance or your Old Age Pension, etc.
(e)   It will avoid you inconveniencing yourself in waiting for the collector.

(f) The service is confidential and the Postmaster will not know your rent.

(g) The Postmaster will accept whatever payment you tender to him.

(h) The method of payment is very simple: all you have to do in making payment is to put your name and address and house reference number on the form when making payment.

I take the liberty of sending you a Giro Payment Book, but if you cannot attend a Post Office or you object to this method of payment will you kindly return the book to this office and kindly state your reasons for objection for not wishing to pay in this manner. Your co-operation in this matter will be appreciated.

Yours faithfully,

C L Jones
Treasurer

Following this letter only seven out of the total of 555 Council tenants refused to adopt this method of payment, but by personal contact and a little improvisation these seven were 'converted' so that the Gower Rural District Council quickly achieved a 100% Giro rent collection.

The Gower Treasurer makes it clear that his approaches to the joint-stock banks had been spurned: 'It should be stated that even before Giro came on the scene contacts were made with the Joint-Stock Banks (with a view to their sending round a mobile bank for rent collection); but there was only one Bank with a branch in the district and they were plainly not interested although subsequent to the innovation of our schemes the Banks have woken up to the fact that an opportunity has been lost.' [7]

Four years' experience appears to have fully justified Mr Jones' initial optimism in the superiority of Giro for rent payments. He estimates in the same Paper mentioned above that 'the savings in collection expenses for his Council amount to £3868 per annum on rates and rents, representing a saving of 27%'. He further goes on to emphasise another important aspect of the non-cash payment system: 'But to be personal and to look at it humanely and ethically the savings are far greater than can be measured cashwise. No longer does a rent collector have to look twice over his shoulder to see if he is being followed. The risk of carrying money today is such a risk that no Treasurer can afford to subject his staff to it; moreover modern means can be adapted to suit us all and thus increase efficiency and reduce costs.' Furthermore, though the Giro system 'like all other known systems will never make good payers out of bad payers it can be stated that the Giro system has reduced arrears at the end of the year, merely by placing at tenants' and ratepayers' disposal a simple method of paying their dues'. [8]

Thus it seemed to the writer to be as pleasant as it was appropriate to make the first of his series of customer-interviews by visiting this rural playground to test whether the tenants' reactions tallied with those of the Local Authority's officials. Like most other country regions the indigenous population of the Gower has been drastically and dramatically thinned of its younger members and consequently it seemed to be most suitable to select Giro customers chiefly though not exclusively from among the older age groups of the area. The tenants visited received no previous notification to mar the spontaneity of their reactions as to the usefulness of the Giro scheme compared with their previous and more traditional methods, the most common of which had been cash payment to the rent collector, or more rarely, personal payment at the Gower Rural District Office in Swansea.

Among the council tenants interviewed were: a young married couple with three children; an old-age-pensioner widow whose sick brother lived with her; a widower whose married son and family lived with him; an old-age-pensioner widower who lived on his own (and managed to keep his garden in spectacularly attractive condition); and a building labourer who had been unemployed for some considerable period—all from social groups D and E and each family already making regular weekly use of the Post Office for receiving welfare benefits. Also interviewed was one of the Sub-Postmistresses who, typically, not only ran the Post Office, but also kept the one and only village shop. In every case the change-over to paying rents through Giro had proved very satisfactory. The tenants found it simple and straightforward and all mentioned that since they had to go to the Post Office to collect family allowance, pensions or unemployment benefit or to do their shopping at the same place, then this made it extremely convenient for them to pay the rent at the same time. Furthermore, they much appreciated no longer having to stay at home to await the arrival of the rent collector and greatly welcomed the facility for paying their rents at *any* Post

Office, when for example they were on holiday, or, as was not uncommonly the case with some of the elderly tenants, when they went to stay, sometimes for up to a few months at a time, at their children's homes in a distant part of the country.

As for criticisms these were surprisingly muted. One of the persons interviewed had been one of the 'reluctant seven' mentioned above. Her opposition turned out in retrospect to be nothing more than a vague fear of the unknown which a few weeks' experience overcame completely. A few of them mentioned that the ready reference which the traditional rent book offered as to the credit worthiness of the fully paid-up tenant and which was useful to show to door-to-door salesmen and smaller shopkeepers was no longer available. Reference to Figure 6.1, which depicts the Giro Rent Form used by the Gower Rural District Council, shows that on the reverse of the form a space is left for notifying needed repairs. The Treasurer voiced some strong criticism of the

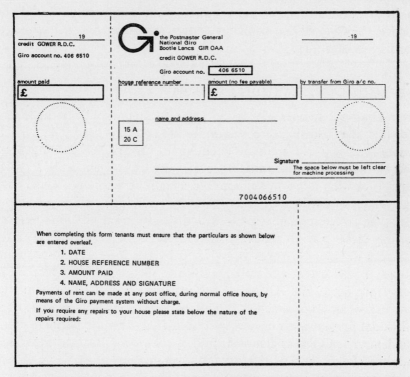

Figure 6.1   Rent through Giro: Gower RDC rent book (front and back)

Giro Authorities who had at one time wished to simplify their procedures by returning to the Gower Authority a single statement combining the total of rents received rather than also returning the individual vouchers deposited at the various Post Offices by the tenants. This would have meant a loss of the useful repair notification service. As the reader might guess, Mr Jones' view prevailed. (Other Local Authorities prefer different arrangements: and as we shall see later, Giro tailors these to suit the peculiar circumstances of the Local Authorities concerned.) There can be no doubt on the evidence of the Gower case studies that on balance the criticisms were far outweighed by the commendations. Anyone who doubts that there was no grass-roots demand for a postal Giro system should study the evidence provided by the numerous rent payment schemes. Similarly for those who question whether the lowest income groups can either make a profitable contribution towards the running of a Giro or themselves directly benefit from its services, the experiences described above offer a convincing and positive answer. In so far as National Giro is the product of the community's social conscience, the Council rent payment system represents one of its most rewarding illustrations.

GIRO AND THE SALARIED CUSTOMER

From among a number of salaried persons interviewed who have Giro accounts, the following three examples are taken: (1) Mr R P, a young twenty-four year old graduate bachelor in his first job earning £1500 p.a.; (2) Mr H B, in his mid-30s, married with two children, a typical example of what it is now fashionable to call the 'executive' class, earning a salary of £4000 p.a.; and (3) Mr F I, holding a senior position in one of the professions, now in his early fifties, married with four children, earning £6000 p.a. Thus having looked earlier in the chapter at a few instances of how Giro was being used by the lowest socio-economic groups, a brief glance will now be given to the manner in which customers from the C and AB social groups make use of Giro to fit their own particular requirements. It will be interesting to see what these individual and business customers considered were the peculiar merits and demerits of Giro as demonstrated by their own practical experience and, in so far as their particular views were typical of the more general body of opinion as indicated by National Giro's own market researches, to see also the degree to which their criticisms, were met by the newer strategies developed within Giro during the year or so following the Government's statement of faith in Giro's future which was issued by Mr Christopher Chataway, the Minister of Posts and Telecommunications, in Parliament on 17 November 1971, and which will be described in some detail in the following chapters. [9]

Mr R P, after graduating in Chemistry at Glasgow, where he had kept a current account with one of the Scottish Clearing Banks, moved south to London for his first post within the Civil Service. He immediately chose to be paid through Giro for a number of reasons. First, while a student he had been charged by the Scottish bank for running his modest account and though the charge was more nominal than real, yet it was felt to be rather irksome. In this respect the bank in question differed from the recent practice followed by the English clearers. Second, a matter to which he gave much stress, his hours of work overlapped bank opening hours which meant that he would find it extremely difficult to get to the bank to withdraw cash without some considerable rush, uncertainty and inconvenience. The Saturday opening of the local Post Office was a boon in this respect. Furthermore, as a single man in his first job, he travelled home from London about every three weeks and also found it equally convenient to be able to draw cash from his home town Post Office, again usually on Saturdays, as well as normally from the Post Office nearest to his lodgings. Since standing orders and transfers are free he made use of these facilities for paying such items as a fixed monthly sum into a savings account with one of the 'Big-Five' Building Societies, enlarged from time to time by a transfer to a share account in the same society as and when he felt he could afford it. His monthly life assurance payments and his annual professional fee were similarly paid by standing orders. Occasionally, he made payment by Girocheque to those without Giro accounts—where, that is, the normally simpler and cheaper transfer could not be made. On the whole he seemed very satisfied with the service and thought it good value for the fixed charge of £1 every six months. He found the statements simple and speedy and as emphasised above was especially pleased with the convenience of being able to draw cash on Saturdays at his nearest Post Office, though he had found that the current maximum withdrawal (without prior notice) of £20 was rather low, since he almost always withdrew the maximum amount. He also considered that payment by

Girocheque, for the sort of small payments which a person of his modest salary would normally make, was hardly better than using the old-fashioned postal order system. As well as wanting a high cash withdrawal limit (without notice) he would also have liked to be able to get this facility from a larger number of Post Offices. He was therefore very pleased to receive a letter from Giro in October 1972 letting him know of their new selective Giro card scheme, which as we shall show later, promised to offer improved facilities of the very kind which his limited experience had already shown to be desirable. [10]

Mr H B, who after considerable experience in marketing and public relations in a variety of institutions now holds a responsible position at the Head Office of a public corporation in central London, provides an example of a Giro customer who appears absolutely determined to make the maximum possible use of its non-cash payment facilities, and in so doing has drastically reduced his own family's need for cash. For his wife and himself (they run a joint account) the cashless society has almost arrived. After income tax, superannuation and similar deductions from his £4000 p.a. salary have been taken into account his monthly net pay of around £250 is credited direct to his Giro account. Although it would not be hard to find an individual or joint account holders who make greater use of the new postal payments facilities, Mr and Mrs H B may be taken as an example of a couple who have come to rely fairly extensively on Giro. They have done this by very carefully drawing up a monthly budgeting system, not only to even out payments throughout the year but also to enable them to use Giro's free transfer and standing order system to the full. Bills for household purposes, e.g. for electricity, for general and water rates, for their tailor, for TV rental, for the monthly mortgage repayment, for his professional fee to the National Union of Journalists, for their joint Automobile Association membership fee, for their savings with their Building Society, for payment to a builder for constructing an extension to their house, for service charges on their dish-washing machine, and even the repayment of a loan from Mr H B's mother-in-law, are all made by Giro transfers or standing orders, most of them by standing orders. His wife draws out cash four times a month from the Post Office near her home, while Mr H B similarly uses the Post Office nearest his own office for the same facility. Their main criticism was with regard to the difficulty which he and his wife sometimes found in making retail shopkeepers sufficiently aware of Giro to open an account so that they could pay through Giro transfers or, when the shopkeepers had no Giro account, to be sufficiently perceptive of the Giro system to accept Girocheques.

He therefore wished to see Giro bring out some form of cheque guarantee card, arguing that since Giro's essential purpose was to reduce the need to carry cash around, then this could obviously be done more effectively by such a guarantee card rather than by extending the existing cash withdrawal facilities from the Post Offices.

Mr and Mrs H B still maintained a modest account with one of the commercial banks, chiefly for occasional payments to creditors who did not have Giro accounts—another pointer to the need for improving the Girocheque system—but their bank account was turned over at a very much slower velocity than their much used Giro account. A further indication of the extensive use made of their Giro account is given by the fact that between the date of opening the account on the 3 January 1970 and the interview date of 8 September 1972 they had received 134 separate statements from Giro—a statement being sent for every credit received and, where no credit appeared on the statement sheet, then a statement being automatically sent for every ten debits. Although they had thus drastically reduced the use of their bank current account, on the other hand their budgeting system had enabled them to increase their deposit account with their commercial bank and so allowed them to benefit from a modest but welcome increase in interest. They did however make a rather trenchant criticism of Giro's inability to allow incidental or accidental overdrafts and contrasted Giro's rather rigid attitude in this matter with the more civilised and relaxed attitude of their commercial bank. Giro is of course prohibited from countenancing an overdraft situation and Mr and Mrs H B felt that this tended to lead to a feeling of insecurity, particularly towards the end of the month, where merely for the sake of a couple of pence overdrawn there was the almost certain danger that a payment through Giro would be stopped, with the inevitably unpleasant and, they felt, undeservedly severe impairment of their good credit rating. They felt that Giro would need to build up a credit rating register so as to distinguish between the relatively few who might attempt deliberately to use the Giro current account facility directly for credit purposes and should therefore be penalised for so doing, and the great majority who merely occasionally and accidentally went into a tiny negative balance for a day or so before their funds, to the certain knowledge of Giro—as for example in the case of the salaries-through-Giro schemes—would again be in a substantial credit balance. [11] On the whole, however, they remained enthusiastic Giro users. In their own words: 'The best thing about Giro is that you know with certainty what the charges are, and also, you know exactly where you stand because of the frequent and clear statements.'

Mr F I, having had a bank account for some thirty years, felt most reluctant to impair such a long-established connection. Furthermore, as someone who had moved house on six occasions during his career, he relied on having bridging loans and occasional overdraft facilities from his bank. Thus, differing from the two previous salaried customers of Giro, Mr F I had neither severed his connection with his bank, nor had he significantly reduced his current account. Nevertheless, there were certain clear attractions regarding Giro which had led him to open his postal account, the chief of which were its cheapness, and above all, its convenience for family budgeting. Since he travelled frequently in the course of his duties, the only time that he seemed to have to discuss the family budget with his wife was at the weekends. Payments and receipts concerning such items as telephone bills, bonus payments and other credits additional to his main salary, mail order business and similar financial matters could be arranged by his wife and himself at home at their leisure at the weekends and the resulting Giro forms dropped into the nearest post box with minimum effort and at little cost. Similarly, the cash withdrawal facility from two named post offices was useful as a fall-back, particularly on Saturdays when his commercial bank was closed. He was of the opinion that in the course of time he might gradually increase his dependence on Giro without however relinquishing to any significant extent his valued connection with his existing commercial bank. In this way he felt he could obtain the maximum advantages offered by both the private and state sector current account banking services. [12]

AGENT DEPOSITS SYSTEM AND THE SMALL FIRM

A brief look at the case of Tickle's Dairies, a firm which supplies milk and other dairy products to some 5000 homes in and around Grays, Essex provides us with a convenient and concrete example of the working of the Agent Deposits system by a typical small family concern.

This firm, which has been run by Mr Tickle's family since 1926, now employs fifteen men on eleven milk rounds—eleven roundsmen supplemented for this seven-day a week service by three rota men and one general mechanic. The reasons why it has adopted the Giro system are complex. As well as carrying on the dairy business, Mr Tickle also runs two small shops supplying general groceries for the neighbourhood and, more significantly, he is also sub-postmaster for the two Post Offices sited within his two shops, one of which, the one through which he conducts his Agent Deposits service, being only 100 yards from his Dairy. Despite the obvious benefit of gaining agency business by using Giro himself, it was however through having to deal with a large and influential customer, the local telephone exchange, which naturally paid its monthly milk bill through Giro, that Mr Tickle was originally persuaded to consider opening a Giro account for his own business. He had become increasingly concerned in recent years at the time-consuming and personally risky methods which he had been forced to use up until he changed to the Giro Agent Deposits system. Although some of his eleven roundsmen are paid by some of the customers every day, most customers naturally enough pay for their milk weekly, fornightly or more rarely at monthly intervals on Fridays or Saturdays. In any event by the time the roundsmen arrive back at the Dairy the banks are closed, though the Post Office is usually still open. Under his former method Mr Tickle was therefore faced with the alternative of either keeping the cash in his own safe or of taking it in the eleven night wallets which had been supplied by his bank, in person by car to the wall-safe of his bank. As both the traffic congestion on Friday and Saturday evenings and the security problems tended to mount over recent years, so the attractions of the Giro Agent Deposits system increased. Upon enquiry, National Giro Centre sent along a representative, trained and experienced in the operation of setting up this system, to study Mr Tickle's particular problems and subsequently drew up a mutually agreed method of operation which has now been working since March 1970. Each roundsman has a book of Agent Deposit vouchers such as that shown in Figure 6.2, on which the daily totals of takings are entered as deposits at the Post Office. The aggregate of each of the eleven vouchers is then entered on a form which is sent to National Giro Centre, the cash being absorbed into the general takings of the postal system. There is therefore much less security risk and complete elimination of the time wasting

145

process of transporting the cash takings by car to the wall-safe of the local bank. 'Previously', in Mr Tickle's own words and confirmed by his accountant, 'we were always carting money about and always feeling insecure.' Now within twenty-four hours (or under the arrangements as from November 1972, within forty-eight hours) a detailed statement of the transactions is returned to the firm. The firm also knows *before hand* the charges made by the Post Office for running the service. 'We have a better control of our money and our statements and can follow up much more quickly than previously any mistakes which may have been made,' said Mr Purdy, who acts as manager/accountant for Mr Tickle.

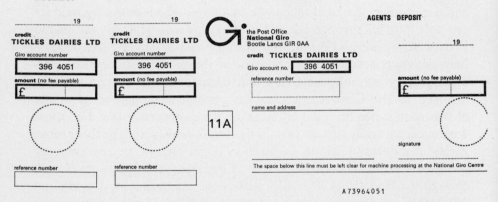

Figure 6.2   Example of an Agent Deposits service voucher as used by a small business firm

Certain difficulties and disadvantages arise chiefly from the receipt of various kinds of cheques which are being increasingly received by the roundsmen, and which the firm find it difficult to incorporate in the *normal* Giro system and this includes even the crossed Girocheques themselves. They realise full well that if special arrangements are made with Giro then Giro could accept these cheques as deposits, but so far as Tickle's Dairies is concerned this would mean an inconvenient duplicating of the present accounting system which they feel would confuse the employees. Consequently, all such cheques, including Girocheques, are deposited with their normal commercial bank. (In this way Giro must be losing in total a considerable amount of deposits which they might otherwise be getting.)

An interesting if somewhat bizarre commentary on an awkward by-product of the way in which we are stumbling towards the 'less-cash

146

society' came to light in the course of my examination of Tickle's Dairies. Out of the 5000 houses served, the dairy receives each week as many as between 200 and 300 cheques of various kinds in payment, and about two-thirds of these are third-party cheques. Generally the milkman is pleased to accept such a cheque instead of having to carry round the monetary equivalent in cash—but he is also often asked to change wages cheques on the spot since he is the first trader with whom the housewife comes into contact on the morning after pay day. It is therefore an ironic comment on the change-over to paying wages by cheque that the small tradesman, in this case the milkman, is becoming more and more a mobile, acting unpaid bank clerk.

GIRO AND BIG BUSINESS

Giro numbers among its most valued customers some of the largest firms in the country and among the largest of their kind in the world: firms which are truly household names not only from the point of view of their size, but also from the nature of their close day-to-day connections with the general public. The fact that Giro has been able not only to capture their custom but to develop increasing amounts of business with them is an indication of an important role which has perhaps been overshadowed in the public mind by excessive preoccupation with Giro as 'the poor man's bank'. As well as being the poor man's bank Giro is also the bank that handles a considerable and growing amount of the cash transmission business of some of the country's biggest businesses. Table 6.1 gives an indication in summary form of some of the more popular services provided by Giro as used by large institutions, comprising a brief selection of local authorities, public boards and commercial companies from among the 30 000 listed in Giro's 'Business Directory'. It should hardly be necessary to remark that, as has been indicated above in describing the Gower rent scheme and Tickle's Dairies, schemes with the same general description may differ significantly in particular cases since the essence of successful marketing is to tailor the general facility to the particular requirements of the customer.

In December 1972 there were some 192 organisations using Giro's Agent Deposits system, ranging in size from Tickle's Dairies to the giant Unilever combine. As our examples of big business usage of this facility the revealing experience of the Associated British Foods Group,

ACCOUNT HOLDER	TYPE OF FACILITY USED							
	1	2	3	4	5	6	7	8
Imperial Chemical Industries	*					*	*	*
Unilever	*					*	*	*
Associated British Foods	*	*	*			*	*	
J H Dewhurst Ltd	*	*	*				*	*
Provident Clothing and Supply Company	*	*	*					
Empire Stores of Bradford			*			*		
Halifax Building Society	*	*			*	*		
North Eastern Gas Board	*	*		*	*	*		
North Western Electricity Board	*	*		*		*		
National Union of Public Employees	*							
Norwich Union	*					*		
Sun Alliance and London Insurance	*			*		*	*	
London Borough of Barnet County Council	*		*	*		*	*	
Department of Health and Social Security	*	*	*	*		*	*	

DESCRIPTION OF FACILITY USED

1 Inpayments/standing orders/transfers
2 Agent deposits
3 Rapid money transfer
4 Rates/rents-through-Giro
5 Pay/pensions/salary-through-Giro
6 Machine readable output
7 Girocheques
8 Miscellaneous, e.g. change-giving/enveloping/addressing/automatic debit transfers, etc

Table 6.1 Typical business customer services

J H Dewhurst Ltd, and the Provident Clothing and Supply Company will be examined so as to bring out the salient features of how Giro supplies a nationwide network handling daily a varied turnover of cash and other payments which run into a total exceeding £1000 million a year.

1. *ABF and Giro*

The Associated British Foods Group under the chairmanship of Mr Garry H. Weston is a vast combine of companies whose principal activities are the manufacture and sale of food chiefly in the United Kingdom, Australia, New Zealand and South Africa. For the year which ended in April 1972, ABF's total sales exceeded £612 million and its profits (before tax and interest charges) exceeded £32 million. Sales in the United Kingdom totalled £450 million where the principal divisions are currently Allied Bakeries operating over fifty bakeries, and 2400 shops—Allied Mills with twenty-one flour mills, Fine Fare with 500 supermarkets plus 500 other shops, Food Securities with fifty-six Alliance Cash and Carry warehouses, nine factories making biscuits, Ryvita and XL Crisps, and the Twining Crosfield group which operates eight tea and coffee factories in Europe. In addition there are a number of other food companies with over twenty-five factories in various parts of the United Kingdom. [13] In order to assist the writer's evaluation of Giro ABF gave ready access to and a lucid explanation of the cash flow system in operation before using Giro, its original usage of Giro and its subsequent wider developments based on its earlier experience. Throughout the interview and in subsequent correspondence the Company stressed that, as in any case should have been obvious with regard to such a large company, it had been essential to obtain the full co-operation of the joint-stock banks in order to carry out its thorough-going reorganisation of its cash deposit, transfer and associated accounting system. In view of the long history of antagonism between the banks and Giro it is refreshing to witness the practical working of a system based on the highest common factor achieved by triangular negotiations between Giro, ABF and its joint-stock bankers.

During the course of 1970 the ABF group carried through a detailed study of its existing cash flow and related accounting system. It found that the speed of cash transit varied significantly in different parts of the country and that, understandably in a company made up of such varied components, the methods of inpayment also differed considerably.

149

In general the study revealed a surprising degree of delay in cash transit before cash already paid could become available at the Company's central account with its London bankers. This meant that ABF was often in the position of having to service substantial and expensive overdrafts while at the very same time in various parts of its organisation considerable surpluses had already been paid in, but which could not physically be brought into the centre, nor documented quickly enough to obviate the need for such overdrafts. 'We therefore felt', said the Company's financial controller 'that we had to find a system which would give us an exact and quick flow of cash. This we believe we have found in the National Giro system.' ABF therefore decided to call in Giro and after a series of successful experiments in Ulster, in Northern England and along the south coast, it went over to a nationwide Agent Deposits system in which most of the companies in the group pay in all their cash (and some of their cheque) receipts into their own respective National Giro account. These separate subsidiary company accounts are cleared by Giro daily into an intermediate 'group' account, and the following day are combined into the main control account of ABF Ltd. Thus once the bakeries' or the shops' or the vanmen's cash-and-cheque takings are deposited in the most convenient Post Office along with the completed Agent Deposits slip (of the same general style as that shown in Figure 6.2, but with space for cheques, money orders and postal orders also), the computer system at Bootle automatically handles all the relevant transfers from the Company's 12 000 paying-in points, complete with full documentation leading to the final stage of rapid transfer of the global sum to the credit of ABF's joint-stock bank account in London. Thus the speeding-up of ABF's cash flow has meant that its centralised deposits in its main joint-stock bank account in the City are, if anything, larger than they would otherwise have been, and arrive in more readily ascertainable and larger amounts without the bank having had the bother of man-handling the many thousands of relatively small, awkward and dispersed cash-inpayments with all the heavy intermediate branch accounting involved. These cash takings are now eagerly, efficiently, swiftly and profitably handled by Giro—a practical and powerful example of the kind of fruitful co-operation between business, the banks and Giro that the Radcliffe Report had hoped for but which, as we have seen, has too often been conspicuously absent. There is no doubt that faster money movement combined with enhanced

150

security, considerable overall economies and much tighter accounting control—this latter factor was repeatedly stressed during my discussions with the Company's financial staff—have been achieved by ABF as a result of the adoption of its particular form of Agent Deposits system. It is worth emphasising that these beneficial results were not achieved merely by grafting Giro on to its existing system, but rather by integrating Giro's Agent Deposits service into a new global scheme painstakingly developed by the Company in conjunction with advice from Giro and from the firm's bankers. The mutually beneficial experience of ABF's relationship with Giro is no isolated example. Safeway, a large and expanding food group which operated some sixty supermarkets at the end of 1972; Dewhurst, by far the biggest retail butchery chain in the United Kingdom, which in turn is part of the Vestey organisation, 'one of the world's largest and more remarkable businesses' [14] and the Empire Stores of Bradford (the last two being pioneers in this respect), also successfully run Agent Deposits accounts with National Giro which are basically similar to that of ABF.

2 Dewhursts and Giro

J H Dewhurst Ltd is a subsidiary Company of the Union International Company Ltd and operates approximately 1550 Retail Butchers Shops throughout England, Scotland, Wales and the Channel Isles. In addition to the shops the Company has thirty-four distribution depots, twelve factories and a slaughterhouse and its own printing works, the whole business being administered from the Head Office at Smithfield through seventy-eight area and district offices. The Company's Chief Accountant in reply to my inquiries wrote as follows:

> The Company was the first National Multiple Organisation to use the services of the National Giro, which commenced in the year of its inception and has continued ever since. Our principal reason for using the National Giro is that in comparison with the banks the post offices remain open for longer hours from Monday to Friday and also on Saturday which obviates the need for our staff to be away from our shops dealing with bankings at what is often the busiest part of a trading day.
> The Company's policy is:
>
> (a) To use the National Giro exclusively for banking shop takings

151

whenever the nearest Crown or sub-post office is not more than 100 yards further from our shops than the nearest bank.

(b) With no exception, to bank all our takings on Saturday with the nearest post office, irrespective of the distance.

By carrying accounts of the type this Company operates, the Post Office receive a benefit in the fact that it often obviates the need for them to transfer fairly large sums of cash from the main post offices to sub-post offices in order to enable the small post offices to pay such items as Pensions and National Insurance Benefits, because they know that every day, with no exception, they will be receiving our takings which are normally consistent, and therefore a great help to them.

We can assure you that throughout our association with the National Giro, we have found them to be most co-operative and helpful and it will continue to be the Company's policy to give them every support provided they can continue to provide a service which is better than that of the banks.

This latter condition is no idle threat, for Dewhurst have occasionally discontinued services which did not come up to their expectations. They also expressed concern regarding proposals to close Crown Post Offices at 1 p.m. on Saturdays 'which can have no other effect than reducing some of the advantages the National Giro has had over the banks'. [15] In replying to this point Giro emphasised that the closure of Crown offices does not inhibit the provision of deposit services, that Dewhurst have agreed deposit facilities to 15.30 hours regardless of whether the public counter is closed, and that similar arrangements are made with a number of other companies.

3 *'Check' trading, agent deposits and rapid money transfer*

The Agent Deposits system thus appears to be particularly suited to meet the needs of chains of retail outlets, and so long as cash and shopping go together so the particular forms of cash-transfer described above are likely to flourish. The Agent Deposits system is however eminently flexible and can also be successfully combined with developing forms of non-cash shopping, as the following example illustrates. The Provident

Clothing and Supply Company Limited, founded in Bradford in 1880, lays claim to being the largest check trading organisation in the world. It is a financial and credit organisation which, like the Post Office Savings Bank and Giro itself, owes its origin and draws much of its inspiration from working-class support. For those who are unacquainted with the 'Provident' (and ignorance possibly indicates a rough line of demarcation between social classes) the company supplies a nation-wide personal credit service through the issue of checks and vouchers to more than $1\frac{1}{2}$ million regular customers. These checks, for amounts up to £20, and vouchers, for more expensive purchases, are used instead of cash for immediate purchase of goods at some 60 000 shops throughout the United Kingdom. The checks and vouchers are 100% guaranteed and redeemable by the shopkeeper at an agreed discount with the Provident Company which employs 16 000 agents operating from 600 branches to make weekly calls at the houses of its customers, mostly on Fridays and Saturdays, to collect the cash repayments on the checks and vouchers. Although the Provident Company makes use of Giro to make payments to Inland Revenue for taxation and certain other similar purposes, its main use is in conjunction with the cash collecting operations of the Company's 16 000 agents, combining its own form of Agent Deposits service with a Rapid Money Transfer system. Like ABF, after carrying out a pilot scheme in Northern Ireland starting in October 1969, and in Scotland from March 1970, the Company put its scheme into general application from June 1970 onwards. The Company's 16 000 agents make an average of between one and two inpay-- ments per week, totalling some 25 000 inpayments to Giro. More than 90% of the Company's total inpayments are channelled through Giro. The money thus deposited within Giro is transferred on a daily basis by use of the Rapid Money Transfer System through pre-determined amounts being transferred on pre-arranged days of the week to specific joint-stock bank branches. Round amounts of £100 000 are 'walked' from Giro's Cheapside office to the City offices of the various banks from where the balances are telegraphically transmitted to the Company's main bank accounts in Bradford and Leeds. The annual turnover of the Provident Group with Giro through Agent Deposits was, during 1972, running at £110 million. According to Mr C J E James, the Group Chief Accountant, the main determining factors which resulted in their adopting the scheme were as follows:

1   The opening of Post Offices on late Friday afternoon and on Saturdays.

2   The location of Post Offices, particularly on housing estates as opposed to banks with their concentration in the commercial sector of towns.

3   The more rapid transmission of funds than has been enjoyed by joint-stock banks.

4   The absence of the problems previously associated with Night Safe Wallets.

5   However, the Company felt that there was a disadvantage which has, in fact, occurred in that the Post Office Giro has less control over individual Post Offices than does the joint-stock bank with its branches and this leads to problems when disputes over amounts of inpayments arise.

This latter problem of Giro having less control over its Post Office counter work than in the case of the joint-stock banks is a matter which is of much more general application than is indicated by the particular remarks of the above Company. It is a matter of considerable concern to Giro itself and although the problem appears much easier to diagnose than to cure, the future growth of Giro depends to some extent on a sharp tightening up of this loose end.

4   *ICI pension scheme*

Having chosen a typical small family concern to begin our illustration of the Agent Deposits system, the country's largest manufacturing company, Imperial Chemical Industries, will be taken as our example in describing one of the more sophisticated Giro facilities for the payment of pensions in which pre-authenticated Girocheques are combined with a computerised reconciliation system based on 'Machine Readable Output' (or MRO for short), enabling large-scale disbursements to be made with an economy of manpower, which nevertheless enabled a tight financial control to be maintained by the Company. Roughly similar systems are in use by Unilever, by the Civil Service, by local authorities, by trade unions and other public authorities with regard to pay-through-Giro and salary-through-Giro schemes, although as has already been stressed, each scheme has variations based on its own special requirements. In many of these other schemes the pay or salary is

154

credited directly into a personal Giro account and withdrawn from a Post Office as and when required by the recipient. In ICI's case the recipient of the pension is sent every fortnight a cheque covering two weeks' pension which is then normally withdrawn in total at any Post Office in the country depending on the pensioner's choice. At the end of 1972 ICI had 25 000 pensioners on its books as registered members of its Workers' Pension Fund: these represent the former weekly paid employees, the salaried staff normally having their pensions paid through credits to their joint-stock bank account, just like the current arrangements for salaried staff. (As is common knowledge ICI used its vast bargaining power with the banks to gain favourable charges—the famous ICI terms.) Of these 25 000 non-staff pensioners around 19 500 are paid through Giro; some 2000 are paid through bank cheques and 3500 through bank credit transfers. In ICI's original agreement with Giro each of the nearly 20 000 Giro cheques had, after printing, to be sent to Giro Headquarters at Bootle for authentication by means of a red embossment on the face of the cheque.

After a while this laborious and time-consuming system (originally felt to be necessary for security purposes) was changed in favour of ICI being permitted to print (on continuous stationery) its own pre-authenticated Girocheques embodying a coded number system which offered an alternative form of security. The fortnightly prints of these 20 000 Girocheques are sent in good time to Giro at Bootle who envelope, address and dispatch the cheques to the individual recipients, who then cash them at any Post Office of their choice. Normally the pensioners cash the Girocheques very shortly after their arrival through the post, acknowledging the receipt of cash by signing the back of the Girocheque. The encashed Girocheques are then sent by the recipient Post Office to National Giro Centre at Bootle where ICI's account is debited and daily and weekly reconciliation accounts on taped Machine Readable Output are sent to ICI followed by the actual paid Girocheques. The encashments can then be compared with the original Girocheque print-out, so, that, in this way, any overdue or unpaid Girocheques or other such discrepancies are quickly brought to light and the Girocheque printings and encashments fully reconciled. By this method ICI dispatches some £200 000 each fortnight; its total pension payments for the year ending 31 March 1972 amounted to £5 506 000. [16] The worker's average pension actually paid was £5·62 per week and the average Girocheque

(£11·24) being very much smaller than the average full service pension of £10·89 per week because many members retire after a relatively short pensionable service. Nevertheless, from such individually modest items Giro has built up an aggregate business of considerable stature.

During the course of my interview with the Secretariat of the ICI's Pension Fund four further aspects of its relationship with Giro would appear worthy of comment. First, they considered that on balance the cost of the scheme was fully justified by the convenience it gave to the pensioner. Second, ICI were pleased that, for an agreed fee, Giro were able to take over the task of enveloping and dispatching the Giro-cheques, a task which they considered as being additional to the services normally expected of Giro. Third, they mentioned that their MRO reconciliation system had recently been examined by another very big organisation which wished to benefit from its experience. Finally, they were pleasantly impressed by the co-operation they had received from Giro and (the interview took place in mid-December) gave a particular instance of such co-operation in that Giro staff had worked through the previous weekend (normally a holiday for Giro staff) in order to facilitate the dispatch of pensions earlier than usual so that their pensioners would be certain to receive their Girocheques in good time for Christmas. Large organisations—whether public like Giro, or private like ICI—are not necessarily inflexible, soulless and unfeeling!

5   Emptying the gas and electricity meters

Many of the above examples have been concerned at varying levels of size and refinement with either cash disbursement or cash collection. One further aspect of the latter must suffice to complete our illustration of customers' usages of Giro's facilities. Among the reasons given by the Provident Clothing Company for using Giro was, as we have seen, the interesting one concerning the wide spread of Post Offices right among the housing estates of the working class, as contrasted with the more concentrated distribution of bank branches in or near the central zones of our towns and cities. It was a consideration of such factors which was responsible for the North Eastern Gas Board and the North Western Electricity Board deciding to go over to Giro for their versions of the Agent Deposits system. These two illustrations show how the problem of handling the bulky and heavy cash collection from gas and electricity meters in the densely populated housing estates of our conurbations may be greatly facilitated by taking advantage of the ubiquitous Post Offices for depositing the cash which is then simply credited via National Giro Centre at Bootle to the account of the Board concerned, thus relieving them of considerable inconvenience, cost and the otherwise growing anxiety on security grounds.

As the country's largest employers the local authorities, like the public corporations, make use of a variety of Giro services including, as we have seen, specially tailored rent-collection schemes (some using the Agent Deposits system), and pay and salary-through-Giro schemes. The extent to which local authorities made use of Giro is indicated by the fact that in November 1972 the number of local authority Giro accounts came to the considerable total of 2175, including 142 Agent Deposits accounts and some fifty using some form of Giro-rent scheme, though the intensity of usage of such accounts varied widely from authority to authority. The above case studies, including the examples of admittedly rather minor but essential services such as milk delivery or emptying the gas and electricity meters, have been chosen to illustrate the range and flexibility of Giro's services, chiefly as seen from the actual customer's point of view.

The supreme importance to Giro of the custom of central government departments is more appropriately considered in the remaining chapters since the degree to which they use Giro depends very largely, though not quite entirely, on major policy matters such as the reorganisation of the method of paying unemployment benefit, the introduction of new methods of taxation like the Value Added Tax, and so on. There is however one aspect relevant to this chapter on customer reactions which was forcibly brought home during my interview with the financial officers of the Department of Health and Social Security, the government department which currently makes far more use of the Post Office in general and Giro in particular than any other department: the Social Security side of DHSS issued 55 million Girocheques in the financial year 1971–72. It so happened that the officer in charge of Girocheque payments had himself, only a year or so before the interview and before his department changed to Giro, been attacked and robbed by an armed gang when taking cash from DHSS in central London to the nearby joint-stock bank. This information was not volunteered: it epitomises the disciplined self-effacement and capacity for understatement of the English civil servant that this pertinent and dramatic

157

incident only came to the surface in a reply by his colleague, who was present with him when I questioned them, to my normal probing at such interviews concerning the security aspect. The security benefits of Giro in reducing the movement of cash have run like a refrain throughout the evidence provided by the above case studies and is perhaps fittingly capped by the personal experience of our typically anonymous and modest civil servant.

SOCIAL PROFILE OF GIRO'S INDIVIDUAL CUSTOMERS

It is now time to round off our individual case studies with a more generalised portrayal of the typical Giro customer based on studies of the private and business sector carried out by various investigators in recent years. The Department of Marketing at the University of Lancaster prepared for Giro during 1971 a two-volume *Study of Attitudes and Account Usage* [17] from which, though not published in full, Giro has released some of the more important findings. With regard to the individual (as opposed to the business) account-holders, their social characteristics are indicated in Table 6.2. Contrary therefore to what

SOCIO-ECONOMIC GROUP	PERCENTAGE OF TOTAL
AB	20·7
C1	32·5
C2	30·3
DE	16·4

Table 6.2   Social profile of Giro's individual account holders 1971

appeared to be the general impression, Giro never has been predominantly a 'poor man's bank', for the statistics show that, even when Giro was still carrying out its original strategy, more than half its private customers (53·2%) were drawn from the higher income groups. Consequently, it should be no surprise to discover that more than two-fifths (41·6%) of Giro account holders have bank accounts. [18] 'This is', say the authors of the Lancaster survey 'a higher proportion than the population as a whole (about 30%). Those respondents who have a bank account are of a much higher social class than the remainder: 76% of those with a bank account are in the ABC category.' [19] Confirmatory evidence as to the typical over-representation of the middle and higher social groups in financial institutions, whether ostensibly 'working class' or not, is given in the evidence submitted by the London Clearing Bankers to the official Committee, under the Chairmanship of Sir Harry Page, to Review National Savings, in which the clearing banks quote from the results of the Continuous Investment Survey carried out for them by National Opinion Polls Market Research Limited. With regard to the clearing banks, the Trustee Savings Banks and the National Savings Bank the investigations showed that 'the lowest socio-economic groups (D and E) are under-represented at all three institutions: the middle socio-economic groups (C1 and C2) are over-represented at all three institutions, but most so at Trustee Savings Banks and the National Savings Bank: and the highest socio-economic groups (AB) are over-represented at Banks and slightly so at the National Savings Bank.' [20] Giro's own market surveys have also confirmed the Lancaster University study's findings with regard to the domestic pattern of the typical account holder. Of Giro's customers some 79·1% are married householders, 73·1% are between the ages of twenty-one and fifty when by far the bulk of spending on the home is made, and 68·5% have children below sixteen, the minimum school-leaving age as from 1 April 1973.

SOME GENERAL CHARACTERISTICS OF GIRO'S BUSINESS CUSTOMERS

The Banker of October 1970 contains an analysis made by the writer of Giro's customers as published in their Business Directory (plus the relatively small number of the ex-directory firms whose names are quoted at the beginning of the directory), when compared with the *Times 500 Largest Companies* and the *Financial Times Top Twenty for Profitability*. A comparison of these three sources would seem to afford strong confirmation for subjective impressions that the larger and more profitable firms, such as the case studies described above, make considerably more use of Giro's facilities than do the generality of firms. Thus, with regard to the *Times 500* index, eight of the first ten, thirty of the first fifty, forty-seven of the first 100 and 147 of the first 500 have Giro accounts; while seven of the twenty most profitable firms are

Giro customers. [21] The 1970–71 edition of the *Times* dealt with a larger group of the 'Thousand' biggest companies. The statistics again seem to indicate that the larger and more successful a company is the more likely is it to have an account with National Giro. Thus seven of the leading ten and fifty-nine of the top 100 have Giro accounts, as also do forty-eight out of the top fifty Building Societies, twenty-one of the top Life Insurance Companies, seventeen of the top twenty-one Finance Houses and eight of the top ten Unit Trusts. [22] In contrast, only some 30 000 of the country's 500 000 limited companies (98% of which are private and most quite small) are as yet customers of Giro, i.e. not more than about 6%. Obviously the potential harvest is great.

REFERENCES

1   KEBLE, JOHN, *The Christian Year, Morning* (London, 1827).

2   MILL, J S, *The Principles of Political Economy*, Vol. II, Book III, Ch. VII, p. 9.

3   WICKSTEED, P H, *The Common Sense of Political Economy* (1946) Vol. I, p. 119.

4   If greater care had been taken to present Giro more in the form of the current account complement to the century-old Post Office Savings Bank with its 22 million customers, the barriers of habit might more easily have been broken. However, the proper relationship between these two institutions is a matter of major policy which is better deferred for the discussion in Chapter 7 below.

5   In pursuance of Section 87 of the National Parks and Access to the Country-side Act, 1949, the National Parks Commission designated some 73 square miles of the Gower as an 'area of outstanding natural beauty' in 1956.

6   JONES, C L, 'Collection of Local Revenue through the Giro'; A Paper presented to the Financial Officers' Association, November 1970, p. 1.

7   JONES, C L, *ibid.*, p. 2.

8   JONES, C L, *ibid.*, p. 4.

9   *Hansard* (17 November 1971), col. 425.

10   As a general rule, in the case of all individuals, firms, local and central government officials interviewed by the author, subsequent correspondence was used as a means of eliciting further information or clearing up points of doubt or difficulty. In this instance Mr R P sent me a letter in early December 1972 volunteering the additional information that the two main complaints that he had made against Giro were being met satisfactorily since the receipt of his 'Giro Gold Card' allowed him free cash withdrawal of up to £30 every two days at any Post Office in the country.

11   The increased loan facilities made available to Giro customers by the Mercantile Credit Company, part of the new strategy announced by Giro in November 1972, should go some way in meeting the complaints voiced by Mr and Mrs H B, without however quite overcoming the problem of marginal end-of-the-month 'unintentional' overdrawing the main Giro current account. Every bank manager quickly becomes aware of the warning signs shown by

any regular pattern of ostensibly 'unintentional' end-of-the-month 'kiting' where these are more than marginal or are tending to increase. The high speed of Giro reduces the opportunities for such 'kiting'.

12 It is again obvious from the bridging loan facilities made available by Astley Acceptances for 'pay-through-Giro' customers as part of Giro's 'new strategy' that the particular complaint made by Mr F I was widely reflected.
13 *Associated British Foods, Annual Reports and Accounts* (1969–72).
14 *Financial Times* (23 December 1972), p. 24.
15 MASKENS, V A, Chief Accountant, J H Dewhurst Ltd, letter received 21 December 1972.
16 Imperial Chemicals Workers Pension Fund, *Report of the Trustees and Statement of Accounts* (London, September 1972), p. 10.
17 MOULTON, J, NEWMAN, J and SUD, R K, 'Giro Account Holders: Study of Attitudes and Account Usages'. Unpublished. Department of Marketing, University of Lancaster (April 1971).
18 *Ibid.*, p. 154.
19 *Ibid.*, p. 154.
20 *Submission by the Committee of London Clearing Bankers to the Committee to Review National Savings* (London, October 1972), para. 25.
21 DAVIES, GLYN, 'Giro's Two Year Hard Slog', *The Banker* (London, October 1970), p. 1074.
22 *Op. cit., Financial Times* (London, 1972).

Chapter 7

Regionalism, the Review and the New Strategy

'The essential need of the country is to gear its policies to the majority of the people who are not lame ducks . . . the majority live and thrive in a bracing climate and not in a sodden morass of subsidised incompetence.' [1]

In all the long series of discussions preceding the first campaign for Giro in the early 1960s it had been taken for granted that there would be a single centre of operations and there was no question but that this would be located at the financial centre of the country within the City of London. For more than a century, particularly since the coming of the railways, there had been a natural tendency for almost all nation-wide businesses to locate their chief administrative and above all their financial head offices in London. In the 1930s anxiety regarding the 'derelict' and the more euphemistically termed 'special' areas coincided with increasing concern with defence requirements to push opinion around towards the desirability of controlling and where possible reversing the powerful centripetal pull of London. 'The concentration in one area of such a large proportion of the national population as is contained in Greater London and the attraction to the Metropolis of the best industrial, financial, commercial and general ability represent a serious drain on the rest of the country', concluded the epochal Barlow Report of 1940. [2]

The Post Office has been among the earliest of the country's major enterprises to take account of the need for decentralisation as part of the reaction against over-concentration in London and the South East. The Bridgeman Committee on Post Office Reform had in 1932 briefly considered the *technical* reasons for some decentralisation of postal

162

activities, and as a result the first major regionalisation of Post Office administration took place in 1936. As the 1930s wore on the national security aspects, particularly that of ensuring an adequate pattern of communications, supplied strong additional reasons for greater dispersal of other economic activities away from the vulnerable London region, a lesson which was hammered home by the events of the war years.

The resurgence of regionalism in economic affairs in the post-war period was however a more complex movement than appears in many present-day accounts of the phenomenon. It is therefore fundamentally important in understanding the reasons why Giro's operations became geographically separated and why National Giro Centre came to Bootle —which were after all political decisions based largely on economic assessments—to disentangle the main threads of regional economic thought during the decade of the 1960s. Despite the considerable industrial diversification which had been achieved in the problem areas of the north and west, absolute industrial growth remained much more pronounced in the London, Midlands and South Eastern regions, so that the economic and financial advantages of having a head office in London and of concentrating financial operations there had never seemed more attractive. At the same time the achievement of full employment appeared by the beginning of the 1960s to have reduced the regional problem merely to a relatively minor matter of mopping up small pockets of unemployment in various scattered parts of the country, a philosophy that took concrete form in the Local Employment Act of 1960 with its emphasis on Development 'Districts' rather than 'Areas'.

The thinking behind this so-called 'new attack on *localised* unemployment' in the early 1960s, just when the final campaign for Giro was being launched, was thus bound to call into question the policy of the mass movement of jobs away from their 'natural' location. [3] After all a national Giro would create between 3000 and 4000 jobs (as we have seen the earlier estimates supposed the higher figure to be something of a minimum) and this in a financial institution which could not, by the very nature of its operations, move its investment and money-management activities out of London.

The first few years of the 1960s saw a vigorous (if mistaken) onslaught by a number of social scientists, geographers, economists and political writers, on the previous generally accepted policy of moving the work to the workers, coupled with attempts to demonstrate the supposedly greater benefits of assisted emigration from the remaining pockets of unemployment in the north and west into the over-full employment areas of the south and east. 'Must we always take work to the Workers?' the title of an article, typical of this school of thought, by H W Richardson and E G West, was being given the negative answer implied by the question by a growing and influential section of public opinion. [4] The joint authors were however rather late in climbing onto this particular bandwagon for by the mid-1960s the stubborn facts, underlined by the experience gained in the operation of the 1960 Act, were already demonstrating the complete inability of such policies to conquer the regional problem. Indeed opinion began to swing back more firmly than ever towards improving rather than dismantling the traditional approach. In a well balanced summary of the economic evidence and opinions of the period Lionel Needleman came to the saner conclusion that 'in Britain attempts to deal with the regional problem by encouraging workers to move where the work is may actually increase rather than diminish interregional differences in prosperity . . . and the alternative policy of bringing work to the workers is basically more sound'. [5]

REGIONAL TUG OF WAR FOR GIRO CENTRE

If a change of government from Conservative to Labour had been, as shown in the previous chapter, a necessary condition for translating the concept of Giro into concrete form, so too the contemporary reaffirmation of the belief that regional problems were after all of major importance requiring solutions on a regional scale rather than being relatively minor, localised affairs, was an essential part of the explanation for the dispersal of Giro's 3500 jobs for its computer centre well away from the London region. Given then that by 1965 there was fairly general support for the official argument that the main employment and income generating effects of establishing Giro meant seeking a site somewhere in the development areas, the question was reduced to considering which of the rival locations should be chosen so as to maximise the net regional benefits. Anyone who has ever been involved in the mechanics of interregional and interdepartmental bargaining with regard to the location of 'plum' factories, firms or institutions will readily attest to the furious nature of the infighting which takes place between the participants, supported by voluminous economic, statistical, and in recent years especially, detailed cost-benefit analyses. [6] The final decision where such large-scale factors are at stake, particularly where the social, economic and politically important matter of thousands of jobs is involved, is inevitably taken at Ministerial or even Cabinet level where the special requirements of the case are not only fitted against what the actual rival sites have to offer, but also the need to keep a fair balance between the competing regions. To its credit the Post Office has been a vigorous as well as an early decentraliser: it set up its Premium Bond Office on the Lancashire coast at Lytham St Anne's in 1956; its National Accounting Centre at Chesterfield in 1963; its Savings Certificate Division at Durham in the period 1963–67 and began the transfer of the Post Office's Research Department to Martlesham in Suffolk in 1968.

The really major regional tug of war however took place with regard to Giro and the Post Office Savings Bank, directly involving a total of around 10 000 jobs. This was probably considered too big a plum for any single region, so there followed a Wilsonian judgement-of-Solomon (similar to that of Macmillan's some years earlier when he divided the new steel strip mills between Llanwern in Wales and Ravenscraig in Scotland). Although the Post Office deserves considerable credit for its sensitivity to regionalism, the actual manner in which it planned for the dispersal of its dual banking functions as between savings account and current account banking involved an unnatural and inhibiting divorce of services that might better have been treated as inseparable. In view of the experience of postal banks on the continent where the tendency, given increased emphasis in recent years, has been to run their Giro and savings business in the closest co-operation, one wonders, with all the goodwill in the world for regional devolution, whether the former Post Office Savings Bank and National Giro Centre should have been so far separated as between Glasgow and Bootle. As we have already seen this geographical separation appears to symbolise an age-old and persistent tendency on the part of the Savings Bank not to be caught up too closely in the hustle and bustle of current account banking as demonstrated in its evidence to the Radcliffe Committee and in its change of name and administration since 1969 into the National Savings Bank under the National Savings Department.

165

The global efficiency of a *Post Office Bank* acting as an individual administration might well have been raised by a massive, combined decentralisation. This would have made possible an easier control over a combined and more specialised 'banking counter', dealing with both current accounts and savings, at most of its 24 000 Post Offices and would have facilitated the development of more effective policies to compete with the other banks, almost all of which, including the Trustee Savings Banks, have increasingly come to realise the crucial importance of combining what the Post Office and the National Savings Bank have insisted on keeping apart. The regional centrifugal forces which sensibly split Giro in two need not also have led to quite such a wide and drastic separation of postal banking.

This is not to decry the undoubted success from the regional point of view of either the Bootle or the Glasgow decentralisation. Mr William Gray, the Lord Provost of Glasgow, paid the tribute to the beneficial results of decentralisation during the course of an official visit in November 1972 to the Cowglen site of National Savings Bank: 'I am tremendously heartened by my visit to the Post Office Savings Bank. Since its establishment here in 1965 it has been a real success story. Today 3750 people are employed, and by 1976 the number will be around 6500.' Mr Gray then went on to use this example as a springboard for his demand, in view of the worsening unemployment situation, for the transfer of a further '20 000 civil service jobs from London to Glasgow'. Thus the 10 000 postal banking jobs that appeared too massive to be offered to or absorbed by any one region in 1965 turned out just a few years later to be a much more easily digestible meal for any of a number of regions which meanwhile had become hungrier for jobs.

Yet at the time when Giro's location was being decided, Scotland, having already been allocated the Savings Bank, could in equity expect little support in any claim for Giro. Wales similarly seemed to have been ruled out for it had been selected as the beneficiary of the move of the Royal Mint from London, where it had been since its establishment by William the Conqueror, to an attractive and highly suitable location at Llantrisant, just a few miles outside the constituency of Mr James Callaghan, who was Chancellor of the Exchequer at the time. Here again a fairly substantial number of jobs were involved, reaching 520 at the end of December 1972, and likely to rise on completion of the second phase of building in the mid-1970s to around 850. The Government's decision to move the Royal Mint out of its traditional site in the capital pre-dated a world trend towards such decentralisation, as was made clear by a number of speeches on the occasion of the Seventh Mint Director's Conference in April 1972 which appropriately included a visit to Llantrisant. (The Royal Mint, always on the look-out to coin a new phase, struck a special medal in honour of the occasion.)

In much the same way Giro's choice of Bootle has been flatteringly reflected in the Midland Bank's selection of the same town as the site of one of its two computer complexes, while in late 1972 Barclays announced a major transfer of head office departments from London to a site at Knutsford, Cheshire, roughly in the same general area, at which site a total of 4400 staff will eventually be employed. Mr W G Bryan, Deputy Chairman of Barclays, stated that the first and foremost reason for the move was the high and rapidly rising level of costs in the South East: 'In the City the (rental) cost to us is more than £1000 a year per head of staff. The equivalent figure in the Knutsford area is no more than £150 a year'. [7] The Post Office was thus something of a leader in office decentralisation and the generally favourable reaction of its management and employees has been paralleled by that of the Royal Mint [8] and further confirmed by the evidence drawn from twenty detailed case studies published by the Location of Offices Bureau. [9] Thus the other major contenders for Giro having been eliminated, the Government's choice of Bootle in the Development Area of Merseyside, a few miles outside the Huyton constituency of the Prime Minister of the time, Mr Harold Wilson, appeared fully justified not only by considerations of equity in regional policy, but also by the special operational advantages it could offer.

BOOTLE AS CENTRE OF OPERATIONS

Giro did however have an overriding locational requirement not demanded to anything like the same degree by the other decentralised postal departments, namely the need for really rapid communications which could cover the whole nation. It needed therefore to be centrally situated, not necessarily in relation to the country's geographical area but rather with particular reference to the country's major business centres. If the London and Midlands areas were ruled out by the Government's regional policies then Bootle was a thoroughly logical choice, situated as it is within the Merseyside conurbation and centrally located

167

as regards the other six conurbations. These seven conurbations with only 3% of the land area contain one-third of the country's population and have 8000 persons to the square mile compared with 400 for the rest of the country. [10] They generate a large part of the private and the major part in value terms of the business handled by Giro. The actual site chosen for National Giro Centre is about 30 miles from the centre of the South East Lancashire conurbation, 50 miles from the centre of the West Yorkshire conurbation, 80 miles from Birmingham in the heart of the West Midlands, 125 miles from Tyneside centre at Newcastle and roughly mid-way between London and Glasgow, 200 and 220 miles distant, respectively, and within easy reach of Crewe the country's second largest railway hub.

In order to give the nationwide rapid 24-hour service originally planned Giro had to be able not only to reach these conurbations, but also other large centres outside the conurbations and still more distant towns like Plymouth, Southampton and Londonderry. National Giro Centre thus lies at the rough centre of a web of more than 24 000 Post Offices conducting Giro business. The Post Office has if anything been rather coy in its claims concerning both the vast number of offices handling Giro business and the peculiarly advantageous distribution of these offices. The actual distribution of the country's 24 000 offices between the main or Crown offices and the subsidiary Post Offices as at October 1972 for England, Wales, Scotland and Ireland is given in Table 7.1. These Crown and sub-offices supply a national coverage of immense value even in a country famous for its branch bank network, for it combines not only strategically sited facilities for the commercial centres of our towns, but also a distinctive penetration into our suburbs and villages giving a degree of locational convenience far exceeding that of the competing banks. This factor of locational convenience—the handiness of having a Post Office just around the corner—came through in all our customer case studies in Chapter 6 and is amply borne out by a number of wider ranging studies of why a customer chooses a particular financial institution to carry out his business. A considerable amount of banking research both in this country and in America confirms that in choosing a branch at which to conduct bank business 'the dominant reason by far has been convenience, by which is always meant convenience of location. Well below convenience in importance has been the intangibles which are independent of location: friendliness of

COUNTRY	CROWN OFFICES	SUB-POST OFFICES	TOTAL POST OFFICES	AREA IN SQ. MILES	AVERAGE AREA PER OFFICE (SQ MILES)	POPULATION 1971 CENSUS (MILLIONS)	AVERAGE POPULATION PER OFFICE
England	1 272	17 249	18 521	50 333	2·7	45·9	2 478
Scotland	216	2 340	2 556	29 798	11·7	5·2	2 034
Wales	133	2 359	2 492	8 017	3·2	2·7	1 083
Northern Ireland	30	725	755	5 206	6·9	1·5	1 986
United Kingdom	1 651	22 673	24 324	93 354	3·8	55·3	2 273

Table 7.1 Post Offices conducting Giro business: national distribution and density 1972

officers and tellers, recommendations of friends, habit, etc. At a still lower point (luckily for many Post Offices in contrast to the more palatial banks) the factor of appearance enters.' [11] The spatial and population density of Post Offices conducting Giro business, as given in the Table 7.1, indicate how well supplied National Giro is in this respect, for no other financial institution in the country, no single bank, nor indeed all the banks combined, can present such a convenient coverage of potential customers. (All the more reason why the Post Office should aim to show itself not merely as a stamp-seller, but as a financial institution, as a bank, combining all its banking functions in a single mutually reinforcing organisation.)

From this network of offices a stream of Giro business converges daily by rail to Liverpool's Lime Street Station, whence it is taken to the Giro sorting office within the Computer Centre at Bootle some 5 miles away. Mail from Northern Ireland is flown from Belfast Airport. Incoming mail is of three main kinds. First, there is the stream of pouches containing documentation of the day's transactions over the counter at Post Offices throughout the United Kingdom, containing paid Girocheques, inpayments, agents' deposits and cash deposits to personal accounts, etc. Pouches may contain anything between one and twenty items, the actual tested as well as the notional average being ten items. These are handled by the Postmaster's Transactions Branch, shown as PTB in Table 7.2. Second, there are the Giro envelopes received direct from account holders containing cheque deposits, transfers, requests for new stationery and so forth, plus documentation sent direct by other banks. These are shown in the table as OSB (Opening and Scrutiny Branch). Thirdly, there are the miscellaneous items such as those addressed to other divisions, for example, new account applications, requests and correspondence relating to accounts and so on. The value of each item can of course vary enormously, but to the computer 'in for a penny in for a pound' or even a million pounds is literally true, so that the input of items gives a rough indication of the volume of work generated by different towns. The Post Office Authorities kindly provided the writer with a detailed 24-hour count of inward items from some twenty-four centres including the conurbations and more distant towns. The results, with the distances from the dispatching centre to Bootle, are given in Table 7.2. The returns from eight large and busy centres around London are combined in the London total, which is

170

TOWN	DISTANCE FROM BOOTLE	POUCHES PTB*	ENVELOPES AND PACKAGES		TOTAL OF POUCHES ENVELOPES AND PACKAGES
			OSB*	MISCELLANEOUS	
Belfast	175 miles	151	62	14	227
Birmingham	94 miles	276	171	201	648
Bristol	183 miles	193	138	18	349
Cardiff	180 miles	134	61	23	218
Carlisle	123 miles	48	26	5	79
Coventry	113 miles	86	35	5	126
Edinburgh	221 miles	177	55	45	277
Glasgow	225 miles	234	56	7	297
Hull	131 miles	107	28	4	139
Leeds	80 miles	221	102	22	345
Londonderry	255 miles	6	4	—	10
Manchester	37 miles	240	155	34	429
Newcastle-on-Tyne	173 miles	176	58	13	247
Plymouth	310 miles	133	50	6	189
Southampton	284 miles	111	59	8	178
Swansea	226 miles	121	24	1	146
Total excluding London	—	2 414	1 084	406	3 904
London	199 miles	811	1 257	647	2 715

Table 7.2 Daily inward flow of mail to National Giro Centre from selected regions: August/September 1972

* The terms PTB, OSB and miscellaneous are as described in the text

171

equal to 70% of that for all the other sixteen selected centres. The figures for London relate to 21 September: for the remainder of the towns the figures relate to 8/9 August 1972, the dates concerned being chosen to reflect typical daily work-loads.

As the world's first fully computerised Giro, the Bootle Centre has naturally attracted widespread attention, particularly from Giros abroad which are in the process of following suit and have been able to avail themselves of National Giro Centre as a model, including for example Norway, which runs what is in some respects the world's most profitable Giro and which has been pleased to take advantage of the unrivalled technical advice given by the staff at Bootle. Within Britain too various groups from among its business and private customers, such as the secretaries of the Giro Users Groups—spontaneous regional organisations of individual Giro customers keen to support this new British banking venture—have visited Bootle to see for themselves how the heart of the system operates. [12] The technical operations inside National Giro Centre would of course require a technical volume to do justice to them. To the non-technical layman it is nevertheless a rewarding, if rather mystifying experience to follow the course of receipt, verification, encoding, transfer between accounts and other of the various forms for processing the documents, followed by the amazingly fast photo-recording and taping of the results, before finally watching the speedy dispatch of the documentation for its outward journey by routes the reverse of those described above.

The physical mass of paper handled should at least remind us that in our present state of technology, electronics has hitherto only supplemented and not yet supplanted our need for millions of pieces of paper, the daily bread of finance. How soon direct electronic payment transfer systems without paper will arrive is a question more appropriately raised in the final chapter. Here it is relevant to note the enormous simplification that would result for vast computer complexes like those of National Giro Centre and of the clearing banks which are still, electronically speaking, in the stage equivalent to those early nineteenth century ships which were elaborately and pessimistically over-equipped with full sails and steam engines. The original plan for dealing with a million items a day and the subsequent experience of the staff enabled National Giro Centre to cope with this enormous daily work load with room to spare for further expansion except at certain troublesome peak periods: for it was soon found that the initial requirement of providing customers with a 24-hour statement service aggravated the peak problem. This remained a matter of considerable concern until a thorough re-organisation accompanying the *Review* allowed a substantial smoothing out of the daily work flow.

LONG REVIEW: GIRO'S 500 LOST DAYS

The first four and a half years of National Giro's operations may be divided into three roughly equal stages, the first being the formative eighteen months during which, for reasons that have already been examined (in Chapter 5), it became abundantly clear to all that its actual growth was not only falling, far behind the original euphoric anticipations, but also failing to meet the much more moderate 1965 White Paper target. The second stage began with the General Election of 18 June 1970 and lasted a full seventeen months during which the new Conservative Government was making up its mind whether or not National Giro was to continue in being and if so what changes would be required in its organisation. Dismay seemed to have given way to despair until at long last the official announcement of the Government's renewed faith in a re-organised Giro was made public on 17 November 1972. The final stage covers the gradual unfolding of the new strategy by a streamlined Giro committed to ensuring viability by July 1977.

Table 7.3 and Figures 7.1 and 7.2 present the main statistics covering the whole period with regard to the growth in the number of accounts and in the value of total and average balances. The vertical lines in the figures represent the General Election and the Reprieve and so indicate the main divisions between the three stages. Since the first stage with a fairly detailed examination of the reasons for the dismally disappointing shortfall in the growth of accounts has already been considered earlier, we begin with the second stage, namely the circumstances surrounding the *Review*. Although a number of prominent Conservatives like Sir Brandon Rhys-Williams and Mrs Hilary Sewell have been among the most adventurous supporters of Giro and although as late as December 1968 Mr Paul Bryan, then the Opposition spokesman for Post Office affairs, confirmed the Conservative Party's official position as one of support for Giro, the Tory Party had long harboured some of its strongest opponents. The latter could hardly be expected to miss the

QUARTER ENDING		BALANCES			TOTAL NUMBER OF ACCOUNTS (PRIVATE AND BUSINESS)			AVERAGE BALANCE PER ACCOUNT £
		TOTAL £M	NET INCREASE/DECREASE OVER PREVIOUS QUARTER		'000s	NET INCREASE OVER PREVIOUS QUARTER		
			ACTUAL	PERCENTAGE		ACTUAL	PERCENTAGE	
1968	December	10	—	—	44	—	—	227·3
1969	March	16	6	60·0	63	19	43·2	254·0
	June	19	3	18·8	75	12	19·0	253·3
	September	24	5	26·3	91	16	21·3	263·7
	December	36	12	50·0	118	27	29·7	305·1
1970	March	38	2	5·6	154	36	30·5	246·8
	June	49	11	28·9	229	75	48·7	214·0
	September	49	0	0	305	76	33·2	160·0
	December	58	9	18·4	377	72	23·6	153·8
1971	March	58	0	0	393	16	4·2	147·3
	June	65	7	12·0	426	33	8·4	152·6
	September	59	−6	−9·2	450	24	5·6	132·4
	December	75	16	27·1	459	11	2·5	163·4
1972	March	69	−6	−8·7	460	1	0·2	149·7
	June	79	10	14·5	465	6	1·1	169·9
	September	70	−9	−12·9	465	0	0·0	149·0
	December	100	+30	42·9	467	2	0·4	214·1

Table 7.3 National Giro: growth in balances and in the number of accounts quarterly 1968–72

Note: For reasons stated in the text care should be taken in interpreting net quarter-to-quarter changes in the number of accounts, especially in 1972 when a considerable number of unused accounts were deleted

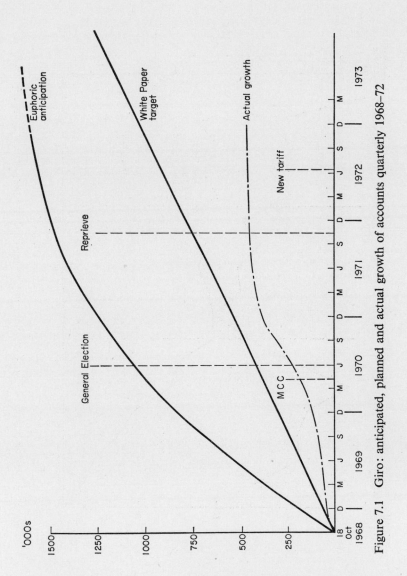

Figure 7.1 Giro: anticipated, planned and actual growth of accounts quarterly 1968–72

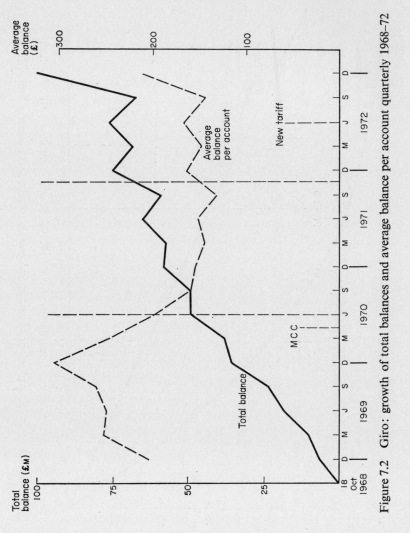

Figure 7.2   Giro: growth of total balances and average balance per account quarterly 1968–72

opportunity presented by the disappointing progress made by Giro in its first year to demand an end to what one of their number, Sir Gerald Nabarro—the Parliamentary member for what had once been Rowland Hill's constituency of Kidderminster—has deprecatingly called 'this Socialist excrescence'. [13] Before Giro had been operating for quite twelve months, Mr J R Sorton, on behalf of the Borough of Poole Conservative Association, put forward the following resolution to his Party's national conference held at Brighton early in October 1969: 'The Conference deploring the substantial losses already made by the National Giro urge the next Conservative Government to close down the Giro, thus freeing the Bootle computer complex for more productive purposes and assisting the Party in its declared aim to reduce the size of the Civil Service.' [14] The motion was not selected for debate so that we have no means of knowing the numerical strength of support for such opinion. Nevertheless, there could have been little doubt in anyone's mind when the Tory Party was returned at the General Election of 18 June 1970 that thereby the future of Giro was cast into a state of considerable suspense.

This middle stage of uncertainty lasted for no less than 517 days. In retrospect one still wonders whether it was really necessary for this officially-induced despondency to drag on for quite so long, particularly when it is obvious that of all institutions, banks are notoriously the most vulnerable to expressions of any loss of confidence from any quarter, let alone from official sources. Even the question as to whether Giro itself was actually under review yet again remained a matter of considerable doubt for some time. Admittedly Mr Chataway, Minister for Posts and Telecommunications, made a statement on 2 November 1970 saying that the postal services in general were being reviewed and that 'the review will look at the social, economic and technological trends which are likely to affect the labour-intensive postal services over the years ahead and try to establish what the choices are likely to be in terms of cost and standards of service'. [15] The fact that Giro itself was being investigated as part of this general review would probably have remained in doubt for much longer despite repeated requests by the Opposition had it not been for the storm which arose over the dismissal of Lord Hall from his position as the first Chairman of the Post Office Corporation. A motion of censure on this controversial matter led to a heated debate in the House on 30 November 1970, during which Mr Ivor Richard, the Member for Barons Court, asked the Government 'for an assurance that the Giro will continue and will be encouraged to expand'. [16] In the course of a long reply Mr Chataway expressed sorrow that the future of Giro had been brought into the dispute and claimed that there was no disagreement between Lord Hall and himself on that matter. Then came the first explicit disclosure that Giro was in fact being investigated: 'There is a review under way of the Giro activities. I have not previously said anything in public about Giro because I was anxious that nothing should be said which would undermine confidence in it. . . . This is a matter which must be under review, but I recognise that it is important to reach a decision as soon as possible. Over recent weeks, I have been having from the Post Office the information, the proposals, the forecasts upon which ultimately we will be able to come to a decision. But what we have to decide is whether and when this service can break even.' [17]

It is a remarkable tribute to the general public's underlying faith in the financial probity of public sector financial institutions that instead of such a doleful announcement leading to a massive closure of accounts and a complete withdrawal of funds, National Giro was able to enrol a remarkably large total of over 200 000 new customers during this period. A glance at the graph will show the curve of accounts rising more steeply between April and the end of December 1970 than at any other time. It is interesting to speculate therefore whether National Giro might not have attained its target rate of growth, as shown by the straight line on the graph of 60 000 accounts per quarter, by the middle of 1971 had the results of the General Election been different. For the last three quarters of 1970 the growth of new accounts exceeded the White Paper target rate by no less than 43 000. This was a sustained boom, not a flash in the pan. No doubt part of the credit for this surprising rate of growth was due to National Giro's agreement with the Mercantile Credit Company, which was announced on St George's Day and put into effect on May Day 1970 (shown as MCC in the Figures), supported by an intensive nationwide advertising campaign using the Sunday Press. Although this scheme was launched just before the *Review*, logically it forms the first part of the new strategy which was being developed in outline within Giro until the dark days of the *Review* not only held up any further really effective planning since such plans could only be transformed into concrete measures if and when a reprieve were granted, but also, after the time-lag shown, unforgivably halted Giro's new progress in its tracks.

The growth of personal accounts during the first part of the *Review* period should not however blind us to its more immediately deleterious effects on *business* confidence, for it is clear from the graph of the average balance of accounts that the growth in the number of accounts during the review period was almost entirely in the small and relatively less lucrative private accounts. The average credit balance per account fell from £214 at the end of June 1970 to its lowest ever point of £132 by the end of September 1971, that is precisely during the period when the total number of accounts grew by 221 000, and this at a time when Giro desperately needed to capture a higher proportion of large lucrative business and institutional accounts. To add to Giro's difficulties the Post Office strike which lasted from 20 January to 8 March 1971 took place right in the middle of this stage. The public's confidence was struck yet a further blow when it became known that the Post Office had commissioned Cooper Brothers, an internationally known firm of accountants, to carry out its own independent assessment of Giro's prospects, for this meant still further delay in coming to a decision.

REPRIEVE—BELATED BUT DECISIVE

According to the *Financial Times*, in general a staunch but not blindly uncritical supporter of Giro, the decision on a reprieve when at long last it was given 'seems to have been a very close-run thing', and, since the Cooper Brothers report has not been published, what evidence there was available to the public at the time pointed in that direction. [18] Giro's cumulative losses had by then amounted to over £19·7 million, and there was clearly no hope of reaching the White Paper target by 1973, even if in fairness to Giro the Government's Review had itself been partly to blame by compounding with uncertainty the mistakes which Giro's political and executive management had made during its first two years. Nor had Giro the veriest hope of achieving the wildly optimistic target of '200 000 corporate accounts by October 1973' which its staunch but less critical supporters in the Public Enterprise Group—an independent, non-political watchdog organisation on the nationalised industries and public corporations—had still been claiming as possible even on the eve of the Reprieve. [19]

After waiting for 517 days it was therefore with very considerable relief that Giro's supporters from all sections of the House and from all parts of the country greeted the announcement made by Mr Chataway, Minister of Posts and Telecommunications, in the House of Commons on 17 November 1971 in the following terms: 'The Post Office Board with the assistance of Cooper Brothers advised against closure. There should be substantial reshaping of the service, improved financial control, changes in marketing policy and in due course a revised tariff structure. On this basis it believes that Giro can be made to pay and can offer a competitive service to the public. In the light of this and the consultants' views, the Government have accepted the Board's conclusion that Giro should continue.' [20] The Minister's statement did not then make it clear within how long a period Giro was expected to achieve viability, but eventually on 22 March 1972 he clarified the objectives more precisely in a statement to Parliament. On the same date the Post Office Users' National Council 'was asked to consider a revised tariff structure for the Giro service aimed at covering direct operating costs within one year and making the service fully profitable within five years'. [21] The new tariffs were not introduced until 1 July 1972; the target date for covering operating costs was 1 July 1973; and full viability, by which was meant the covering of all variable costs and all associated overheads, was to be achieved by 1 July 1977.

Nowhere was the relief that greeted this unambiguously positive statement of confidence in Giro's long-term viability more pronounced than in Bootle itself where the news that over 3000 jobs had been saved was all the more welcome since its current rate of unemployment was 6·7%, while Merseyside as a whole was suffering from 51 000 unemployed. The wider regional and the narrower financial aspects of the cost-benefit equation were closely intertwined, for a sound regional economy cannot be built on the basis of unsound institutions. Thus in retrospect there was obviously some advantage for Giro in having had its 'ordeal by accountant', not only for the valuable specific items of advice it gave on many practical points, but also because of the broader inference that might legitimately be drawn, namely that Cooper Brothers would hardly have recommended the continuance of Giro merely as an expensive way of absorbing labour. It was vital to Giro's case for a reprieve that both the Conservative Government and the independent consultants believed firmly that Giro could be made into a profitable and commercially competitive business.

NEW STRATEGY

The third stage in Giro's eventful life began with the Reprieve—a re-birth which necessitated a new approach to its operations, to its costing and to its marketing, based on its own experience, the Post Office Board's review and the consultants' report. Three aspects of this new strategy involving structural changes, a new tariff and a more selective marketing policy, will be examined in turn. First, a number of structural reforms were carried out during 1972, the main aim of which was to reduce total costs and improve the work-flow. Giro stationery and Post Office procedures were greatly simplified. Office staff re-organisation enabled a more streamlined and productive labour force of 3000 to do work which previously absorbed 3500. Whereas Giro had formerly employed 150 representatives in local head postmasters' offices it changed to a system of requiring only one-third that number by using its own representatives at regional headquarters. Perhaps the most important single reform on the cost side came in connection with a change from a standard 'same-day' or 24-hour statement service to one of a 'next-day' or 48-hour service.

Up to November 1972 the country was divided into six Giro sectors numbered inversely according to the postal dispatch times required to achieve delivery of statements by first post on the day following receipt and ledgering at Bootle. Customers' envelopes were imprinted with their Sector number. In order for all parts of the country to enjoy this rapid 24-hour service it was obviously a case of last in, first out. Scotland was numbered One, the South West and East Anglia Two, The South East Three, Wales and the Midlands Four and London, with its express rail connections, Five. The near-by North and Northern Ireland (which latter as we have noted enjoyed an air-mail service) were numbered Six. The old system required updating the incoming ledger six times per day in conjunction with the six regions resulting in a series of relatively short batches for this sectoral mail with its accompanying peaks and troughs, instead of the much more economical, smoother, longer run of ledgering and computer processing which has been the case since the new system came into operation on 1 November 1972. The new system also has slightly lengthened the stay of credit balances within Giro and although this aspect is very welcome, it was the cost-reducing benefits of the scheme rather than its revenue-increasing potential that was the prime reason for the change.

Rationale of the revised tariff

A further unfortunate result of Giro's long period in limbo was its enforced continuance of a scale of charges for its services which had been based on prices and income levels obtaining in the early 1960s and which therefore completely failed to reflect the subsequent increase in the rate of inflation. A table of Giro's original charges and the revised tariff that came into operation on 1 July 1972 is given in full in Appendix B. Giro's original charges were on balance already too low when it commenced operations in October 1968, since they had been fixed as early as 1965 when the White Paper was published. There could hardly have been any other business in the country that was charging the same prices in 1972 as in 1965. In the four years before Giro began operations, from 1965 to 1968 inclusive, the average monthly index of retail prices rose from 112·1 to 125·0 or by 11·5%. In the four years 1969 to 1972 inclusive the index rose from 131·8 to 164·3 or by 24·7%. [22] The date of Giro's establishment coincided rather unfortunately with the watershed that divided unanticipated or creeping inflation from that of strongly anticipated or trotting inflation and Giro's rather inflexible price-fixing mechanism is not geared to dealing with such rapid inflation.

Thus Giro, having saddled itself with a scale of charges barely appropriate at best to a mild type of creeping inflation was forced to operate with such fixed charges in a quite different environment of trotting inflation, so adding substantial but unexpected losses on top of those which had been expected, if underestimated, in its early years. The clearing banks' criticism that Giro's low charges constituted unfair competition was therefore justified more by subsequent inflation than by any deliberate intention by Giro's managers. When bank charges are hidden, vague, uncertain or even in part at the manager's discretion, they can obviously be much more flexibly adjusted in line with changing needs than where they are definite, clear, published and uniformly fixed nationwide: and this distinction becomes of heightened importance when the pace of inflation quickens. The ending of the 'cartel' in 1971 has further increased the flexibility of individual bank charges, whereas it still remains largely true of Giro that any charges are a matter to be decided by civil-service type committees internally, are obviously subjected to close government scrutiny, and in addition as a statutory obligation they have to stand up beforehand and subsequently to the critical examination of the Post Office Users' National Council, and as a moral obligation to similar examination by the Councils for Scotland, Wales and Northern Ireland. All four Councils, inflation or no inflation, have a vested interest in keeping the charges as low as possible. Thus what in the case of the banks may still be done rather privately, quickly, flexibly and discriminatingly, can, in the case of Giro normally be done only after slow deliberation, uniformly and in the full glare of publicity, so that anything other than minor adjustments are inevitably postponed until they appear as part of a packet of changes that look larger than they really are. With regard to medium and large business accounts Giro like the banks of course always exercised a degree of flexibility in its charges, often tailoring its services to the particular requirements of the firm concerned.

The first revised schedule of Giro charges in seven years thus reflected two different but related aspects; first, policy decisions taken as a result of the general pressures of inflation, which caused the general level of charges to be raised substantially; and secondly, as a particular consequence of the Review itself, which indicated the need for a change in relative prices involving the introduction of charges for certain services which were previously free. The new charges were therefore formulated so as to dovetail with Giro's new marketing strategy. Despite all the changes however the basic Giro services of deposit, transfer and standing orders between account holders remained free to most users—a cherished and fundamental Giro principle which has been only slightly dented by the overriding need for selective marketing.

Selective marketing

The outside expertise which was brought in to help form the new marketing strategy confirmed the more selective approach to which the logic of events pointed. The tariff of standard charges as originally proposed illustrates this selectivity in that it penalised the customer whose account fell below £30 by imposing a penalty charge for every debit thereafter. This penalty was not to apply to one section, those who received their pay through Giro. It is obvious simply from a glance at the table of revised charges that Giro management was even more keen to attract these favoured customers than it was to remove the troublesome and loss-making low-balance accounts. This same privileged group was able to enjoy free stationery and reduced charges and other

183

facilities not shown in the table of tariffs, such as 'bridging loans' to cover the gap between the sale of one house and the purchase of another and favourable rates on the improved 'loans-through-Giro' scheme which had been arranged in conjunction with the Mercantile Credit Company and which had proved so successful when first introduced in May 1970. The original scheme allowed Giro account holders eligible to the Company to borrow up to twenty-four times their agreed monthly repayment: the revised scheme increased the revolving credit limit up to thirty-six times the monthly repayment, with 'pay-through-Giro' customers enjoying a rate of interest currently $1\frac{1}{3}\%$ per month compared with the standard rate of $1\frac{1}{2}\%$. Similarly the current rates of interest on Mercantile Credit fixed term loans for Giro account holders, e.g. $9\frac{1}{2}\%$ for 12 months, was reduced by 1% for the favoured 'pay through-Giro' account holders who are obviously a better risk. The bridging loan facility available through Astley Acceptances, a subsidiary of Mercantile Credit Company, removed a hindrance which held a number of potential Giro customers too tightly to their commercial banks.

These links between the private and public sector thus enabled the constraints which previously tied Giro exclusively to current account banking to be overcome in a path-breaking fashion and although in the more competitive environment existing since mid-1971 Giro would be unlikely to experience the same quick surge in the growth of accounts that occurred after the original scheme was announced, the resultant steadier growth should be much more prolonged and might well be widened by forming links with other merchant banks, building societies, insurance companies and so on. It is also of interest to note that Giro's first joint venture with the private sector was perforce with what was then one of the 'secondary' or peripheral banks but that from January 1971 Mercantile Credit Company, along with a small number of other leading financial houses, was granted full banking status. [23]

The Agent Deposits system, pioneered by National Giro and developed in Britain to a much greater extent than has been the case with any other Giro including Europe's largest, was obviously a feature selected for emphasis in the new marketing strategy and, as we have seen, around 200 organisations already make use of it. Similarly, various Rent Collection schemes have been aggressively marketed by a team of experts from Giro who visited local authorities covering every region in the United Kingdom in the period following the Reprieve.

The Giro Gold Card which allows its holder to withdraw up to £30 every other working day from any Post Office in the country was selectively distributed, particularly to 'pay-through-Giro' customers in the latter part of 1972, and if Giro's experience justifies it, the card will be made much more generally available later. The Gold Card is a cash withdrawal card and not a cheque guarantee card or credit card. Giro's cautious approach in this contrasts with the blanket coverage of its newest and largest plastic competitor, 'Access', which was sent by its sponsoring joint-stock banks to some 3½ million customers ready for its launching on the 23 October 1972. Finally, mention might be made of the 'relaunch' issue of *Giroscope* as an integral part of the new marketing strategy. The general theme of this quarterly Giro magazine is home management, and with an issue of 400 000, Giro claims it to have the largest British circulation of any magazine of this type. The new custom with its more lucrative balances and its increased charges have helped considerably in boosting Giro's revenue, which, however depends not only on total balances and on charges, but also to a very large extent on the managerial skill with which its day-to-day investments are controlled. Consequently it is now necessary to look at the main aspects of the working of Giro's money desk.

MONEY MANAGEMENT AT CHEAPSIDE

The Post Office Act 1969 (Part III, section 40) states that 'The Post Office shall be deemed for all purposes to be a bank and a banker and to be carrying on the business of banking and a banking undertaking'. The intention was absolutely clear: the institution was to be given the full status of a bank, and it is crucial to any reasonable assessment of the role of Giro to realise that it was set up specifically as a bank, with the power to become something appreciably more than the money transmission service to which some of its critics would narrowly confine it. On the other hand the legal provisions which thus clearly defined its banking status in the widest terms also, in contrast, laid down certain imperative constraints, mainly to do with its investment policy, within which the bank has to work. Thus the same Act ruled that so long as the Post Office provides a banking service it shall be its duty to secure that its liabilities to its customers are matched only by such assets as are specified in considerable detail in Schedule 2 of the Act. Briefly this stipulated that such assets were to be comprised of two groups: first, liquid assets consisting of cash, current accounts at other banks, money at call or repayable within fourteen days placed with the Discount Market or local authorities, and Treasury bills; and second, a less liquid group made up of local authority securities and loans up to five years and short-dated government securities. These constraints appear at first sight to be debilitatingly narrow, but a useful escape clause was, sensibly, attached to the very tail of this section of the Act which allows investments in 'assets of such other classes as may from time to time be designated . . . by the Post Office with the approval of the Treasury'. Table 7.4 gives the composition of these assets quarterly in 1971 and 1972.

Compared with the joint-stock banks, Giro's powers over its assets are seen to be considerably circumscribed. Nevertheless, it is in a very privileged position when compared with other public sector institutions, for example the National Savings Bank, the ordinary department of which still has no option but to invest all its holdings in government securities. Furthermore, Giro instead of passively handing over its funds to the National Debt Commissioners, manages its own investments from its London office, that most unbanklike building wedged into Cheyne House at Cheapside within walking distance of the Bank of England and the head offices of the country's main financial institutions. It is thus actively involved in the day-to-day management of a growing balance of funds which after fluctuating between £49 million and £79 million for the two years following June 1970 rose sharply—almost triumphantly—to a peak of £110 million on 21 December 1972 and registered the highly significant figure of £100 million at the close of the year. Giro's money desk already operates twenty telephone lines to the City's main money market institutions; eighteen of these lines were put in by the Discount Houses or Local Authority brokers themselves, and, as an indication not only of Giro's own confidence in its future, but also of the more telling confidence of the City brokers in Giro, it was about to fit up another ten lines in 1973 to give it even wider coverage and a sharper competitive edge.

A glance at Table 7.4 shows the highly liquid composition of Giro's assets, averaging over 40% during the two year period though these end of month figures somewhat exaggerate the degree of liquidity since they are normally higher than during the rest of the month. The Treasury

186

	31 MARCH 1971		30 JUNE 1971		30 SEPT. 1971		31 DEC. 1971		31 MARCH 1972		30 JUNE 1972		30 SEPT. 1972		31 DEC. 1972	
	£ 000's	%	£ 000's	%	£ 000's	%	£ 000's	%	£ 000's	%	£ 000's	%	£ 000's	%	£ 000's	%
Liquid Assets:																
(a) Cash	4 078	6	770	1	1 625	3	1 003	1	317	1	2 669	3	2 554	4	3 509	4
(b) Call and short notice	18 400	32	24 325	37	17 730	30	29 425	39	22 555	33	34 940	44	18 940	27	40 780	41
(c) Treasury and local authority bills	1 150	2	413	1	—	—	1 904	3	2 968	4	1 978	3	983	1	1 494	1
	23 628	40	25 508	39	19 355	33	32 332	43	25 840	38	39 587	50	22 477	32	45 783	46
Investments:																
(d) Local authority loans	18 480	32	18 530	29	16 530	28	13 830	18	14 080	20	14 680	19	21 920	32	26 365	26
(e) Other (mainly local authority stock and bonds)	8 187	15	8 420	13	7 926	13	6 083	8	6 058	9	4 282	5	5 681	8	7 615	8
(f) Government securities	7 580	13	12 246	19	15 754	26	23 070	31	22 864	33	20 398	26	19 217	28	20 463	20
	34 247	60	39 196	61	40 210	67	42 983	57	43 002	62	39 360	50	46 818	68	54 443	54
Total	57 875	100	64 704	100	59 565	100	75 315	100	68 842	100	78 947	100	69 295	100	100 226	100

Table 7.4   National Giro: growth and distribution of assets quarterly 1971 and 1972

laid down Giro's minimum liquid assets percentage as thirty-five initially, but reduced this to 28% in July 1969 and to 20% in November 1972, at which time the Treasury also permitted Giro to hold up to 20% of its total securities in the medium-dated category, that is with a mean maturity of not more than ten years. The reason for Giro's high level of liquidity is therefore clearly not because of Treasury strictness, but rather is based on Giro's own commercial judgement which reflects both the unprecedentedly high rates of interest available during this period on fairly liquid funds and also the fact that there are considerable seasonal and day-to-day variations in the total balances available to Giro. Furthermore, it must be remembered that, different from practically every other bank in the country, *all* deposits in Giro are immediately withdrawable on demand (though as we have seen there is a limit to the cash which can be withdrawn over the Post Office counters).

Table 7.5 shows the source of these balances as they grew during 1971 and 1972, distinguished as between the two main categories of public and private sector balances. With regard to these two main divisions, public sector deposits now represent just over half of the total, whereas at an earlier period the percentage was much higher. The sub-divisions show clearly that the Government itself has not been wildly extravagant in making deposits in Giro and there has been no discernible growth in such deposits throughout the period shown. The deposits by local authorities are seen to be very volatile and only the deposits of the public corporations among this sector have shown any considerable growth. With regard to the private sector, deposits by the financial institutions are low and stable, but company deposits trebled between the beginning and end of the period shown, largely as a result of the strong growth in Agent Deposits. Deposits by individuals and partnerships have also shown a welcome and steady increase in trend.

Among the questions that arise from examining these statistics are the extent to which the Government itself makes use of Giro, a subject which will be discussed in the final chapter, and also whether Giro might not attract a larger proportion of business accounts for longer periods in view of the fact that the individual values of such accounts are much more weighty than those of private accounts. Two avenues which might profitably repay exploration are the possibility of Giro's entry into the interbank market, and even more important, whether Giro might deal in and issue its own negotiable certificates of deposit—

SOURCE OF DEPOSIT	31 MARCH 1971 £M	30 JUNE 1971 £M	30 SEPT. 1971 £M	31 DEC. 1971 £M	31 MARCH 1972 £M	30 JUNE 1972 £M	30 SEPT. 1972 £M	31 DEC. 1972 £M
Public sector:								
(a) Government	16	10	12	14	15	12	10	15
(b) Local authorities	2	12	2	10	2	13	3	17
(c) Public corporations	14	16	17	17	18	19	19	21
	32	38	31	41	35	44	32	53
Private sector:								
(d) Financial institutions	3	2	2	2	2	2	3	3
(e) Companies	4	5	5	6	5	6	7	12
(f) Individuals and partnerships	18	20	21	26	26	27	28	32
	25	27	28	34	33	35	38	47
Total	57	65	59	75	68	79	70	100

Table 7.5 National Giro: growth and distribution of deposits quarterly 1971 and 1972

Source: Bank of England Quarterly Bulletin, Vol. 13, No. 1 (March 1973), p. 86. The rounded totals for March 1971 and March 1972 are slightly different from the fuller figures published by National Giro

as is already being done successfully by some of the former secondary banks, for example the Co-operative Bank. Giro CDs might be of two kinds, the first type (Giro National CDs) similar to those in the existing market with a minimum limit of £50 000. These could well be supplemented by tapping what seems to be an existing gap by issuing a smaller series of CDs (Giro Regional CDs) with a minimum of £10 000 with intervals of £10 000 to £50 000. The marketing of these might be aimed particularly but not exclusively at the smaller and medium firms most of which do not have head offices in London.

Some direct method of attracting such large sums from business and institutions and retaining those already attracted through Agent Deposits and so on, would appear to be advantageous to Giro, if only the necessary permission were to be forthcoming. Closely related to this question is the degree to which Giro should continue to be officially restrained in its marketing and investment policies in an era when its competing private sector institutions have been given a free rein. Although this might at first sight appear to be merely an academic question at least until Giro becomes fully profitable, yet it might well affect the speed with which such viability is attained. It is a subject to which we must return in the final chapter, where the statistical omens for Giro's immediate and long-term future will be investigated. Perhaps a look at the longer, more varied and prosperous experience of Giro abroad will help us in interpreting these omens. [24]

REFERENCES

1   DAVIES, JOHN, Minister for Industry, *Hansard* (4 November 1970).
2   *Report of the Royal Commission on the Distribution of the Industrial Population*, Cmd. 6153 (London, January 1940), para. 171.
3   See, for example, the article by Professor A. T Peacock and Mr D G M Dosser, 'The New Attack on Localised Unemployment', *Lloyds Bank Review* (London, January 1960), pp. 17–28.
4   RICHARDSON, H W, and WEST, E G, 'Must we always take work to the Workers?', *Lloyds Bank Review* (London, January 1964).
5   NEEDLEMAN, L, 'What are we to do about the Regional Problem?', *Lloyds Bank Review* (London, January 1965), p. 58.
6   A brief indication of some of the relevant theoretical issues is given in my 'Regional Economic Civil War', *University of Strathclyde Regional Studies Bulletin*, No. 4 (Glasgow 1966), an abstract view fully borne out by subsequent practical experience as the first Economic Adviser to the Secretary of State for Wales in the period 1968–70.

7 'Barclays Bank Offices for Cheshire', *Financial Times* (London, 5 October 1972).

8 Mr R A Yates, Superintendent of the Royal Mint, Llantrisant, reports that 'The Mint has been welcomed in Wales with enthusiasm' and comments further that 'Attendance, in an area that often receives adverse publicity about absenteeism has been very good', *100th Annual Report of the Royal Mint* (H.M.S.O.: London, 1970), pp. 46–7.

9 *Case Studies of Decentralised Firms* (Location of Offices Bureau: London, 1972).

10 BUCHANAN, COLIN AND PARTNERS, *The Conurbations* (London, 1969), p. 11.

11 WEART, S, 'The Right Size Branch', in *Banking* (June 1961), quoted in Eilon, S, and Fowkes, T R, 'The Role of Convenience in the Bank Branch Selection Process', Chapter 14 of *Applications of Management Science in Banking and Finance* (London, 1972), p. 215.

12 'Group Secretaries Visit Giro Centre', *Giroscope* (London, Winter 1972), p. 26.

13 *Hansard* (21 July 1971), col. 1435.

14 SORTON, J R, Conference Agenda Motion No. 1240, Conservative Party National Conference, Brighton (October 1969).

15 *Hansard* (2 November 1970), Oral Answer No. 25.

16 *Hansard* (30 November 1970), col. 982.

17 *Ibid.*, cols. 992–3.

18 MCLACHLAN, S, 'Reprieved Giro Faces Reshaping', *Financial Times* (London, 18 November 1971).

19 'Watchdog Group's Plea for Giro', *Financial Times* (London, 16 November 1971).

20 *Hansard* (17 November 1971), col. 425.

21 *Post Office Users' National Council, Annual Report* 1971–72 (H.M.S.O.: London, 1971), para. 27; see also *Hansard* (22 March 1972), cols 1478–80.

22 *Monthly Digest of Statistics* (February 1973), Table 171. For a more detailed survey of this problem of the impact of inflation upon Giro's pricing policy see Davies, G, 'Giro Unchained and Recharged', *The Banker* (May 1972), pp. 657–62. The index for February 1973 was 172·4.

23 The other financial houses granted full banking status in January 1971 were United Dominion Trust, First National Finance, Lombard North Central and the Hodge Group.

24 The publication of the Hardman Report confirms the view given earlier in this chapter that Scotland was not really in the running so far as the location of National Giro Centre was concerned: 'Glasgow has done well out of dispersal so far (having received the largest dispersal of the previous exercise, the National Savings Bank, which will total some 7000 posts).' *The Dispersal of Government Work from London*, Cmnd. 5322 (H.M.S.O.: London, June 1973), para. 31.

Chapter 8

Giro Abroad: Growth, Density and Profitability

'Imitation is the sincerest form of flattery.' [1]

IMITATIVE PATTERN

Modern Giro was created in Austria in 1883 as an avowed improvement upon the British Post Office Savings Bank system which had already been in existence for some twenty-two years and had become increasingly admired abroad as a model to be adapted to each country's particular administrative requirements. Austria's distinctive achievement remained unnoticed for rather a long time, but after twenty-three years its example led to a second wave of Giro formation on the Austrian model. Far-away Japan in its typically adaptive mood and Switzerland, Austria's next-door-neighbour, both set up their Giros in the same year, 1906, followed by Germany in 1908, Luxembourg in 1911 and Belgium in 1913. The start of the third wave which was to bring in all the major continental countries may be dated from the Municipal Giro which the City of Amsterdam established with considerable enthusiasm and foresight in 1917. This paved the way for the Netherlands as a whole to establish its postal Giro in 1918. This latter year also saw France and Italy put into practical operation their own long-prepared postal Giros which, but for the First World War, would almost certainly have been established some three or four years earlier. The examples of Denmark in 1920 and Sweden in 1925 completed this third wave of Giro formation.

By the mid-1920s therefore most of the richer countries of continental Europe as well as Japan were already operating their own postal Giros, while campaigns in favour of such a system were being pressed hard not only in Britain but also in a number of other countries. There was however a long delay before further international progress was made: the Doldrums of the 1920s and 1930s involved not only Britain, but were international in extent. Eventually the fourth wave brought in the remaining Scandinavian countries of Finland (1940), and Norway (1942), movements which occurred, rather surprisingly, during the course of the Second World War. In the decade after the end of the war, a fifth wave led to Giros being established, or re-established in indigenous form, in the emergent, newly independent countries which had previously been directly or indirectly in touch with such a system, for example, the former French, Belgian and Dutch colonies. It also included the interesting example of Israel which set up *ab initio* its own small Giro system in 1953. The belated conversion of the United Kingdom to National Giro in 1968 inevitably prompts the question as to whether or not this will start a sixth wave in countries now without Giro, particularly those in the English-speaking world which appear to have a built-in resistance to such a system. This matter is however better postponed until we have examined some of the salient features of the development of Giro in a number of different countries, underlining the lessons which appear to be most relevant to common problems of cost, density and profitability; the relationships between the Giro, the banks and other financial institutions; and the vitally important matter as to the degree of use made of Giro by other government departments.

Thus, while it is clear that deliberate imitation has played a powerful part in causing countries to adopt Giro, imitation alone is patently not enough to explain its widespread growth and persistence in diverse environments. Granted that Giro is an eminently exportable institution, only its intrinsic merits including an inherent versatility could account for its widespread adoption by countries with such widely differing basic economies and such contrasting financial superstructures as Holland and Italy, Sweden and France, Germany and Denmark, Belgium and Japan, Norway and Switzerland, Israel and Madagascar, and so on. Was Britain, and is the rest of the English-speaking world, so unique in arranging its finances that what has served so well for others is of little or no use to themselves? No country that has taken up a Giro system and has tried and tested it has abandoned it.

On the contrary in every case despite the inevitable opposition of

193

vested interests, the system has become part of the financial establishment and in most countries has shown a vigorous growth that appears far from coming to an end. Unlike the hostility towards National Giro, the very existence of which institution was untimely called into question by officialdom for nearly a year and a half, the public's long familiarity with Giro on the Continent has bred a general air of contentment without however engendering any noticeable degree of complacency. Constructive criticism is continually leading to modifications and improvements in institutions which have a public duty not only to complement but also to compete with the other financial institutions whether in the public or in the private sector. Obviously, in the space of a single chapter only a few glimpses can be given to illustrate the rich diversity in the application of the common financial principle that is Giro. After giving brief country-by-country descriptions of the salient features of postal Giro in Austria, the Netherlands (including the highly successful Municipal Giro of Amsterdam), and the four Scandinavian countries, we shall follow this with a more general functional and analytical comparison of major Giro systems covering size, growth, density and profitability. The choice of these particular countries is based chiefly on the fact that the history of their development and current practices has much to offer by way of example as to how National Giro itself might develop. The huge Giro systems of France and Germany have been rejected for separate treatment partly because their size and role differ significantly from that likely to be achieved by National Giro, but principally because any really adequate description would require far more space than could be allocated in a work concerned mainly with the British Giro system. [2]

AUSTRIA LEADS THE WAY

The political decline of the Austro-Hungarian Empire coincided with an astonishing efflorescence of intellectual achievement in the arts, in music, in the sciences, particularly the newer sciences like psychology, and in administrative innovation. Edward Crankshaw, an authority on the history of the Habsburg Empire, in a recent re-assessment of its achievements considers that 'the Monarchy has not been kindly treated by historians . . . by dismissing the last phases of this extraordinary institution as being unworthy of serious contemplation we dismiss at the

	FOUNDED	POPULATION		GIRO ACCOUNTS		DENSITY	
		NUMBER IN '000s	RANK	NUMBER IN '000s	RANK	NUMBER OF ACCOUNTS PER 1000 INHABITANTS	RANK
Netherlands	1918	13 175	6	2 764	3	209·7	1
France	1918	50 950	5	7 156	1	140·5	2
Luxembourg	1911	340	14	41	14	120·3	3
Belgium	1913	9 695	7	1 026	4	105·8	4
Sweden	1925	8 070	8	628	6	77·8	5
Switzerland	1906	6 220	10	436	9	69·1	6
Western Germany	1908	61 750	2	3 369	2	54·6	7
Denmark	1920	4 935	11	200	10	40·5	8
Norway	1942	3 895	13	141	11	36·1	9
Finland	1940	4 710	12	121	13	25·7	10
Austria	1883	7 400	9	135	12	18·4	11
Italy	1918	53 900	4	518	7	9·6	12
Japan	1906	98 920	1	875	5	8·8	13
United Kingdom	1968	55 711	3	467	8	8·3	14
City of Amsterdam*	1917	1 041	—	267	—	256·4	—

Table 8.1 Size and density of postal Giro in Europe and Japan 1971–72 [3]

* A Municipal Giro and hence not ranked with the other postal Giros

same time a considerable sector of our own past which still bears heavily on the present'. [4] Crankshaw firmly believes that most previous writing on this subject underestimates the positive achievements of the Austro-Hungarian Empire (among which surely the invention of postal Giro should figure prominently). According to A J P Taylor 'The Austrian Empire was a vast collection of Irelands' which could be ruled only by the deployment of an army of skilled and devoted civil servants. [5] 'The bureaucrats still had a great state to administer', for example, 'Bohemia had in Prague an administrative machine larger than the British civil service which in London conducted the affairs of the United Kingdom and of the British Empire.' [6]

Typical of such hard-working and far-sighted civil servants was Georg Coch, founder of the world's first postal Giro, whose name is suitably commemorated in Georg Coch Platz in Vienna, where now stands the headquarters of the Austrian Post Office. As is the case in most Giros, the Austrians created and still run theirs as part and parcel of their postal savings bank. It is indicative of the warm personal support for the new ideas presented to him by his bureaucracy that the first depositor in the new Austrian postal bank was the Emperor himself, and those who are only too prone to think of Giro simply as the poor man's bank should reflect on the standing of the world's first Giro customer. Even the *London Times* reported the event in the following brief lines: 'Post Office Savings Banks on the English model have been opened in all parts of Austria. The number of deposits accepted in Vienna and the provincial towns is reported to be remarkable. The first depositor in the chief office in Vienna was the Emperor'. [7]

In my inquiries into the profitability of continental Giros, the Austrian authorities pointed out to me that already by its second year 1884–85 the combined Austrian Savings Bank and Giro had moved into a profitable situation to assist the general finances of that hard pressed state. It is perhaps understandable in view of the fact that it is far older than any other Giro that Austria's appears to be one of the very few to show some signs of saturation of its market in so far as the *number* of accounts is concerned. Its highest post-war total was reached in 1946 with an end of the year figure of 188 168 accounts. In the difficult post-war period the number of accounts fell rather drastically to 115 403 by the end of 1948. By 1954 the total had slowly picked up again to 131 774 and since that time the figure has remained between 130 000 and 140 000, being 135 229 at the end of 1971. A glance at Table 8.1 giving the size and density of postal Giros shows that the oldest are not necessarily the largest proportionately to population. Austria ranks only as eleventh in this league, most of her major imitators having out-stripped her in this regard, a not unusual phenomenon.

This relative stagnation in the number of accounts fails however to do justice to the persistently rising trend of the business being financed, for example, the number of inpayments which was less than 20 million in 1946 rose to over 100 million in 1960 and reached its highest point in 1971 with over 120 million inpayments. This increased business was made possible by the change-over from manual operations to automa-tion during the 1960s; a rather long process which began in 1960 and was not completed until 1972. [8] This pattern of slow growth in the number of accounts and reasonably fast growth in the business financed by them is paralleled in the savings section of the bank. The number of savings accounts rose from 603 600 in 1962 to 879 500 in 1971, an in-crease of 46% compared with the total value of savings which more than doubled rising from 2·77 to 6·17 thousand million Shillings in the same decade. Within the Giro or 'postal cheque' system as it is com-monly known in Austria (and a number of other continental countries) one of the fastest growing sectors was that concerned with external payments, which also doubled during the same decade. The Austrian Savings Bank Annual Reports for 1970 and 1971 recognise the increased importance of marketing, given the more competitive current financial situation and give evidence of a determination[6] to widen the functions of the PSK beyond its original conception . . . so that the world's first Giro, created by Georg Coch, might again provide the classic example of integrated marketing'. [9] Luckily for the world, Austria did not merely imitate the British Post Office Savings Bank, but being forced into innovation by dire necessity, grafted upon it a versatile current account and credit transfer system that has stood the test of time for nearly a century and has expanded over much of the western world, including eventually even the recrossing of the Channel to Britain.

GIRO IN THE NETHERLANDS

(a) *Amsterdam's Municipal Giro*

In many respects the operation of both the Dutch postal Giro and

197

Amsterdam's Municipal Giro afford striking examples of how such credit transfer systems should ideally be run. According to the American periodical *International Management* the newly automated Dutch postal Giro system is 'unmatched in the world'. [10] The European continent has always allowed a larger role for municipal banks than has Britain, where Birmingham's Municipal Bank, founded in 1916, a year before Amsterdam's Municipal Giro, stands out as the sole major exception to a persistent official refusal in the United Kingdom to recognise the complementary part that such banks can play within a national banking system. Even on the Continent, however, the spectacle of a municipal Giro is so unusual that the initiative of the Amsterdam authorities in this regard deserves at least a brief mention. By 1969 it had secured 250 000 account holders and by May 1971 the number had grown to 267 000, which out of a population for the urban area of Amsterdam of 1 040 000 gives it a coverage of one person in every four—by far the highest Giro density in the world. Despite this spectacular success the municipal authorities have no intention of resting on their laurels. The declared policy of the Amsterdam Giro, according to its Report for 1969, is 'To reach all citizens and not just a section of them'. [11] To help it to expand its custom still further it asked the Netherlands Institute of Public Opinion to carry out a market survey on its behalf in November 1969. This showed that 66% of all heads of families questioned held an account with the Amsterdam Giro and that 81% of account holding respondents stated that they enjoyed 'Excellent or very good service'. [12] Communication between the municipal clearing institute and its 267 000 account holders is carried out by its own delivery service. Payment orders are collected on a daily basis from some 500 blue letter boxes, marked 'Gemeente-Giro', located on public roads and spread out over the entire city. Daily statements are delivered to the homes of the account holders, and a network of fifteen offices and over 100 agencies are at the disposal of the account holder for immediate cash transactions (withdrawals and deposits). In addition to the normal current accounts, the municipal Giro also offers facilities for savings accounts. Both current and savings accounts bear interest, the latter obviously at higher rates, though the current account interest is limited to personal account holders and is not available for firms. As well as its main credit transfer service the Amsterdam Giro also provides personal loans, foreign currency, travellers cheques, transfers of funds abroad and a

	WEST GERMANY	NETHERLANDS	NORWAY	FRANCE	BELGIUM	UNITED KINGDOM	SWITZERLAND	FINLAND	SWEDEN
Profit/loss:									
1968	£4·851m	£1·829m	£1·266m	−£10·3m	−£14·7m	−£6·0m	£2·0m	£1·0m	£5·0m
1969	£4·282m	£2·394m	£1·733m						
1970	£6·481m	£2·946m	£2·334m						
Population* (millions)	58·315	12·875	3·850	50·280	9·645	55·711	6·220	4·710	7·940
Annual average* profit/loss per head of population	£0·09	£0·19	£0·46	−£0·20	−£1·52	−£0·11	£0·32	£0·21	£0·63
Number of Giro* account holders ('000s)	2469	1802	101	6877	1014	146	387	120	574
Profit/loss per* account holder	£1·73	£1·33	£17·16	−£1·50	−£14·50	−£41·10	£5·17	£8·35	£8·71

Table 8.2 International comparison of profitability of postal Giro services 1968–70 [14]

* For the year 1969

cheque guarantee card. It also has a number of automatic cash dispensing services and in addition to the 500 fixed boxes, Giro post boxes are carried on the front of all the municipal buses, a simple but telling example of the cost-reducing possibilities in such a concentrated urban market. The Treasurer of the City of Amsterdam acts also as the Director of its municipal Giro, which is the main financial agent for all that local authority's services. Thus almost all of the payments and revenues of the municipal authorities are channelled through their municipal Giro, which itself is linked with the Dutch postal Giro system. The main link however is a direct one to the central bank—the Bank of the Netherlands.

There is little doubt that the Amsterdam Municipal Giro has been a resounding success, whether measured in narrow financial terms or in terms of a social audit, though since the Giro finances are part and parcel of municipal finances, the authorities were not able to provide me with detailed separate profit figures. 'The picture that emerges most clearly as a result of the Netherlands Institute of Public Opinion's research into the Amsterdam Giro is that of an institution known in Amsterdam and its surroundings with an assured reputation for its practical and quick service'—a reputation which deserves to be more widely known and appreciated. [13] Its freedom in providing such a wide range of customer services must surely be the envy of its nearest British counterparts—including in this comparison not only National Giro, but also its close competitors the Trustee Savings Banks and, of course, the Birmingham Municipal Bank.

(b) Dutch PCGD

The first practical signs of interest in setting up a postal giro in Holland were given by its Federation of Chambers of Commerce and Industry in 1904, an organisation which repeatedly pressed its case in the following fourteen years. Powerful academic support in favour of a Dutch Giro was given two years later by De Bosch Kemper in *De Economist*. [15] Perhaps the most powerful argument was however the fact that by 1914 Holland was surrounded by countries which had already set up postal Giro systems—Germany in 1908, Luxembourg in 1911 and Belgium in 1913. The weight of argument and example began to tell. Just a year after Amsterdam, its commercial and financial capital, had shown the way, the rest of Holland followed by setting up its particular form of postal Giro known as 'Postcheque en Girodienst' or 'PCGD' for

200

short, which began operations on 16 January 1918. At first the system was decentralised and operated from some 370 separate Post Offices each of which kept accounts as well as acting as a payments and transfer office. The system grew slowly at first, enrolling only 14 000 customers in its first year. It took until 1923 to reach 100 000 customers at which point the decision was taken to centralise the system at the Hague and to bring in, what was for that period, the last word in automatic handling procedures. Having achieved these 100 000 customers, it managed in 1924, six years after its formation, to pass its break-even point and make a modest profit. It passed the 200 000 customer mark in 1932 and by the outbreak of the Second World War had reached 365 000 accounts. In 1969, when, as we have seen, the Amsterdam Giro enrolled its 250 000th customer, the PCGD celebrated the acquisition of its 2 millionth customer, despite having had to hold back its campaign for new customers during part of this period because it was in the throes of computerisation and therefore was not so free as it otherwise might have been to engage in aggressive marketing. However, having successfully carried through its main computerisation programme, it has now returned to the fray and has attracted $\frac{3}{4}$ million new customers in little over two years. With the number of accounts currently being $2\frac{3}{4}$ million, this is, with the exception of Amsterdam's Municipal Giro, easily a world record in customer density, while only France and West Germany exceed Holland in the absolute number of postal giro customers. To handle the transactions generated by this growth of custom without increasing delay the PCGD has set up a new regional office at Arnhem and since May 1966 all new accounts have been handled at this office.

In view of the fact that many other postal Giros, particularly those of the Scandinavian countries to be examined later, are dependent to a very significant degree on the custom of central and local government, it is of interest to see the relatively small part played by government balances in the Dutch Giro, and the correspondingly large role played by private and business accounts. A breakdown of the number of accounts into eight categories and the balances held by these accounts is given in the following Table 8.3, in which it will be noticed that the private accounts total well over 90% in number and in value terms are well over 40% of the totals. Thus private firms and individuals together supply 96·4% of the total number of accounts and 71·4% of the total balances. In this

201

way the Dutch Giro has penetrated deeply into almost every sector of family and business life throughout the country.

DESCRIPTION	NUMBER OF ACCOUNTS %	BALANCES %
Private individual accounts	91·4	44·4
Private business firms	5·0	27·1
Foundations and social institutions	2·5	4·7
Insurance companies, pension funds, etc	0·3	3·1
Educational institutions	0·3	2·1
Central government	0·2	8·3
Credit banks	0·2	8·5
Other accounts, e.g. foreign account holders, postal accounts used by the Giro service, Netherlands Bank, etc	0·1	2·8
Total	100·0	100·0

Table 8.3 Distribution of accounts and balances by category: Netherlands Postal Giro 1971

In the four years between 31 December 1968 and 31 December 1972 the Dutch postal Giro added well over 1 million customers—so much for the myth of saturation of the market. Some indication of the extent of this achievement is given by the fact that this is just about the length of period coinciding with the existence of Britain's National Giro, during which, from a population of 55 million, four times that of Holland, we have been hard-pressed to muster 467 000 customers. Admittedly, this also indicates the more difficult financial environment facing Giro in Britain and yet it should afford some encouragement as to what it is possible to achieve once a certain momentum of business is attained. During the same period the daily balance remaining in the PCGD has grown by 81% from 3839 million guilders to 6938 million guilders, the latter at current rates of exchange being equivalent to £978 million, giving an average balance per account of about £350. With such large numbers of the population already having Giro accounts it is no great struggle to induce private enterprise, business firms, insurance companies, welfare societies and clubs to open Giro accounts.

If really widespread usage, coupled with profitable returns, are valid criteria for international comparisons of progress then Holland's Giro must rank as the world's most successful. Nearly all social grants such as old age pensions, health service payments, unemployment benefits, holiday bonuses and so on, are made through Giro. An important feature of recent growth has been its success in attracting salary payments through Giro. The Dutch Giro Card allows its owner to withdraw cash not only from any Post Office in Holland, but also from any Post Office in a number of other countries, including the United Kingdom, the card being guaranteed by the Dutch Giro to include such cash withdrawals abroad. This meant that Dutch Giro users had a facility in the United Kingdom, which before National Giro introduced its own Gold Card in 1972, was better than anything National Giro's own customers possessed. Last but not least, mention may be made of the Giro sweepstake, where the account holder's Giro number serves also as his sweepstake number.

Of course, not quite everything in the Dutch garden is perfect: three areas of recent conflict may briefly be alluded to, although to enlarge upon them would be to cavil unnecessarily in view of its overall success. These are, first, the doubts about whether it is wise to compete aggressively with the savings banks and commercial banks in offering competitive rates on current accounts or in offering personal loans, and second whether the Government should allow the PCGD higher interest on PCGD funds deposited with it and allow it greater freedom from liquidity and investment constraints, which the PCGD believes would enable it substantially to increase the not inconsiderable profits indicated for past years in Table 8.2. Thirdly, many of the officials in PCGD wonder whether a fuller integration of postal savings and Giro business would lead to substantial benefits on the cost-efficiency side (the model it has in mind in this regard is possibly that of Sweden). Dr C J Schotsman, Director in Chief of the Money Services section of the Dutch Post Office, writing on *Future Difficulties* in the authoritative 430-page book published to mark Giro's Fiftieth Anniversary, considers that 'an integration of the administrative processes of the Giro and the GPO would be most beneficial to the cost structure. It is interesting to note that in 1906, twelve years prior to the setting up of the Postal Cheque and Giro Service, an article was published in the (Dutch) Economist pointing out the usefulness of just such an integration'. [16] Before turning to look at the Scandinavian systems it is fitting to finish this

203

account of the Dutch Giro on a less controversial note with a reminder that it is the world's first postal Giro to have achieved the remarkable distinction of having the equivalent of one in five of its population as depositors, which as Table 8.1 shows is considerably higher than that of any other country.

GIRO IN SCANDINAVIA

(a) Denmark's Postgiro

Denmark was the first of the Scandinavian countries to go for Giro, which began on 1 January 1920, the year of Danish reunification after its territorial losses in the war of 1864. The origins and operation of Giro in Denmark differ in a number of interesting ways from those of other countries. In contrast to the situation at the time in Britain, it was the executive head of the Danish Post Office, Mr V O Kiorboe himself, General Manager from 1905–25, who pressed its merits. His views were luckily shared by the Minister of Posts and Transport, Mr J Hassing Jorgensen—and the fact that he happened to be a banker was, as we shall see, more an encouragement than a hindrance. Another highly placed postal official who strongly supported Giro was the General Secretary of the Post Office, Mr O C Hollnagel Jensen. Mr Jensen was, incidentally, the son of a 'money postman', i.e. one whose job it was to be entrusted with the carriage of registered mail. The General Secretary, therefore, had his feet very firmly on the ground regarding the detailed operations of the Post Office and in particular realised just how obsolete the previous Danish system of cash transfer was in comparison with what Giro could offer. Another rather curious peculiarity was the fact that in Denmark it was the commercial bankers who were, with the heads of the postal authorities, the staunchest supporters of the postal Giro. The main reason for this, according to Mr Gert Hammerby, the Danish historian of its fifty years of development, was that the banks considered '*large* payments to be their proper business: small amounts in transit were merely a nuisance which could very willingly be left to the Post Office. Thus the Post Office had to solve the problem (of increasingly heavy cash transfers) that others had left. Against this background the modern postal Giro emerged'. [17]

In view of British experience it may be hard to believe that Denmark provided the unusual spectacle of the General Manager of Copenhagen's oldest bank, Mr C C Clausen of the 'Privatbanken', engaging in public debates urging the merits of the proposed postal Giro system. In this he was ably supported by the Professor of Law at Copenhagen University, Dr L A Grundtvig who, luckily for the cause of Giro, was also General Secretary of the Danish Chambers of Trade. In this latter capacity he was particularly useful in calming the fears of the small shopkeepers, especially those in the provinces. As well as the opposition of the small traders, who feared that a postal Giro would harm them by stimulating the growth of mail order firms, there was a more widespread fear that Giro would drain money away from the provinces into the capital, that it would unnecessarily increase the bureaucracy and strengthen the state's influence over the monetary system. By far the strongest opposition, however, came from the Savings Banks, who were not only unfavourably disposed to Giro itself, but were very much more concerned lest the door would thereby be opened for a dreaded Post Office Savings Bank. This side of the opposition has remained unrelenting for over half a century, for Denmark, with the exception of Switzerland, remains the only country in Western Europe which has failed to set up such a bank.

Gradually, however, the opposition was worn down and when Mr Jorgensen, Minister of Posts and Transport, introduced the Bill into Parliament in 1919 authorising the Post Office to set up their Giro, it passed through without difficulty. Despite provincial fears, the decision was taken right from the beginning to centralise operations in Copenhagen—'the cheapest and most practical method for a country the size of Denmark'. [18] Growth was slow, although the Post Office had managed to induce 1193 firms and individuals to join in advance, a figure which by the end of its first year had grown to some 3000. The reasons for such sluggish growth in its early years were largely due to a general feeling that advertising was somehow improper for a government organisation. 'Even as late as 1927 it was considered to be a most daring experiment when Giro took part in the Trade Fair then being held in Copenhagen. Older visitors expressed indignation at the sight of postal officials actually handing out advertising matter.' [19]

In contrast to the situation in the other three Scandinavian countries and especially in Norway and Finland, State departments in Denmark were at first reluctant to use their own Giro, rather like National Giro's first two years in Britain. Consequently, it took some twenty years for the Danish Postgiro to reach the figure of 55 000 accounts.

At that time the experts were firmly predicting that '100 000 account holders would be the highest one could ever expect to get in Denmark'. [20] This 'ceiling' figure was eventually reached in 1957, after thirty-seven years, but to confound the experts (who in financial matters are constitutionally prone to pessimism), instead of flattening out, the pace quickened, the second hundred thousand being reached in 1972 after only fifteen years.

The average account tends to be more fully utilised in Denmark than in most other countries: its daily turnover in 1972 was well over 2000 million kroner (£135 million) or more than the total annual figure for its first full year in 1920. This heavy usage has enabled it consistently to return a reasonably high profit from a relatively low number of accounts, the more active use raising the average balance per account. Nevertheless, Denmark's Postgiro pursues an active recruitment policy, the salient features of which were fully explained to the author in an interview with the head of the section concerned, Mr V T G Jensen, at Aarhus, Denmark's second city, in August 1972. [21] Of the many marketing methods used in recent years, including the use of 'Giro-Girls', who attracted more attention than custom, strikingly successful results had been achieved through concentrating by means of an initial letter and follow up interviews, with those households possessing telephones who were not already Giro customers. With regard to the future Mr Jensen anticipated keener competition with the banks for deposits—the Danish Giro's example of paying interest on its accounts has, as we have seen, been followed by a number of other countries, especially Holland—and even keener competition for salary group payment schemes. Whether the Danish Post Office will ever have a Savings Bank of its own remains a very live political issue, interest in which has inevitably been intensified by neighbouring developments in Sweden, where the Giro and savings sections of the postal system have recently been brought more closely together.

(b) Giro in Sweden: comprehensive competitive postal banking

The main point of interest which comes through to anyone comparing Giro systems in the 1970s is that Sweden has at last done the logically sensible thing by explicitly creating a Post Office Bank as a commercial undertaking to carry on in joint harness the savings and money transfer business of the community. Consequently it is this vital aspect, which

206

should be of relevance to the future development of Giro in a number of other countries including Great Britain, which will mainly be looked at in this section, after first giving a brief outline of some of the other main features in the growth of Swedish Giro up to the present.

As in Denmark, support for Giro came from among the higher ranks of the Post Office itself, including Mr Julius Juhlin, the Postmaster General, who was appointed Chairman of the 1917 Postal Cheque Committee which recommended in favour of a multi-centred Giro. However, when Sweden eventually set up its system in 1925 they sensibly followed the single-centre example set by Denmark. In contrast to Danish experience, however, most of the public departments joined within the first year and their large and lucrative accounts have continued to be a strong support ever since. Swedish Giro's Fortieth Anniversary practically coincided with the achievement of half a million accounts, since which time a further 150 000 accounts have been added. The rate of growth in the value of deposits was treble that of the number of accounts, total deposits rising by 133% in the decade 1960–70, compared with a 44% growth in the number of accounts.

Following a series of official reports a revolutionary Post Office Bank Act was passed in December 1969, the essence of which was to give the new bank as far as possible the same freedom and the same obligations as the private enterprise banks, so as to make competition between all forms of banking institutions both equitable and effective. The Act helped to bring about still greater co-ordination between the Post Office Bank's two sections (the Savings Bank and Giro) and also between these and the other state-owned bank, Sveriges Kreditbank. 'By making use of all the Post Office's service points the Bank can give its customers throughout Sweden full facilities for convenient saving and a fast payment service.' [22] The logic of Swedish experience thus confirms the theoretical point emphasised in earlier chapters, namely that the essence of money and of its successful management lies not in separating money-for-spending from money-for-saving, and therefore not in separating Savings Banks from Giros (as in Britain), but rather in emphasising their closely parallel development. The Boards of the Postal and Kredit Banks have certain common Directorships with the express purpose of collaborating in fields where the joint use of their resources can strengthen their competitive power and promote their development.

A few examples of this across-the-board facility must suffice. There has been a very substantial increase in the 'postal pay accounts' recently to around 300 000, a form of personal account which is a combination of both a savings account and a Giro account. The Post Office Bank also provides for a variety of personal loans and in conjunction with Sveriges Kreditbank established in 1971 a jointly-owned mortgage company, 'Bofab', so as to increase its competition with the private sector building finance companies. Whether measured in terms of deposits or branches (if we include its 2600 post offices) the Post Office Bank is the largest bank in Sweden. Newly re-equipped to act with almost complete commercial freedom rather than being closely bound by conventional civil service restraints, it faces the future with considerable confidence. The Swedish authorities' interpretation of the international swing towards greater competition among financial institutions has thus meant the removal of constraints not only from the private sector, but also from the public sector, so that both parts of the Post Office Bank, having long achieved a profitable situation, have been given not only greater nominal independence, but in their combined form have been given much greater commercial freedom to act as the most formidable competitor to the other Swedish banks.

(c) Giro in Finland's Postipankki

Whereas, as we have seen, the First World War delayed the onset of Giro in a number of countries, the war of 1939–45 precipitated the over-hesitant postal authorities in Finland and Norway into deciding in its favour. Since the experience of these countries, even more than that of Sweden, illustrates to a high degree the important part that support from Departments of State can give to raising activity to a profitable level, it is this aspect which will be highlighted in this section.

Although Finland's Giro did not become fully operational until March 1940, it had already begun in a small way from 13 October 1939. The circumstances of the war and especially the disruption of communications, accelerated its growth since from the outset 'it became possible to make withdrawals without notice from all post offices in the country. . . . The final break-through occurred after the war when the Treasury used Postipankki's savings books for paying repatriation benefits to soldiers returning from the war and when compensating people moving from areas lost in the war'. [23] It is worth recalling that this use of the bank facilities of the Post Office is precisely that which was advocated in 1940 by Dr A Fischer in Britain, but which as we saw (in Chapter 4) was completely and universally ignored at the time. The Savings and Giro sections in Finland have always worked closely together, so that like Sweden, the Finnish authorities decided in 1970 to combine both functions in a single Post Office Bank. English readers will be delighted to learn that at the same time the bank's name was changed from 'Postisäästöpankki' to 'Postipankki'. Obviously, in a largely rural economy like Finland's, which in 1972 had a population density of only thirty-six persons per square mile with 45% of its population still living in rural areas, postal banking can afford to operate in small scattered communities, where private banks would find it unprofitable to establish branches. This has meant that nearly half (47% in 1972) the total banking offices in the country are those operated by the Post Office Bank. [24] Every local authority and Department of State has an account with the Bank: consequently it is not surprising that so has almost every private firm. An advertisement in the London *Financial Times* at the end of 1972 giving a 'Special Report on Finland' went so far as to claim boldly that 'Every Finnish Firm has a postal giro account' [25] though the head of the Economics Department of the Postipankki, Matti Korhonen, more modestly claims that it is 'used by almost all business enterprises in Finland'. [26] Of Giro's 121 000 accounts nearly 11 000 are state accounts. By far the greater part of the Treasury's transactions are carried out through Giro. The Treasury's proportionate contribution to Giro's total average daily balance amounted to 28·8% in 1971. [27] Finally, the Finnish Postipankki is more independent of the Post Office than are corresponding institutions in most European countries.

(d) Giro in Norway 1942–72: big profits from small numbers

In March 1908 the Norwegian Foreign Office sent to its Home Office a letter which it had received from its Legation in Berlin informing it 'of a new postal cheque service which the German Post Office was then introducing'. [28] Nearly thirty-five years of prolonged debate on the merits of the system were to ensue before Norway decided in its favour and in the event the German military occupation had come first. Not long after the occupation had begun came the Ordinance of 16 March 1942, authorising the Post Office to set up its Giro, which began operating early in 1943 'in circumstances far different from those which its supporters had hoped for'. [29] Although its growth, measured in the number of accounts, was very slow in its first decade—less than 10 000 by the end of 1947 and still less than 21 000 by the end of 1952—yet the Norwegian Giro has shown an almost unbelievable ability to return useful surpluses on its accounts from its very first year of operation onwards, despite such a relatively low total of customers: 65 000 Kr in 1943 and 160 000 Kr in 1944.

This remarkable profit record will be examined more fully below, but here it is appropriate to note that the main reasons for such returns lie in the fact that Giro manages to attract very large average balances from its customers, more than one-third of the total number being business firms, and also that the Treasury allows it reasonably high rates of return on its investments, the great bulk of which are either direct loans to the Treasury or government investments. Thus, although compared with its Scandinavian neighbours the Norwegian Giro has enjoyed considerably less freedom, in other respects it has managed to achieve a commendable success within the constraints of its constitution. The high ratio of business accounts is also largely responsible for the surprising fact that the Norwegians keep much more money in their postal Giro than in their Post Office Savings Bank: thus in March 1972 the total deposits in the Post Office Savings Bank came to only 2876 million Kr (approximately £166 million at the then central exchange rate of 17·3 N.Kr to £1) compared with more than twice that amount 6166 million Kr (approximately £356 million) in the postal Giro. Norway's Giro with 160 785 customers at the end of 1972, about one-third that of Britain's National Giro, yet managed to pull in about four times the British total of deposits. The main financial statistics summarising this success story are given in Table 8.4. Very close links have developed between the United Kingdom's National Giro and Norway's Giro since 1970. National Giro has arranged substantial payment facilities for many Norwegian firms with business interests in Britain and it has also acted repeatedly as an agent for Norway's Giro in the purchase of foreign exchange, where it has been able to quote finer rates than have been obtainable in Oslo—an indication that the ability of the London office to earn money and act as an agent for European Giros is shrewdly appreciated by one of the world's most profitable Giros.

NORWEGIAN KRONER

	31 DECEMBER 1970	31 DECEMBER 1971
Liabilities:		
Deposits—		
From the Treasury	446m	533m
From the Banks	183m	376m
From other sources (mainly business and private)	3178m	3841m
Total deposit liabilities	3807m	4750m
Assets:		
Deposits with Norges Bank	—	66m
Government Bonds	1339m	1865m
Loans to the Treasury	2120m	2570m
Other assets	348m	249m
Total assets	3807m	4750m
Profit for the year (Sterling equivalent)*	40·0m (£2 312 138)	67·7m (£3 913 294)
Number of accounts	133 939	146 177
Average deposit per account (Sterling equivalent)*	28 423 (£1643)	32 495 (£1878)
Average profit per account (Sterling equivalent)*	298·5 (£17·25)	463·1 (£26·77)

Table 8.4 Norway's Giro: a statistical summary of its financial position in 1970 and 1971

* The rate of exchange has been taken at the central rate of 17·31 Norwegian Kroner per £1, a rate which if anything understates the current sterling equivalent, particularly since the floating of the £ in 1972 (m=1 million)

Sources: 1 Norges Bank Economic Bulletin, Vol. XLIII, No. 4 (Oslo, December 1972)
2 Information on profit and number of accounts supplied by the Norwegian Postal Authorities

PROFITABILITY, DENSITY AND THE SOCIAL AUDIT

Almost all the main Giros kindly answered a questionnaire (given in Appendix C) by the author on the thorny subject of the viability of their institutions. The questionnaire was purposely made as brief and as specific as possible, so as to concentrate on the question at issue (profitability) but to do so in a way that might overcome some of the problems regarding the difficult question of joint costs in a service which is shared so closely with other saving and postal services. Countless pitfalls, however, have to be avoided in trying to make a comparative assessment of profits where not only the legal rules and regulations, but also business customs vary so much from country to country. The main difficulty, which the answers to the questionnaire could only partly overcome, lies in the fact that most countries do not publish profit and loss accounts for Giro alone, these being amalgamated with those of other postal services, most commonly and sensibly, the postal savings banks. Moreover, even in those instances where separate surpluses or deficits can be unearthed, including the information made available by the various Giros in answering the questionnaire, the widely differing accounting methods make any direct quantitative comparisons misleading unless the special circumstances of each case are taken into the reckoning. The enlargement of the European Economic Community has raised the question of the compatibility of national accounting methods to a high level of political urgency. An interesting summary of some of these problems is given by Monsieur Claude Jeancolas in a recent issue of the European business magazine *Vision*. After stating boldly the obvious fact that 'the standardisation of European accounting and reporting procedures is still in its infancy', M Jeancolas goes on to conclude that despite all that is being done in official circles to achieve compatibility 'official action to standardise accounting practice among countries must remain an ultimate long-term aim. It will be a long and hard task'. [30]

Nevertheless, the replies obtained from the questionnaire together with the published information in the Annual Reports of the Giro and postal services of the countries concerned, constitute at least a rough framework of reference with regard to which one might consider whether one should ever expect a postal Giro system to yield a profit and what importance, if any, one should attach to this slippery concept. It is immediately clear that above a certain critical number the size of Giro is no guide to its profitability. The size and density of Giro varies widely even among countries where the system has long been established. A glance at Table 8.1 shows four countries, each with over 1 million accounts. France easily leads with more than 7 million accounts, over twice the size of its nearest rival Germany which has nearly $3\frac{1}{2}$ million accounts. These, together with the Netherlands which has $2\frac{3}{4}$ million accounts and Belgium with over 1 million, form the European core of the Giro system. Japan, Italy and Sweden follow with between $\frac{1}{2}$ million and 1 million accounts, followed in turn by Switzerland and the other Scandinavian countries and Austria. It is interesting to see how the current UK figure, having expanded from 146 000 in 1969, is already approaching the half million mark—a figure considerably in excess of that which has enabled Switzerland and the Scandinavian countries to operate very profitably in the past, though of course a correspondingly larger figure will be necessary in our case so long as our proportion of business and government accounts remains low.

The statistics on density enable us to make allowances for the differences in population and so give us a rough index of the impact of Giro on the business life of the various communities, with Holland, including, as we have noted, Amsterdam's Municipal Giro, emerging as the country with by far the greatest penetration by Giro. Holland's postal Giro density of 209·7 per 1000 inhabitants is distantly followed by France and then by Luxembourg and Belgium, all four countries being in the top league with over 10% of their population having Giro accounts. It is rather remarkable that Austria and Japan, despite the fact that their Giros are ninety and sixty-seven years old, respectively, are towards the bottom of the league as regards the density of accounts, which makes it all the more creditable that National Giro's density after four years probably already approached that of Japan and Italy, whose Giros were founded in 1906 and 1918, respectively.

Table 8.2 records the statistics on profits earned by Giro as supplied in answer to my questionnaire for the period 1968–70. A comparison of the results would appear to indicate that if the average profit per account is taken as the criterion, it was the Scandinavian countries which were the most profitable, led probably by Norway, which apart from ourselves is the youngest of the European Giro systems. An examination of the results for Holland, Germany and Switzerland similarly indicates that they all appear year by year to return reasonably sized profits from the operations of their Giros. Book-keeping losses on the Belgian service would be considerably reduced and in the French case probably transformed into a substantial surplus if commercial rates of interest were gained on their Giro credit balances kept with various departments within the state system. Japan's Giro accounts are included

213

along with a number of others in a 'Special Services Account' which together yielded annual profits of between £8 million and £10 million in the three years 1968–70. However, even after sixty-six years Japan's postal authorities admit that 'Our Postal Giro has not seemed to be at a profit as yet' though the progress of automation 'we hope will make the Giro service a profitable one in the future'. [31] With such well-established services the net social value of Giro has obviously been taken for granted—even by Japan, the most commercially competitive nation in the world—and there has been little public pressure for full disclosure of the kind that in the United Kingdom has amounted almost to indecent exposure, where excessive pre-occupation with the amount of loss, inevitable as such losses are in the early days, inhibited consideration of the proper policies conducive to eventual profitability.

In almost all countries the profits could have been greater and the losses considerably reduced were it not part of a deliberate policy resulting from two main factors, first the natural tendency for some Treasuries to reduce the rate of interest allowed on Giro balances below the market rate, and secondly, the determination to expand the social and less profitable sides of Giro as soon as opportunity offers. Typical of the first point, the Annual Report of the Netherlands Giro (PCGD) for 1969 complains strongly of the low interest rate allowed on its compulsory balances with the Treasury—on which it was then granted only 1·5%, whereas it might have earned 5·25% had it been allowed to invest the greater part of these balances in Treasury Bills. The social and welfare aspects may be illustrated by recent experience in Denmark and Sweden. Their Giros have been keen to develop special welfare services even though they were perfectly aware that the costs would be high since only a small minority would use them. Thus both countries recently introduced services for the blind whereby blind customers send in their orders by telephone and have their accounts returned promptly in braille. Rather similar social services are also provided for pensioners. Thus when the Giro system is strong enough its social conscience can be generously exercised, even though by so doing it deliberately reduces its profits.

In Britain's case the urgent requirement has been not so much to develop its social conscience but rather to postpone such considerations until after it has been able to expand its hold over large and rich customers. The electronic revolution has tended to saddle all modern

Giros with very high overheads and so has made demands for an increased number of accounts and/or an increase in the size of accounts all the more urgent. In every case except Britain's, however, these heavy overheads were diluted by the fact that they had already penetrated their markets and had achieved a fair density. National Giro's difficulties arose largely from the fact that it was the first Giro in the world to be established subsequent to the electronic revolution which meant that the heavy costs associated therewith had to be absorbed in what was bound to be a low average density for the first four or five years.

If National Giro can double its present number of accounts to around 900 000, or at least to 750 000 customers by 1977, giving it a density rate of between thirteen and sixteen per 1000—a target which past experience might suggest as being quite realistic—National Giro should arrive firmly in the black, providing only that its proportion of salaried, business, central and local government customers is high enough. Obviously, the higher the proportion of large business, local authority and government department accounts, the lower the total number of accounts required to achieve viability. The five years to 1977 will therefore be crucial, especially with regard to capturing the 'quality' accounts, the proportion of which hitherto has clearly been too low. The revolution of the tax system which is now proceeding in continental Europe, including their belated introduction of PAYE and their advanced introduction of VAT, in enabling their Giro systems to capture a large and lucrative market. The National Economic Development Office's Report on *Value Added Tax* gave our own authorities a broad hint in stating that 'Denmark and Sweden have all payments made through postal Giro', a hint which so far, however, has been ignored, for the British 10% VAT which came into operation on 1 April 1973 has no such sweepingly simple payment stipulation. The Inland Revenue believes it is doing quite sufficient by merely making passive provision for Giro payment if required by the tax-payer. [32]

There is considerable interest abroad among the foreign Giros concerning British experience and all of the respondents to the questionnaire gave as their opinion that, surplus or no surplus, the Giro system was fully justified as potentially the most logical and efficient of payment systems. Obviously, one would not expect a statement from Giro authorities themselves to point to any other conclusion, but it would seem clear from our examination of the evidence that once a sufficient

215

number of business and government accounts have been attracted so that the size of the average balance kept with Giro is increased, then there would appear to be little ground for concluding that Giro services are bound to operate at a loss. Some manage to be highly profitable, most appear to be moderately so, and in those few instances (including Japan) where financial losses are shown these are considered by the authorities to be adequately compensated by their social or fiscal benefits. The final picture, therefore, which emerges from this brief glimpse of the experience of Giros abroad is one which is not without encouragement for Britain's National Giro, which after all is still in its formative years. To talk, therefore, as Mr Bruce-Gardyne, MP for South Angus, has done of 'a bankrupt bucket shop operation' is needlessly to condemn in advance an institution which is likely to play a substantial and profitable role in the financial institutions of the Europe of the Nine within a reasonably short space of time. [33]

REFERENCES

1   COLTON, CHARLES CALEB, Lacon: *Reflections*, Vol. 1, No. 217 (1820).
2   For those who wish to be referred to the salient features of these important Giros their Annual Reports give a verbal as well as a statistical coverage. As well as these Reports, which for the German Giro is particularly detailed, there are the publications issued to mark the fiftieth and sixtieth anniversaries of the French and German Giros, respectively. That for France, a prestigiously attractive publication by M Ives Guena, Minister of Posts and Telecommunications, was issued in 1968 and gives a fairly detailed history of the origin and development of the world's largest Giro, *Les Cheques Postaux 1918–68* (Paris 1968). Like most such official publications, however, they naturally tend to be somewhat uncritical in their approach.
3   Figures refer to mid-1971 except in the case of the Netherlands and the United Kingdom which refer to 31 December 1972, which latter date slightly improves their relative positions but makes no difference to their rankings.
4   CRANKSHAW, E, *The Fall of the House of Habsburg* (London, 1963), p. vi.
5   TAYLOR, A J P, *The Habsburg Monarchy* 1809–1918 (London, 1948), p. 22.
6   TAYLOR, A J P, *ibid.*, p. 158.
7   *The Times* (Saturday, 13 January 1883).
8   See *Austrian Post Office Annual Report* for 1970 (Vienna, 1971), p. 18.
9   *Ibid.*, p. 17.
10   Quoted in *Een Halve Eeuw Postcheque en Girodienst*, edited by Reinhoud, H (Utrecht, 1968), p. 434.
11   *Amsterdam Municipal Giro Annual Report for the year* 1969 (Amsterdam, 1970), p. 3.
12   *Ibid.*, p. 3.
13   *Ibid.*, p. 3.

14 The Table is based on information supplied by the national postal authorities in reply to the author's questionnaire. The rates of exchange are those current for the years in question.

15 KEMPER DE BOSCH, 'Postal Cheque and Giro Bank', *De Economist* (Amsterdam, 1906).

16 SCHOTSMAN, C J, 'De Exploitatie van de Postcheque-en Girodienst', in *Een halve Eeuw Postcheque en Girodienst* (Utrecht, 1968), Ch. 5.

17 HAMMERBY, G, *Postgiro i 50 Aar* (Copenhagen, 1970), p. 4.

18 HAMMERBY, G, *ibid.*, p. 4.

19 HAMMERBY, G, *ibid.*, p. 17.

20 HAMMERBY, G, *ibid.*, p. 18.

21 In contrast to Mr F P Thomson's experience who complained in his book on *Giro Credit Transfer Systems* (p. 155) 'that the Danish Postgiro Administration repeatedly refused to provide statistical information about their service', I am pleased to state that the Danish authorities not only supplied me with all the information that I required, but went out of their way to arrange the interview referred to, in which a full and frank discussion of policy took place.

22 *The Swedish Post Office Annual Report for* 1970 (Stockholm, 1971), p. 11.

23 KORHONEN, M, 'Postipankki in Finland', *Bank of Finland Monthly Bulletin*, No. 8 (Helsinki, 1971), p. 3.

24 KORHONEN, M, *ibid.*, p. 4.

25 *Financial Times* (London, 28 December 1972).

26 KORHONEN, M, *op. cit.*, p. 4.

27 *Postipankki in Finland, Annual Report for* 1971 (Helsinki, 1972), p. 8.

28 *Postgiro 25 Aar* (Postgiro Office; Oslo, May 1968), p. 9.

29 *Ibid.*, p. 11.

30 JEANCOLAS, C, 'Now Where did that Euro-Profit Get To?', *Vision*, No. 19 (June 1972), pp. 53 and 58.

31 MIYANO, S, Head of International Services Division, Ministry of Posts and Telecommunications, Tokyo, in answer to Questionnaire, 12 October 1971.

32 National Economic Development Office, *Value Added Tax* (H.M.S.O.: London, 1971), p. 41.

33 BRUCE-GARDYNE, J, MP, *Hansard* (9 February 1972).

Chapter 9

The Future of Giro: Money on Tap

'Experience is the name we give to our past mistakes:
reform, our name for future mistakes.' [1]

RECEDING CASHLESS SOCIETY

With regard to the technology of money transfer there is probably
much truth in the paradox that the peaks of the longer-term future are
easier to perceive than the misty low ground which comes within the
compass of our more immediate vision. There is general agreement with
regard to the longer-term aim of developing versatile economic and
ubiquitous money transfer systems so that payment and credit facilities
operated by the individual at home through video-telephone, by the
executive at his office or by the housewife at the shop, all linked directly
to a central computer centre, will in future be virtually on tap, enabling
immediate validation and payment within agreed credit limits for
practically every one in western society and possibly including even
the richer persons living in the urban areas of the less developed countries. Disagreement arises as to exactly when this picture of a universal,
direct credit system will actually arrive within widespread everyday
usage in such a way that it will largely replace rather than merely
supplement existing cash and paper transfer systems. In a few localities
in the United States prototypes of this system are already in operation,
while the Federal Reserve Board has itself sponsored a series of high
level studies for incorporating such systems over much larger areas
under 'SCOPE', its special committee on paperless entries. [2]

In the mid-1960s the so-called cashless society was thought to be just
around the corner, and technical feasibility was taken too readily to

218

mean social and economic acceptability. Mr David Rockefeller, Chairman of Chase Manhattan Bank, New York, a bank that has long been in the van with regard to computer applications for banking purposes, stated in Cardiff in the course of a lecture on the future environment of worldwide banking that 'We were assured in 1965 that the necessary technology already existed to implement this (paperless) system and that it would surely be in place and functioning smoothly by 1975. It is now 1973 and though there are various bank-to-bank electronic payment systems in operation, none has reached down to the individual consumer level'. He went on to say that despite the willingness of the banks to move ahead with electronic payments, the public had been reluctant to follow: 'Opinion polls in the US show that up to 75% of the people surveyed want no changes in the present cheque handling system'. [3]

SAILING-SHIP EFFECT

Reference has already been made to the fact that, electronically speaking, the present paper-chasing computer systems operated by the banks and Giro form merely a transitional stage of uncertain length, rather like the position with the early steamships, where steam merely supplemented rather than replaced sails. This comparison with the history of the development of the steamship is relevant also in another important aspect, namely that the threat of steam brought about such a remarkable improvement in the quality of the sailing ship that the economic life of this apparently obsolete mode of transport was extended for considerably longer than had seemed at all possible in the middle of the nineteenth century: both the number and the quality of sailing ships were increased. This 'sailing-ship effect' is very much in evidence in the current improvements in the present paper transfer systems supplemented by electronic recording; improvements which have postponed the advent of the impatiently awaited cashless society to a rather more distant future than was thought probable only a few years ago. 'During 1965, when Americans were writing 17 billion cheques, few could imagine handling today's 23 billion annual rate without the entire system collapsing under a mountain of paper, (yet) operations management tell me', said Mr David Rockefeller in the article quoted above, 'that we could, if necessary, handle twice the present volume of cheques using current technology.' [4]

Even the currently fashionable substitute term, the 'less-cash society' is hardly compatible with the greatly increased demand for currency of all forms in recent years; for *more* rather than fewer notes, coins and cheques have been needed, despite the substantial growth of new methods of money transfer, including some 6 million credit cards current within the United Kingdom at the end of 1972. Increasing real affluence and the mirage of inflation have both been partly responsible for this increased supply of cash, but there also seems to be some evidence that Milton Friedman and the monetarists are perhaps right in thinking— what the man in the street has always thought—that money is a luxury, the demand for which is elastic and therefore increases more than proportionately with increases in national income. [5] Thus if we look at the Bank of England statistics for currency in circulation during the decade 1963–72 inclusive, the estimated circulation of coins increased from £212 million in December 1963 to £359 million in December 1972 or by 69%. The growth of notes during the decade was almost exactly of the same order, namely from £2613 million in December 1963 to £4380 million in December 1972 or by 68%. [6] The same kind of increases have been taking place in the number of cheques cleared, though their total values have increased very much more rapidly during the decade. Changes in the composition of the clearings made through the London Bankers' Clearing House, partly because of mergers and changes in methods, enable only rather rough comparisons to be made. The published figures show that the total number of items in the debit clearing, predominantly cheques, passing through the Bankers' Clearing House rose from 488 million in 1963 to 788 million in 1972, an increase of 62%. Their total value, however, more than trebled in the same period from £302 338 million to £1 071 621 million. [7]

Experience in the USA is similar. In an article published in a banking review early in 1972 entitled 'Whatever Happened to the Cashless Society?' the writer showed that 'the US has become if anything a more-cash-than-ever society' and that 'even after allowing for today's larger population and for inflation so-called real per capita holdings of cash are more than 50% higher than in 1939. Coins are now well over double the amount that circulated in the early 1960s.' [8] The Federal Reserve Bank of Atlanta, one of the States which has already experimented with local 'cashless' systems also published in 1972 the results of a detailed analysis of trends in currency and cheque payments.

This study showed a six-fold increase in the number of cheques between 1941 and 1971 and estimated that this latter total would almost double again in the short space of time to 1980. Furthermore its survey indicated the rather surprising fact that even among the same income groups people who used credit cards drew more cheques than those who did not have credit cards. The study concluded that 'This growth will undoubtedly force a change in the payments mechanism in the near future'. [9]

The parallel German experience is reflected in the Deutsche Bundesbank's view that 'in the course of the 1970s the number of credit transfers, cheques and automatic debit transfers will rise to more than twice its present level' and therefore 'this trend makes it imperative to adopt new streamlined methods, based on the resources of modern technology, to handle cashless transfers'. [10] In January 1973 the bank published an explanation of the basic features of the voucherless procedure which it was in the process of installing first for serving the larger banks, firms and public authorities, since it was convinced that 'in the field of bulk payments the growth rate of cashless payments, which is already high, will increase more than proportionately'. [11] Thus although improved paper cheque and Giro systems will enable us to cope with growth in the immediate future, pressures already discernible would seem to indicate that the plans for paperless systems now being put into operation bank-to-bank will be widely extended probably during the 1980s so as to include the greater part of transfer payments by the ordinary bank and Giro customers. Before turning to look at some of National Giro's plans for its own future, we may first glance briefly at what is undoubtedly one of the most path-breaking of recent technical inventions with enormous possibilities for the future development of direct payment systems in the longer term.

LASER: MAKING LIGHT WORK OF MONEY TRANSFER

When T H Maiman invented the laser in 1960 it was dubbed 'a solution in search of a problem'. [12] Perhaps in no field will problems rise more quickly to demand the sort of solution that the laser can so generously provide than in communications, including money transfer. Mr James Martin of the International Business Machines' Systems Research Institute, New Jersey, according to his authoritative work on

221

Telecommunications and the Computer believes that Britain might have a considerable advantage in the development of cashless systems compared with the United States, if only it seizes its opportunities. 'The development of such systems could be easier in a country like England than in the United States, because in England the General Post Office owns and operates all telecommunications and the nationwide, computer-run Giro banking system. The commercial banks are also largely nationwide. . . . If only England could invest courageously in technological innovation, it could make spectacular use of the new computer techniques. The country is geographically small and data highways of massive capacity could interlink it at a fraction of the cost of those in the United States.' [13] The increasing congestion in conventional money transfer systems could be enormously relieved by the timely arrival of the laser. Thus, according to *Fortune*, March 1973, 'The use of light waves for communications represents a quantum jump to an entirely new level of transmission. Whereas a co-axial cable or micro-wave system can transmit some 100 *million* bits of information a second, a laser beam can transmit over 100 *billion* bits per second. This tremendous increase in capacity, achieved by an economy of means that marks a new level of technology, opens a new era of potential expansion for all kinds of communications.' [14]

The long-term future for so-called transfers therefore looks very bright. National Giro was the world's first fully computerised nationwide money transfer system: whether it can live up to the promise implied above by Mr Martin, one of the world's leading experts in this field, and become one of the first of the major paperless systems will however depend not only on technological progress but even more directly on the successful extension of its custom on the basis of its existing technology within the more immediate future. As we have seen, the omens at the end of 1972 and the beginning of 1973 looked strongly encouraging.

GIRO'S DEVELOPING DATA TRANSMISSION NETWORK

The entire field of data communication and terminal deployment is continually under examination throughout the Post Office, and Giro's plans are necessarily dovetailed with the related activities of other sections of Post Office business, thus enabling very considerable joint cost advantages both in research and operation. Future developments may consequently be described under two categories, first internal Post Office projects and secondly the external direct links which Giro will increasingly be making with its own customers. Regarding the internal developments it is likely that all Crown Post Offices and many of the larger sub-offices will be directly wired for data transmission between 1976 and 1980, with most of the smaller offices joining the network in the following decade. Linking National Giro Centre with Post Offices throughout the country will enable the direct capture of Giro business at the counter, including the recording and immediate receipt of deposits, the withdrawal of cash from dispensers inside (and probably also outside) the Post Office and of course the immediate validation of customers' credit standing.

Externally there are three main developments already in train to link the larger businesses, government departments and the banks to National Giro Centre. We have already described (in Chapter 6) the various existing computerised links with big business firms and local authorities. It will be a natural progression to make such highly computerised linkages in a more direct manner, obviating the need for exchange of paper and tape. Government departments, particularly the Department of Health and Social Security and the Department of Employment, are setting an example to other departments regarding inter-computer planning of Giro business in a manner which will enable direct money transfer on an even larger scale to take place within the foreseeable future. With the joint-stock banks, the Trustee Savings Banks, the Building Societies and the larger financial houses setting up their own computer networks it is highly desirable to say the least to make sure that the systems used are fully compatible at their interface, so that the various sectional networks may eventually be combined in a much more general system. Such a network would obviously be very much to Giro's advantage. It was for this reason of trying to achieve the highest degree of compatibility between the various cashless payment systems being devised by other users that the Deutsche Bundesbank felt that 'its approach to the automation of cashless payments should be published' in 1971 some years before realisation since it wished to 'enable all interested parties to take the project into consideration at an early stage when drawing up plans of their own'. [15] Finally, for the more distant future a network of selective retail outlets will supply terminals for use with the individual Giro customers' magnetic strip encoded card (or some similar form of authentication) so as to complete Giro's nationwide system of direct transfer payments.

GOVERNMENT DEPARTMENTS AS GIRO CUSTOMERS

So much then for the enchanting landmarks discernible in the more distant ranges of future money transfer. It is necessary however in this concluding chapter to return to the more prosaic economic factors which will help to determine the achievement of full viability by National Giro by mid-1977. Prominent among these is the degree to which the Government itself makes use of the infant bank. The general policy is clear: to allow the question of whether or not to use Giro to be a matter for the individual departments to decide for themselves in accordance with two vague guide-lines of 'convenience' and 'economy'. In other words only if the use of Giro would be easier and cheaper should any change in existing arrangements be made. The trouble is that although this sounds eminently sensible, it fails to take into account the heavy weight of inertia which exists in government departments to an extent at least equivalent to that in the private sector of the economy; and after all, it is a public sector bank, and as such might well expect greater departmental efforts to give its services a fair trial. Although the British Civil Service has many virtues, even its most ardent protagonists would hardly claim enterprise, in the old-fashioned economic sense of entrepreneurship, to rank among the most prominent of these. For entrepreneurship means not only risk-taking, but risk-taking spurred on by the sporting chance of obtaining really high personal profits; and it is still difficult to get the daring implied by one side of entrepreneurship without the reward implied by the other side. Such factors may perhaps continue to condition achievement in government departments and public corporations, despite current fashionable emphasis on running them as if they were commercial concerns and however much economic viability is raised to a high priority as a policy criterion.

Consequently, it is not surprising that the attitude of various government departments towards Giro has been very patchy, some being enthusiastic users and others being completely negative in their attitude and seemingly unaware of the very considerable advantages that neighbouring departments are reaping from using Giro. Financial journalists could hardly help noticing this and though the following statement by Mr James Poole of the *Sunday Times* Business News Section was made before the present Government's firm announcement of its renewed faith in Giro, it is nevertheless an understandable reflection on this pervasive, negative attitude: 'Government and civil service have been disbelievers in Giro from the word go. It hardly helped to have the Paymaster General setting up a similar central computer to handle inter-government and welfare payments.' [16] Perhaps the best way to convince laggard departments is however to indicate the positive achievements of co-operation between Giro and departments such as those of Health and Social Security and of Employment. The extent of the use being made by the Department of Health and Social Security may be gauged from the fact that during the financial year 1971–72 the Department issued 54 690 596 Giro orders, totalling some £543 603 000, the average value of each order thus being approximately £10. Plans already in being, involving particularly close co-operation with the Department of Employment, will greatly extend the already substantial scale of usage made by this department of Giro's services.

It is not merely a question of using Giro for making payments previously made by other means, but rather of taking the opportunity which Giro provides of re-organising the whole pattern of the services provided by these departments. Thus from 1971 onwards the Department of Employment began its most important re-organisation for sixty years with the objective of separating the administration of the employment service from that of the provision of unemployment and related benefits. The change-over from the payment of unemployment benefit in cash to postal payment by Girocheque (which we noted as being in operation in rural areas such as Gower in the late 1960s) was adopted on a nationwide scale in 1972 and completed by the end of June 1973. The abolition of the dole queue represents a silent social revolution for which Giro can claim a large part of the credit.

The final phase in the programme involves the processing of all claims and the production of all payments by computer. The computerised system will gradually be extended from the London region to cover Wales, the Midlands and the whole of Southern England by September 1975 using the Department of Health and Social Security's computer facilities at Reading. The remainder of Britain will be covered during

1975–76 when a second computer at Livingston in Scotland comes into operation. The Department of Employment will thus be able to provide a much more specialised and professional job-service than before with a reduction in staff and, at long last, the end of the dole queue which previously over-shadowed, in more ways than one, its employment service. Being 'on the Giro' instead of 'on the dole' may not be at first sight a flattering image for Giro; however, one does not have to believe Goebbels' dictum that there is no such thing as bad publicity in order to appreciate that Giro's popularity and the public's awareness of Giro is bound to be increased by its deep penetration into the everyday working life of a major part of the still largely unbanked working-class population of Britain. A new scheme for the postal payment of rent allowances by Girocheque in connection with the Housing Finance Act of 1972 was also introduced later that year and by November 1972 local authority orders for 5 million cheques had been placed. These developments involve *additional* balances of several hundreds of millions of pounds passing through Giro annually.

The value of such payment traffic to Giro might be enhanced if it were part of a more pronounced shift within the United Kingdom towards monthly payments. In France the drive for changing directly to monthly payments from weekly seems to have been pressed more strongly than in this country. The French process of 'mensualisation' of wages began after the Second World War in French industry, at first in respect of highly skilled employees, but was sharply accelerated by the personal initiative of President Pompidou in May 1969 and has been extended down the income scale so that by 6 October 1972 Prime Minister Messmer announced the 'mensualisation' of minimum wage payments. A number of British employers, including the British Steel Corporation, have sent their experts to study the French system at first hand. Somewhat related to these changes are the recent and belated movements in Britain away from its traditional attachment to piece-work and its over-indulgence in overtime. These recent changes in traditional industrial practices have thus removed some of the inhibitions which previously hampered the development of 'pay-through-Giro' and similar schemes as preferred alternatives to weekly cash payments. In view of these developments the tone of the official report of the Committee of the National Joint Advisory Council on *Methods of Payment of Wages*, published in July 1972, with its over-emphasis on gradual and piecemeal evolution towards monthly payments sounded old-fashioned and lacking in urgency. [17]

CHANGING ATTITUDES OF CUSTOMERS AND COMPETITORS

The patchiness of the use made of Giro by central government departments is repeated in the case of local authorities where again one meets the whole spectrum from positive enthusiasm to an apparent refusal even to consider using Giro at all. Nevertheless, Giro was operating some 2338 local government accounts by April 1973. The re-organisation of local government into larger units from 1974 onwards following the Radcliffe–Maud and Kilbrandon Reports will force the major authorities to take a new look at their financial arrangements, a process which should at least remove any remaining inertia that may hitherto have played its part in preventing some local authorities from tackling this formidable task. The example of those local authorities which have already made substantial use of Giro for rent collection and agent deposits should focus the attention of the new larger authorities precisely towards those sectors where Giro has been able to show itself to advantage. The re-organisation of the finances of central and local government and the growth of agent deposits on a rising trend to a current rate of £1000 million per annum, are examples of developments that could not have been foreseen with any clarity a few years ago.

If such new and expanding uses were largely unforeseen, at least in method and extent, when Giro was set up, in other respects confidently anticipated custom did not materialise. Perhaps the most disappointing of all such confidently expected responses lies at the door of the trade unions, particularly in view of the long history of pressure for a Giro exerted not only by particular unions, but also by the TUC. A study of the Reports of the Chief Registrar for Friendly Societies, combined with National Giro's Directory of Business Customers (and confirmed by the author's correspondence with the trade unions concerned) showed that only one of the head offices of the eight largest unions in the country had an account with Giro in 1972, while extremely few of their branch offices held an account either. The exception is the National Union of Public Employees which runs an active account used chiefly for credit transfer and staff salary purposes. The five and a half million members

227

of these eight unions represent around 60% of the total trade union membership and include such powerful and influential giants as the Transport and General Workers Union, the Amalgamated Union of Engineering Workers, the General and Municipal Workers Union, the Electrical Electronic Telecommunication and Plumbing Union and the National Union of Mineworkers. Judged by this attitude then so far as the country's major trade unions are concerned, with a few notable exceptions, National Giro might just as well not have been founded. [18] Thus contrary to general expectations, National Giro has turned out to be neither the poor man's bank nor the trade unions' bank, despite the fervour of working-class support for the cause of Giro before it came into existence.

In pleasing contrast to this situation with regard to the larger trade unions is the change in attitude shown by the joint-stock bankers, who have become much more resigned and co-operative towards National Giro in recent years. We have already stressed this aspect in showing how firms like Associated British Foods have co-operated in a triangular relationship with Giro and their own joint-stock banks in formulating their particular variant of the Agent Deposits service. As early as February 1971 the change in attitude had become noticeable, when Sir John Thomson, Chairman of Barclays Bank Limited, stated in his Annual Report: 'Reluctant as we always are to lose any customers, it may be that the National Giro will satisfy the needs of some of those who require no more than a simple money transmission service'. [19] The new co-operative attitude on the part of the clearing banks became more apparent with the advent of the new era of freer competition in mid-1971 and the realisation that the competitive impact of National Giro was far less, so far as the clearing banks were concerned, than the competitive pressure exerted by other banks, especially the American banks. If we look at Giro's £100 million of deposits in December 1972 in the context of over £65 430 million which the banking system as a whole held as deposits in the United Kingdom at the time, or compare the £16 187 million of the London clearing bank deposits with the larger total of £17 515 million of deposits in American banks in the United Kingdom, then the role of Giro as a competitor with the clearing banks is placed in a more rational perspective than was the case when exaggerated claims were commonly and forcibly expressed when Giro was first established.

228

Which SIGNALS SATISFACTION

The Consumers' Association, an independent non-political organisation set up to guard the interests of the ordinary consumer, carried out a survey during the autumn of 1972 of the convenience, efficiency and costs of the services provided by the London and Scottish clearing banks, the Co-operative Bank, the Trustee Savings Banks and National Giro. The results of this comprehensive survey involving members with a total of nearly 4000 bank accounts, were published in *Money Which* of December 1972. Despite certain sharp criticism of Giro's shortcomings on the score of the relative helpfulness of its counter staff and its customers' needs for 'authentication' of cheques in certain circumstances—two awkward points which repeatedly stick out like sore thumbs— on balance the survey indicated conclusively that Giro's popularity with its customers exceeded that for any other bank, and very considerably exceeded that for the 'Big Four'. Thus 87% of the respondents stated that they were 'very or extremely satisfied' with its service, compared with an average of 74% for all the other banks, Giro's figures being some twelve percentage points higher than that of the highest of the Big Four and thirty points higher than that of the lowest of these four. Similarly with regard to the question as to whether the respondents 'would certainly recommend the bank' National Giro's customers replied with a convincing 83%, being by a clear margin the highest score, some twenty points higher than the average for all the other banks, twenty-four points higher than the best performance for the Big Four and forty-one points higher than the Big Four's worst figure. [20]

These divergences are so wide that they point to a difference in customers' subjective standards of satisfaction—and there are no agreed absolute standards—that is clearly of substantial significance. *Which* noted that one of the possible reasons for this clear superiority was the interesting fact that 76% of their respondent members who had National Giro accounts also had at least one other bank account and 'so could use Giro mainly for the things it does well'. [21] It may also be of relevance in this connection to remind ourselves of similar expressions of satisfaction in the case of continental Giros, where public sector banks appear in the present social climate to be more generally acceptable than those of the private sector simply because they are in public ownership and control. Thus Dr H G Advokaat, Economic Adviser of the Amsterdam–Rotterdam Bank, Holland's biggest private bank, writing in *The Banker* of December 1972 believed that: '*There is far more public acceptance of savings banks and the Postal Giro system than of the general banks, which are seen as strongholds of capitalism by many*', an attitude 'which is deeply ingrained . . . and by no means confined to this country'. [22] Dr Advokaat not unnaturally considered this attitude to be immature and mistaken, but one which nevertheless needed to be reckoned with in planning for the future of retail banking. Whatever one's viewpoint, the converse would appear to be that public sector financial institutions like Giro have an in-built advantage in competing with those of the private sector, a factor which may be rather useful in lubricating the rapidly increasing inter-European money transfers now being planned. Domestically, however, the value of this support should not be exaggerated, as the examples just given concerning the changed attitude of the trade unions convincingly demonstrate. In Giro's present and immediate future circumstances a pound of old-fashioned profit is worth far more than a plethora of modern political platitudes, while the community's rising curve of real affluence promises more for the future growth of Giro than do vague changes in social attitudes even where these are distinctly favourable. Probably a stronger force than this vague opposition to 'capitalistic' banks is the belief that public sector institutions can generally help to stimulate the commercial banks into more effective competition for the consumers' benefit, a fact that was put clearly by Mr Paul Bryan, the Conservative Party's official spokesman on Post Office matters in the early stages of Giro: 'The competition which will be provided is one of the reasons why we wish it well'. [23]

PAGE REPORT AND GIRO: AN OPPORTUNITY MISSED

The Chancellor of the Exchequer, Mr Anthony Barber, in his Budget Speech of 30 March 1971 announced his intention of appointing an independent committee to review National Savings and its related institutions. The Committee, under the Chairmanship of Sir Harry Page, reported on Budget Day 1973 and its controversial findings were published somewhat belatedly in June of the same year. [24] Its terms of reference appeared from one point of view to exclude Giro, a current account bank, for they confined the Committee to an examination of *savings* institutions. Yet, since the Committee was also required to

230

consider the future role and development of money transmission and to examine the relationship of the savings institutions to other financial organisations, some specific analysis of Giro was unavoidable. After admitting that 'This reference to money transmission has caused us some difficulty because it is not a major activity of the savings organisations . . . but is the only function of the National Giro service, which does not form part of the National Savings conglomerate' [25] the Committee compromised by dealing with Giro rather summarily in only two or three pages. It may also have considered that Giro, with its short history and repeatedly long reviews, had already been overexposed.

The Page Committee plainly regretted the fact that Giro and the National Savings Bank had been physically and administratively separated, despite their common dependence on the network of Post Offices which also still separately handle the old postal and money order systems: 'If we had been charged with the task of establishing a State operation to cover current account banking, we would hardly have recommended the establishment of three independent systems.' [26] The Report goes on to state that since they had not been so charged and since the establishment of a single coherent postal banking system was a remote, long-term consideration, then 'In our recommendations we confine ourselves to the short term and urge that the management of the National Savings Bank and National Giro should be given directions to explore how far collaboration without merging can take place so that there is a minimal duplication of standing order systems and so that something approaching a single State system of money transmission can be evolved.' [27]

In fairness the Page Committee saw that 'in the longer term a merger between (the) two organisations might be the solution to the problems of both . . . though the longer development at Bootle and Glasgow goes on, the more remote is any possibility of the emergence of what could be a coherent and comprehensive State banking/saving service.' [28] Since in the nature of things such far-ranging command papers on National Savings and money transmission are rare birds, it is all the more unfortunate that the Report missed this opportunity of focusing much more attention on the relative advantages of combining National Giro with the National Savings Bank to form a powerfully effective public sector bank which could, like its successful continental

231

counterparts, offer a wide range of transfer, deposit, saving and lending services to compete more effectively across the board not only with the profit-seeking private sector banks, but also with the 'mutualised' financial institutions such as the Building Societies and the Trustee Savings Banks. The Page Committee recommended that the Trustee Savings Banks under a new designation, the Trustee 'Mutual 'Banks, should be granted a substantial measure of freedom to enter new lines of activity and thus develop into a vital 'third force' in British banking. The Committee's controversial forward-looking plans for the favoured Trustee Banks stand in plain contrast to its more dismal treatment of the National Savings Bank which was to remain essentially unchanged and strictly confined within all the irksome and old-fashioned Treasury constraints.

The Page Report in giving the Trustee Savings Banks more than they asked for compensated by giving the National Savings Bank even less than it feared. Competitive freedom must not however be a formula fit only for the private and 'mutual' banking sectors: equity and efficiency alike demand that a greater measure of freedom should be extended to the public sector as well. Despite the manifold benefits of fuller competition it will be a bleak day for public institutions and for the community at large if freedom to compete is lavishly encouraged by Governments for every financial institution excepting only those within the public sector itself. The moral is clear, and as Giro approaches closer to its goal of full viability, so should the authorities be ready to remove Giro's remaining constraints, where these are felt by its management to restrict its freedom to compete on equal terms with its powerful rivals, whether these are private sector banks or those of the newly liberated 'third force', the Trustee Mutual Banks.

NATIONAL GIRO: ITS SIGNIFICANCE AND PERMANENCE

A few Building Societies still carry in their title the term 'permanent' to distinguish them from a previously common alternative kind of 'terminating' society. Banks have not found it necessary to describe themselves as permanent because they are not expected to be temporary institutions, although many have turned out to be ephemeral. However, not a single postal Giro having once been set up has as yet been terminated and in real terms, once over their formative years, all appear to be reasonably viable institutions. National Giro as judged by the tastes of its consumers has abundantly justified the hopes of its protagonists and as judged by the acid test of viability has already made considerable progress since adopting its new strategy. As a living organism it has been developing in ways not entirely anticipated by its founders. In particular, with three-quarters of its individual customers also having accounts with other banks and who by and large tend to use Giro selectively as part of a rather sophisticated system of managing their personal finances, it is serving a different market in different ways from that which was described in the White Paper of 1965 as being intended 'for many people with simple needs and no bank accounts'. [29] Its immediate future role will clearly be to seek profitable custom wherever it can find it, rather than straining to adopt an uncomfortable and unprofitable pose as the poor man's bank. Once full viability is achieved a re-assessment of strategy in favour of the unbanked may then be justified: but that situation lies in the more distant future.

In the meantime National Giro is faced with its urgent task of achieving full viability by July 1977. By March 1973 it had already succeeded in covering its operating costs and by July 1973 had comfortably exceeded the initial target which had been set for it by the authorities at the time of the reprieve. National Giro is an institution with long antecedents and a brief but eventful and controversial history. There can be few other banking institutions that have had to undergo such a series of official investigations during their formative years, but having emerged through these trials and having already demonstrated the success of its new policies, there can now be no doubt that National Giro has carved out for itself a significant and permanent place among Britain's financial institutions, a place which may in time grow to rival that of the National Savings Bank of which National Giro is logically the other half.

It seems appropriate therefore to close our study of the first public sector bank to be established in Britain for over a century by allowing the Chairman of the Post Office, Sir William Ryland, to share the penultimate word with Sir John Eden, Minister for Posts and Telecommunications. When the Post Office announced its new policy in March 1972 the Chairman concluded simply: 'Giro is here to stay, to serve its customers and to stand on its own feet.' [30] Luckily for Giro's cause the Minister, armed with the statistics for the first year of Giro's operations under its new strategy, was able to furnish convincing evidence of its profitable progress. In a statement to the House of Commons in July

1973 the Minister could not help admitting this marked change in Giro's fortunes: 'The short-term target agreed with the Post Office by my predecessor required Giro to make a positive contribution to Post Office finances within a year of introducing new tariffs on 1st July 1972. I can now inform the House that this target has been achieved.' [31] The long, hard, lean years were over, so confirming in the end the bitter-sweet truth of that comforting old adage:

'In all labour there is profit.' [32]

REFERENCES

1   The first part of the saying, slightly modified, is from Act III of *Lady Windermere's Fan* by Oscar Wilde (London, 1891).
2   For example see: (1) 'The Cashless Society Comes Closer', *The Financial Times* Friday 6 October 1972), where schemes in Long Island, Atlanta and California are briefly described; (2) the *Annual Report of the Federal Reserve Bank of Atlanta for* 1972 in an article concerning 'Improving the Payments Mechanism' gives details of a number of developments including a 'point of sale funds transfer system' which allows merchants and consumers to settle financial transactions on either a cash or credit basis via a direct link to the five participating commercial banks.
3   ROCKEFELLER, DAVID, 'The Future Environment of Worldwide Banking', *Third Jane Hodge Memorial Lecture* (UWIST: Cardiff, 2 February, 1973), p. 3.
4   ROCKEFELLER, DAVID, *ibid.*, p. 4.
5   For the classic empirical study of the relationship between wealth and the elasticity of demand for money see Selden, R T, 'Monetary Velocity in the United States' in Friedman, M *Studies in the Quantity Theory of Money* (Chicago, 1956), pp. 179–257.
6   *Bank of England Quarterly Bulletin* (March 1967), Table 4, and (March 1973), Table 4.
7   *Bankers' Clearing House Annual Reports* 1963 to 1972.
8   *Morgan Guaranty Survey* (New York, February 1972), pp. 10–11.
9   *Federal Reserve Bank of Atlanta, Monthly Review* (February 1972), pp. 18–22.
10 'The Future Automation of Cashless Payments', *Deutsche Bundesbank, Monthly Report* (Bonn, February 1971), p. 55.
11 'The Future Automation of Cashless Payments through the Voucherless Exchange of Data Media', *Deutsche Bundesbank, Monthly Report* (Bonn, January 1973), p. 17.
12 BROWN, R, *Lasers: A Survey of their Performance and Applications* (London, 1969), p. 4.
13 MARTIN, JAMES, *Telecommunications and the Computer* (New Jersey, 1969), p. 17.
14 LESSING, L, 'Communicating on a Beam of Light', *Fortune* (Chicago, March 1973), p. 119.

15 'The Future Automation of Cashless Payments', *Deutsche Bundesbank, Monthly Report* (Bonn, February 1971), p. 55.
16 POOLE, J, 'Last Post for Letters and the Giro?', *Sunday Times* (London, 7 November 1971).
17 *Methods of Payment of Wages; Report of a Committee of the National Joint Advisory Council*, Department of Employment (H.M.S.O.: London, 1972).
18 *Report of the Chief Registrar for Friendly Societies*, Part 4, Trade Unions (H.M.S.O.: London, 1971), p. 11.
19 THOMSON, SIR JOHN, *Barclays Bank Limited, Report and Accounts for 1970* (February 1971), p. 32.
20 'Bank Accounts', *Money Which* (December 1972), pp. 204–6.
21 *Ibid.*, p. 204.
22 ADVOKAAT, Dr H G, 'Retail Banking in the Netherlands', *The Banker* (London, December 1972), p. 1600. Italics in original.
23 BRYAN, PAUL, M P, *Statement made at Fifth Sitting of Standing Committee D on the Post Office Bill* (10 December 1968).
24 *Report of The Committee to Review National Savings*, Cmnd. 5273 (H.M.S.O.: London, June 1973).
25 *Ibid.*, para. 391.
26 *Ibid.*, para. 398.
27 *Ibid.*, para. 400.
28 *Ibid.*, para. 400.
29 Cmnd. 2751, *A Post Office Giro* (H.M.S.O.: London, August 1965), para. 6.
30 RYLAND, SIR WILLIAM, National Giro, *Statement on Giro Price Changes* (22 March 1972).
31 *Hansard*, 16 July 1973, col. 2.
32 Proverbs, ch. 14, v. 23.

Appendix A

Extracts from the Earliest British Publication Advocating a Giro

'THE POST OFFICE
THE CASE FOR IMPROVEMENT DEVELOPMENT AND EXTENSION
AS ADVOCATED BY THE
UNITED KINGDOM POSTAL CLERKS' ASSOCIATION

'*Issued for the information of Business Men, Chambers of Commerce, City Councils, Friendly Societies, Trade Unions, the Trading Community and the Press.*'

FOREWORD

With a view to bringing before the public the possibilities of the British Postal Service as a means of providing the business community and the general public with facilities for the transaction of business, the United Kingdom Postal Clerks' Association has been collecting and tabulating evidence and information concerning the postal services of other countries.

This pamphlet outlines the most remarkable feature of Post Office activity which has taken place during the last five years, viz., the development of the Post Office Banking Business of several countries and the improved facilities for the transmission of monies, known as the *Postal Cheque and Transfer Service.*

The importance of the subject from a business standpoint has impelled the Postal Clerks' Association to place this matter before the public with a view to directing attention to postal affairs, so that the Post Office Authorities may be induced to improve and develop the service on the lines advocated.

The Chairman of the Postal Clerks' Annual Conference, Mr Albert Varley, of Manchester, in his Presidential address at Leicester, 1911, said:

236

"The policy of this Association is in the direction of an improvement in, and extension of, the work of the Post Office. The Department is altogether behind Continental nations in the scope and value of its Services. In Savings Bank and Insurance facilities, in provision for Transfer of Monies, for Debt Collection, for Cash on Delivery, the British Postal System lags woefully behind, and the times are waiting for a great development along these and other lines. This Association has started a movement which has in view the linking up of Trade Unions and other Public Bodies with a demand for progress in this direction. A statement will be presented to the Postmaster General, pamphlets will be supplied to our members, deputations will wait upon various influential authorities, and it is hoped to educate the public in the possibilities of the extension of Post Office work."

The United Kingdom Postal Clerks' Association will be pleased to send a deputation to Chambers of Commerce, Trade Associations, or Public Authorities, to further outline and explain these proposals for an improved Postal Service.'

The pamphlet then went on to explain in some detail the growth of Giro abroad, or, as it called the system: *The Postal Cheque and Transfer Service.*

'This remarkable development of Postal work originated in Austria, and has merited world-wide attention. Several countries have adopted and improved the system, whilst others have the matter at present under consideration.

As the following statements shew, this natural outcome of the Post Office Money Order and Savings Bank Services gives enormous advantages to the public.

The system is already international in character . . .

The adoption by the British Post Office of a Postal Cheque System would confer immediate advantages, for on the cost of each payment there is a saving of at least 50%. Many of the large firms and organisations would save hundreds of pounds annually, and every member of the public would benefit from the improved method of business.

The facilities offered are so useful that practically every trader, large or small, and thousands of private people open Cheque Accounts.'

There then followed 'A Summary of the Rules and Methods of the System as adopted in other Countries' with actual examples of suggested Postal Cheques and Pay-Cards. The pamphlet finished with the following statement:

'The United Kingdom Postal Clerks' Association claims that a case has been made out for the adoption of the Postal Cheque System by the Post Office in this country and calls for the co-operation of Public Authorities, Chambers of Commerce, Trade Unions, Friendly Societies, and the business community generally, urging them to pass resolutions calling upon the Postmaster General to adopt the Postal Cheque and Transfer Service, and to forward such resolutions to him.

Further information and particulars can be obtained from Mr Albert Varley, General Secretary, Postal Clerks' Association, 39 Gainsboro' Street, Higher Broughton, Manchester.'

Appendix B

Giro's Original and New Charges

NATURE OF SERVICE	ORIGINAL CHARGES 18 OCTOBER 1968 TO 30 JUNE 1972	NEW CHARGES FROM 1 JULY 1972
Deposits to own account excluding deposits by agents	Normally no charge	Normally no charge
Transfers (including standing orders)	No charge	No charge
Girocheque services:		
Cash on demand (up to £20)	4p	8p*
Cashable at post offices		
(i) up to £50	4p	10p
(ii) over £50	10p	10p
Crossed Girocheques	3p	6p
Inpayments by non-account holders	4p	10p
Stationery:		
Cheques (20)	5p	10p*
Transfer/deposit slips (20)	5p	10p*
Envelopes, postage paid to		
Giro Centre (25)	5p	10p*
Debit transaction charge†		
(balance below £30)	—	5p*

* Not payable by those enrolled in 'pay-through-Giro' schemes.
† The Debit transaction charge was not brought into effect on 1 July 1972, and up to the present (April 1973) has not been implemented.

Appendix C

Questionnaire on Profitability of Giros

Postal Giro Services in . . .

1. Do you publish Profits or Losses for your *Giro services alone*, that is separate from that of any other postal bank services?

Yes ☐   No ☐

2. How are these Profits/Losses defined?

3. According to this definition please supply the information indicated:

	PROFIT		LOSS	
	ACTUAL AMOUNT (PLEASE STATE CURRENCY)	% RATE OF RETURN ON CAPITAL	ACTUAL AMOUNT (PLEASE STATE CURRENCY)	% RATE OF RETURN ON CAPITAL
1968 1969 1970				

4. Are your Giro services charged the full economic costs for the use made of other postal offices, officers, postmen, mail deliveries and collection, etc? It would be helpful if you could kindly indicate how you deal with this problem.

5. 'Joint costs': How are the costs estimated for services which you share (joint costs) with other branches of the postal or other government departments?

6. How many years after your Giro was started, did it take for it to become a profitable service?

7. Would you consider the Postal Giro service to be sufficiently useful to justify its continuance to the public, even if it continued to make a loss?

240

Index